WALLS *of* ALGIERS

WALLS *of* ALGIERS

NARRATIVES OF THE CITY THROUGH TEXT AND IMAGE

EDITED BY

ZEYNEP ÇELIK,

JULIA CLANCY-SMITH,

AND FRANCES TERPAK

THE GETTY RESEARCH INSTITUTE, LOS ANGELES *in association with*

UNIVERSITY OF WASHINGTON PRESS, SEATTLE AND LONDON

This book is published in association with the exhibition *The Walls of Algiers: Narratives of the City,* curated by Zeynep Çelik and Frances Terpak at the Getty Research Institute (May 19–October 18, 2009).

© 2009 J. Paul Getty Trust
Printed in Canada
Designed by Ashley Saleeba
14 13 12 11 10 09   5 4 3 2 1

GETTY RESEARCH INSTITUTE
1200 Getty Center Drive, Suite 1100
Los Angeles, CA 90049-1688

UNIVERSITY OF WASHINGTON PRESS
PO Box 50096, Seattle, WA 98145
www.washington.edu/uwpress

The paper used in this publication meets the minimum requirements of American National Standard for Information Sciences—Permanence of Paper for Printed Library Materials, ANSI z39.48-1984.

Library of Congress Cataloging-in-Publication Data

Walls of Algiers : narratives of the city through text and image / edited by Zeynep Çelik, Julia Clancy-Smith, and Frances Terpak. — 1st.
p. cm.
Includes bibliographical references and index.
ISBN 978-0-295-98868-9 (pbk. : alk. paper)
1. Architecture and society—Algeria—Algiers—Congresses. 2. Algiers (Algeria)—Congresses. I. Çelik, Zeynep. II. Clancy-Smith, Julia Ann. III. Terpak, Frances, 1948- IV. Getty Research Institute.
NA2543.S6W35 2009
307.760965'3—dc22   2008048359

COVER: *Panorama of Algiers Taken from the Lighthouse,* Théodore Müller after a daguerreotype by F. Geay, handcolored lithograph, c. 1845–50 (printed by August Bry, Paris; Getty Research Institute, 2007.PR.101**)

FRONTISPIECE: "Ancient Residence of the Secretary of the Bey," section through the courtyard, Pierre Trémaux, lithograph (*Trémaux Parralléles des edifices anciens et moderns du continent africain* [Paris: L. Hachette, 1861], p. 13)

CONTENTS

ACKNOWLEDGMENTS

Walls of Algiers originated from a workshop organized by Zeynep Çelik and Frances Terpak and held at the Getty Research Institute (GRI) in May 2004. Several scholars working on the city from different perspectives were brought to the GRI to profit from the primary materials on Algeria—particularly visual sources—held in the department of Special Collections. Many of the chapters of the current book are versions of the papers delivered at that workshop. We would like to thank Gail Feigenbaum, Karen Stokes, Alison Langmead, Karin Lanzoni, and the entire staff of the Special Collections for making this event possible. The presenters benefited greatly from the issues raised by the small, but learned, group of colleagues who attended the workshop; we would like to express our gratitude to Roger Benjamin, Irene Bierman, Nabila Oulebsir, and David Prochaska for their feedback. At the conception stage of the workshop, Ali Djerbi's contribution was indispensable; we owe him the title of the book as well. The senior staff at the Canadian Center for Architecture in Montreal, in particular Nicholas Olsberg and Helen Malkin, also played significant roles in formulating the first ideas on an exhibition and a book on Algiers.

The editors acknowledge the intellectual generosity of Seyla Benhabib, Karim Boughida, Jean-Louis Cohen, and especially Susan Slyomovics, who answered our many questions as we put together the volume. Elaine Mokhtefi translated two chapters from French with great expertise.

At the Getty Research Institute, Michelle Brunnick, Jean Kim, and Sharon King provided us with invaluable assistance, while Jobe Benjamin, Christine Nguyen, and John Kiffe supplied our many requests for photography.

At the University of Washington Press, Michael Duckworth, then acquisitions editor, accepted the project with genuine enthusiasm, and Beth Fuget and Mary Ribesky took it over from him graciously. Pamela Bruton copyedited the manuscript with meticulous attention, and Ashley Saleeba readily understood the importance of the images to the essays in designing the book. At the Getty Research Institute, Gail Feigenbaum and Julia Bloomfield were instrumental in building a productive collaboration between the Getty Research Institute and the University of Washington Press.

Coediting frequently tests the limits of scholarly collaboration. Working *à trois* on a project as distinctive and complex as this one, while at times a daunting enterprise, has instead provided an opportunity for intellectual camaraderie. Nevertheless, that camaraderie would not have been possible without the forbearance and engagement of the four other authors of this volume—Eric Breitbart, Omar Carlier, Isabelle Grangaud, and Patricia Lorcin—who responded to incessant requests for this or that with good cheer throughout this arduous process.

NOTE ON TRANSLITERATION

Consistent transliteration for modern Algerian history poses a number of problems because there is no single agreed-upon system among scholars. Proper names and place-names as well as the terms for institutions come from a range of languages—classical Arabic, dialectal Arabic, Berber, and Ottoman Turkish. To complicate matters, proper names and place-names often came into English or other European languages through the vehicle of French transliteration, which was not consistent and frequently deformed the original Arabic, Berber, or Turkish. Therefore, the transliteration of terminology in this volume is the product of compromise, as is true of all published work on North Africa for this period. If there is an alternative spelling of a foreign word, the alternative spelling will be noted when that word is first used in this volume.

We have decided to rely upon the following system. If a term, such as the Arabic word for "city"—*madina*—has entered into the *Oxford English Dictionary* in another variant form, in this case *medina*, then the *OED* spelling is employed. If the word is clearly Arabic, as opposed to a French derivation, diacritical marks are used to indicate long vowels, the *ayn*, and the *hamza al-wasl*. For Turkish words such as *bey* or *dey*, which refer to political titles and have also entered the *OED*, these are used instead of the more accurate Arabic transliteration, *bay*. The name Husayn Dey, the last Ottoman ruler of Algeria, is rendered Hussein Dey because this is the most commonly used spelling. Finally, place-names or geographical references are generally rendered in French transliteration because these were adopted in atlases, such as *The Times Atlas of the World*.

WALLS *of* **ALGIERS**

INTRODUCTION

Zeynep Çelik, Julia Clancy-Smith, and Frances Terpak

Travelers arriving by ship in the port of Algiers prior to July 1830 would have remarked that urban spaces, activities, and residents were contained within the walls of the Ottoman-Arab and Islamic city perched on a hill overlooking the Mediterranean. France's invasion of 1830 utterly transformed the city's social organization, meaning, and aesthetic. The logic of empire and settler colonialism demanded that the French military demolish mosques, markets, walls, and neighborhoods and that the colonial party in Paris work to convince citizens to emigrate to France's newest possession and, when this did not suffice, to lure non-French Mediterranean subsistence migrants to the country. By the fin-de-siècle, if not before, the walls of Algiers stretched in a metaphorical sense across the Mediterranean and the Maghreb thanks to the movements of people, things, and ideas, including programs that regarded city planning and urban renewal as the crucible of modernity. Those walls also extended across the Sahara to Dakar and other cities in French West Africa where colonial administrators, missionaries, investors, and urban planners emulated the Algerian model. In the interwar period, the city represented a space of experimentation in modern urban forms, ideologies, and practices culminating during the last decade of the occupation in massive social housing projects—most famously, the "200 Colonnes," which is the centerpiece of the Climat de France development, by architect Fernand Pouillon. With the advent of worldwide decolonization after World War II and the 1954 outbreak of the revolution, Algiers became the symbol of global struggles for independence, justice, and dignity as well as the tragic emblem of the colonial city torn asunder.

At the outset of the twenty-first century, as the moral legitimacy of nation-states and national identities are challenged from different directions, as some borders become less porous and others open up, as the practices of empire acquire cataclysmic dimensions, and the global economy constructs new implacable hierarchies, those histories that still connect Western imperial powers with their former colonies in Asia and Africa invite us to think about present-day dilemmas. Algeria, the most turbulent yet most cherished French colony, is a particularly charged case study that carries universal messages. The country's enduring status as the site of legendary confrontations was recently confirmed by two memorable incidents. In January 2003, on the eve of the Iraq War, the Pentagon screened Gillo Pontecorvo's masterpiece, *The Battle of Algiers* (1965), among American military strategists, manipulating the film's message to inform U.S. government war tactics in the Middle East. In April 2005 Alistair Horne made a heroic, if quixotic, attempt to use the past to talk about present-day imperial folly by sending then Secretary of Defense Donald Rumsfeld a copy of *A Savage War of Peace*, Horne's classic account of the Algerian War, which elicited a "savage response" from the head of the Pentagon.[1]

Algiers, the capital of French Algeria and a prominent battleground of the decolonization war that took place between 1954 and 1962, stands out among colonial cities. From 1830 to 1962, Algiers served as a platform and testing ground where intricate strategies were developed in response to confrontations and negotiations between colonizers and colonized, and all the people in between who had settled in Algiers. The results of these colonial experiments—successes and failures alike—often played a determining role in shaping imperial structures and relationships in other French territories *outre-mer*. What were the historical processes that transformed Ottoman Algiers, the "Bulwark of Islam," into "Alger la blanche," the colonial urban showpiece—and eventually counter-model—of France's global empire? More important, what are the conceptual and theoretical approaches that can help translate the social and spatial biography of a city whose evocation even today conjures up enchantment as well as incomprehensible violence?

"Urban process," a concept introduced by the late architectural historian Spiro Kostof, provides a framework: the proactive and reactive social, political, technical, and artistic forces that generate a city's form never cease.[2] Starting with the premise that these forces and spatial productions are intertwined, the authors approach the city from different vantage points. Their wide-ranging, but intersecting, essays span the disciplines of social and cultural history, art and architectural history, urban studies, and history of film, ultimately coalescing into a comprehensive vision of Algiers that operates in multiple registers. Nevertheless, the common emphasis is the analysis of the city's discourses: the selection, documentation, and presentation of visual and textual data—for example, in a particular photography album, archive, or urban design project.

The authors of the different chapters come from a range of disciplines, and while their approaches allow for triangulation, each author at the same time pursues an interdisciplinary methodology of his or her own fashioning. Collectively, the essays engage in a discussion as scholars from various disciplines search for ways of crossing boundaries and constructing meaningful bridges to other fields of inquiry. This juxtaposition unravels the issues faced in pursuing interdisciplinary research on common subjects by two social historians, a cultural historian, a film historian, an art historian, and an urban historian, each engaged in a parallel, although not identical, inquiry. Visual evidence and visual culture play a central role in all of the chapters: visual documents are used as primary sources and are given equal value as textual sources, representing a new approach in urban history.

To follow and grasp the nature of the dialogues between the essays, it may be worthwhile to zoom into a key space in Algiers, the current place des Martyres, the site of the precolonial souks, demolished immediately after the French occupation to make room for a place d'Armes and later renamed place du Gouvernement. The authors study this urban fragment and its defining architecture, highlighting specific issues that range from the medley of people that crowd it, the institutions that occupy it, the symbolic associations with which it is endowed, its place in the image of the city, its shifting representations in visual and textual media, its physical transformations, and the political agendas behind them. The resulting picture traces the daily life of ordinary citizens or subject populations within ambitious urban design experiments. Moreover, by charting the emergence of a civil society in colonial spaces and built environments, the inherent conflicts between the original intentions of colonial design decisions and the social practices of city dwellers molded by actual conditions emerge to reveal cases of exploitation and repression. Accordingly, visual documents are often cross-referenced. For example, a photograph of the balustrade at the edge of the place du Gouvernement (fig. 3.13) is analyzed by the different authors from different perspectives: as a display of ethnic population mix; as the regularization of public space; as an elegant boundary demarcating the major city square that provides panoramic views; as a site of recreation where residents, tourists, and artists enjoy a captured image of the bay from the dark chamber of a camera obscura positioned on the balustrade; or as historical evidence for the growing power of photography to disseminate a certain image of Algiers in the metropole.

Many themes cut across the chapters to weave a diachronic narrative. Among them, strategies of military occupation and expropriation of the colonized on many levels—land, material possessions, and culture—stand out: the forcible remaking of the urban fabric, the imposition of new institutions, waves of immigration that rendered the Algerians strangers in their own land, the creation of a colonial archive that facilitated seizure of property, and methods of representation drawing upon advances in visual technology. While the emphasis in most of the chapters is on the colonial period, which witnessed the most profound transformations due to radically new strategies and urban forms, we also offer telling glimpses of the governing mechanisms of the Ottoman period and of the modifications in colonial policies after independence in 1962 to suit the new political and ideological climate. By connecting the precolonial, colonial, and postcolonial eras through urban spaces, we draw an alternative framework and enlarged field of vision for an area of inquiry that has too often suffered from a fragmented perspective. Current attempts, whether in Algeria or in other former French or European colonies, to reclaim "colonial cities" face formidable difficulties and challenges due to the durability of colonial interventions and the resulting social dislocations.[3]

Linked to the invention of colonial categories, inherent themes emerge, such as the neighborhood unit, human "types" (e.g., the "Jewish man" and the "Moorish woman"), the Algerian house, and urban scenes (e.g., streets of the Casbah). It is critical to understand that these were not innocent categories but rather representations informed by violence and the destruction of social worlds. The obstinate, almost incantatory, reiteration of the cultural constructs throughout French rule engraved them in image, text, discourse, and ultimately the European *mentalité* as shorthand references to the colony, to the empire, and to Islam. Tied to the creation of symbolic sites and practices, the very same categories would be endowed with other meanings by Algerians throughout the entire colonial period, particularly during the war for independence from 1954 to 1962; ultimately these meanings were folded into the sociocultural and spatial norms of the independent nation.

Since the dialogues between the chapters form a web, and not a rigid linear trajectory, we chose to organize the book in three parts to highlight selected aspects of the history and historiographies of the city of Algiers through peoples, images, and places, followed by a critical review essay in which Patricia Lorcin addresses the main trends in the extensive literature on Algiers. Under the

"Peoples" category, Julia Clancy-Smith investigates the social chaos of the early colonial period created by largely unorganized migrations to, and settlement in, the city from southern Europe and the Mediterranean world. Immigration and the disorders of military rule triggered changes in the daily uses and understandings of urban spaces and the people, activities, and social categories associated with those spaces. She complicates the binary construction of "French and Algerian" by inserting southern Europeans and Mediterranean folk of indeterminate national origins into the city, along the way speculating on their puzzling absence in much of the travel literature and visual culture. Filling the streets, squares, and neighborhoods of Algiers with men and women from different cultures and classes, she makes a strong case for incorporating understudied issues such as individual and group behavior patterns in public spaces, codes of dress, and even sounds into the writing of urban history.

In Algiers, as in other North African cities, the social and cultural meanings of the medina, or "traditional urban core," for its inhabitants were distorted by the combined forces of Orientalism, imperialism, and settler colonialism. Universally cast as "backward" or "backward looking," if at times charming, the medina was often portrayed by Europeans as dark and menacing, even as a space of sexual deviance.[4] By 1900 the "old city" in Algiers sheltered largely impoverished artisans and increasingly rural peoples who had been driven from villages to urban areas and who were socially and culturally disoriented by the effects of modernity and colonialism. That the medina and its adjacent neighborhoods nurtured within their confines one of the most salient indexes or signs of modernity—forms of associative life that existed largely outside the family and state—is a startling conceptual advance made by Omar Carlier. Like Clancy-Smith, Carlier emphasizes the multiethnic character of the inhabitants of Algiers, but during a later period (between the two world wars) when the formation of a civil society was under way. Tracing the emergence of sports clubs, music clubs, and religious and political organizations, he points to a new social vitality that owed much to cross-cultural exchanges among ethnic or religious groups and between French citizens or European residents and colonial subjects, as well as interactions with other Muslim states or societies. He anchors the institutions of the civil society in their specific locations in the historic center, maintaining that Algerians repossessed their city during this period by embracing modern kinds of sociabilities. Carlier brings a rare level of intimacy to urban history by narrating the stories of specific individuals whose decisions, actions, and life trajectories signaled a moral reconquest of the capital city by its Algerian inhabitants marginalized by the colonial regime.

In the "Images" section, Frances Terpak argues that the new genre of the historic panorama allowed viewers to duplicate the experience of actually entering the captured city and to take possession of it metaphorically. By partially erasing the boundary between observer and observed, the panoramas of Algiers permitted a sort of voyeuristic participation in military occupation and thereby functioned as a propaganda device to convince the French public and elected officials in Paris to continue to bankroll a military adventure begun in 1830. Terpak goes on to analyze the shifts in representations of Algiers wrought by changes in visual media as the printed image gave way to photography. She maintains that photographers' persistent depiction of symbolic and political sites for the French viewing public links the early history of photography with that of Algiers.

Moving from the scale of the city to the intimacy of the domestic space, Zeynep Çelik traces the increasingly privileged place given to the "Algerian house" in colonial political discourse and visual culture. This house, whose aesthetic and spatial attributes were further flattened in colonial architectural practice, came to stand in for all of native society, particularly in reference to Islam and women. Infused with Orientalist fantasies, the textual and visual depictions of the Arab house aimed to expose, rationalize, and conquer the spatial unit that sheltered and preserved the core of indigenous society. The obsessive focus upon the home and hearth, however imagined and constructed, was far from an innocent enterprise in terms of colonial laws, policies, and praxis. The riposte of the Algerian family was to conceal the household from the colonizers' gaze, as, in parallel fashion, Islam had served as refuge. Much changed during the 1930s when rural immigration from the *bled* (countryside) into the city, driven by catastrophic demographic expansion in the midst of a global economic crisis, belied the centenary's boastful claims that Algeria would eternally remain French. The social dislocations and violence that propelled Algerian families out of the dangerously oversaturated Casbah, suburbs, and villages and into the *bidonvilles* (squatter settlements) ultimately came with a political and moral price.

Complementing the writings on photography and violence, Eric Breitbart expands on the power of visual representation by turning to films; he probes the ways in which movies engraved the image of Algiers in collective consciousness, holding the city captive, while enhancing and transforming it. He identifies a dominant association with the historic city (the Casbah) as a prison of sorts, relayed by films made during both colonial and postcolonial periods. He also points to divergences: if the Casbah appears as a place of shadows and fears, occupied by marginal people in colonial cinema, it is turned into a site of resistance and dissent in postcolonial productions. Thus, the moral economy of visual and social violence was inverted and replaced by another. Pontecorvo's *The Battle of Algiers* is the film par excellence that presents the city itself as a main actor during the war for independence. It needs to be stressed that the origins of the notion of Algiers as a place of warfare go back deep into the preceding century when the French military drew upon new forms of image making by using the photograph and panorama theater to legitimate conquest and despoliation. However, the story of war, memory, and cinema still reverberates in the present time. Mehdi Charef's 2007 film *Cartouches gauloises* is emblematic of how a new generation chooses to remember the terrible events of 1954–62 through the eyes of children living in the midst of war and violence.[5]

The enduring symbolic power of *The Battle of Algiers* was recently spotlighted by New York–based artist Dennis Adams with implicit reference to the Iraq War in a work titled *Double Feature* (shown at the Kent Gallery, New York, 27 March–26 April 2008). Through a series of "constructed images" that insert the figure of Jean Seberg from Jean-Luc Godard's *Breathless* (1960) into stills from the *Battle of Algiers,* Adams uses the fluidity of the photographic medium to reference Godard's own style of referencing other film classics and to comment on how the immediacy of the news medium shapes perceptions of the modern war. Seberg, the young American selling the *New York Herald Tribune* on the streets of Paris, is, in the words of the artist, "recast as an allegorical figure wandering the war-torn streets of Algiers, where she traces the fault line between the roles of messenger bearing the news and frontline witness to its making" (fig. I.1).[6]

The third section, "Places," comprises an essay each by Isabelle Grangaud and Zeynep Çelik. Grangaud's topic is the neighborhood, or *hawma*, and its precolonial, colonial, and postcolonial definitions. Revisiting the notion of the city quarter, she reveals the processes through which the colonial state constructed an urban archive that classified and categorized indigenous legal documents to facilitate the appropriation of land, structures, and spaces. She suggests that the precolonial *hawma* embodied a semiconcealed social and mental landscape (with its own unspoken customs and rules—and secrets), which might have had ragged edges but whose center was known to all claiming membership. Significantly, the inner workings of the *hawma* present historians with methodological challenges precisely because its very existence was so dependent upon what might be termed a daily culture of *oralité*.[7] On the basis of documents in Arabic from the Fonds Ottomans in the National Archives in Algiers, Grangaud argues that this older collective notion of *hawma* was partially erased by the colonial regime, which was intent upon drawing boundaries that accentuated streets,

I.1 *Double Feature #38*, Dennis Adams, composite film still, 2008 (courtesy Dennis Adams and Kent Gallery, New York)

access, and therefore social control. With its implicit maternal associations, the *hawma* has direct relevance to the study of social memory. The importance of a shared center, recognized perhaps only by the "citizens" of a particular *hawma*, resonates with Jacques Berque's earlier work showing that North African tribes reckoned kinship and belonging in similar fashion—from a genealogical core outward.[8]

Çelik's essay also bridges the three historic eras. She takes an urban fragment, the place des Martyrs (place du Gouvernement), and surveys the transformations it underwent, connecting them to shifts in power structure from the Ottoman period to the colonial and postcolonial ones. An urban design project from 1969 that underlines the continuing colonial entanglements, as well as the national ambiguities regarding the historic heritage, brings the discussion to the years immediately following independence. In an attempt to reach back to the precolonial past while addressing the prodigious social and economic concerns that haunted Algeria, the plan offered to regenerate the heart of the city in an architectural language that harked back to the colonial period. Of course, Algeria's postcolonial condition is not restricted to the country's national boundaries but crosses the Mediterranean. Once again, Dennis Adams's art provokes historic associations. To underscore problems regarding immigrants in present-day France, Adams turned to the passage from the colonial to the postcolonial era in his 1989 project with an approach that finds an echo in this volume. *The Algerian Folie* was commissioned for an exhibition at the Centre Pompidou in Paris entitled Magiciens de la terre, which proposed to bring artists from the "first" and "third" worlds together for the first time. Adams used archival photographs taken in 1962 that showed statues of French military officers on a beach in Algiers just before they were transported to France in an act of rescue. He "reconstructed" the truck seen in one of the photographs, on which he reloaded the statues, now in the form of translucent prints, illuminated from the back. Transporting to Paris the literal symbols of French colonialism that had dotted the public squares of Algeria, his installation reflected on the potential neocolonialism of the exhibition (figs. I.2 and I.3).[9]

Concluding the volume, Patricia M. E. Lorcin's panoramic essay analyzes critical junctures in the history of Algiers from the "corsair centuries" to the postcolonial era and weaves those moments into wide-ranging, often contradictory, portrayals of the city, principally from the pens of "outsiders." The chapter takes us on a centuries-long literary journey that runs in parallel, yet intersecting, fashion with the previous essays. From the earlier captivity narratives to bourgeois travel accounts, from artistic renderings to ostensibly colonial scientific studies, representations and visions of Algiers tended to ignore or muffle the voices, dreams, and aspirations of its indigenous inhabitants. Yet, the final section of Lorcin's chapter demonstrates that in recent decades, this earlier pattern has been transformed by Algerian artistic, literary, film, and scholarly production. Nina Hayat's 1995 memoir-novel *La nuit tombe sur Alger la blanche*, which captures the daily struggles inherent in cultural hybridity, brings, in Lorcin's words, "the Janus-faced imagery of Algiers, a city of light and torment, full circle." Hocine Mezali's history of Algiers (*Trente-deux siècles d'histoire*) from Roman times to the present stands as further testimony to how the "citizens" of today's Algiers have taken back their city's past, present, and future.

The Walls of Algiers is neither a definitive work nor a grand tour that pretends to view the city's structures, spaces, histories, and inhabitants in their entirety but, paralleling Adams's art, is intended to provoke questions. One of the principal methodological arguments made in all of the chapters is that the courtyard, corner, terrace, *hawma*, or *bidonville* might reveal more about urban processes—ruptures, reappropriations, or accommodations—than large-scale surveys. Recognizing that the way in which questions are formulated may even be more critical than the answers, the essays grapple with fundamental methodological issues: For example, how do architecture, spatial arrangements and allocation, and physical forms serve as social and political documents? This

I.2 Dismantled colonial statues at Camp Sirocco, Algeria, silver gelatin photograph, 1962 (courtesy Dennis Adams)

question becomes especially daunting in the absence of textual documents, most notably evidence and commentary from the "inside," from the Algerian perspective. If architecture is left as primary evidence, how does the historian read and interpret it, dissociating it from the meanings given by colonial representations, yet capitalizing upon them? How do we break free from the guided or supervised receptions imposed by colonial image making in order to perceive other social facts and realities? How can the erasures in text or image be recovered and interpreted historically? In other words, how can we acknowledge the violence inherent in colonial urbanism while recognizing that the "citizen-dwellers" of the quarter or neighborhood had imagined and mobilized a "sovereign" city sector relatively free from colonial violation, or that new forms of association, such as sports organizations, could bring together, if only momentarily, individuals from different strata of the colonial hierarchy?

The image of old Algiers that remains with us suffers from its legendary status, the end result of a centuries-long process of sedimentation that cre-

I.3 *The Algerian Folie*, Dennis Adams, color photograph, commissioned for the exhibition *Magiciens de la terre* by Centre Pompidou, Paris, 1989 (courtesy Dennis Adams and Kent Gallery, New York)

ated often-contradictory layers of meanings and associations. Today's Casbah is commonly equated with decay, poverty, and lack of social opportunity—as is true of many "traditional city cores" around the world—albeit intertwined with traces of its earlier aura. Its prospects seem grim, to the degree that some preservationists predict that the entire quarter could be uninhabitable in the near future.[10] The city's physical frame no longer seems able to recover from the abuses brought by long periods of neglect and damage. Nevertheless, even as the dense fabric of the Casbah gradually disintegrates due to the increasing number of "holes" caused by crumbling buildings, the political symbolism of the Casbah and the sad beauty of its ingenious urban forms struggle to preserve the heart of Algiers. Of course, the sufferings of the Casbah are not isolated but permeate the entire city, extending from the flight of middle- and upper-class families to ever-extending suburbs, to issues of security and failing infrastructure. The questions raised in this volume, and the approaches the authors employ, do not pretend to offer solutions to the urgent present-day problems revolving around the preservation, restoration, and renewal of a historic urban core and with it an entire city. Nevertheless, we hope that a nuanced and critical understanding of the city's many pasts will inspire new ways to imagine its future.

NOTES

1   See Maureen Dowd, "Empire of Novices," *New York Times*, 3 September 2003; and Maureen Dowd, "Aux Barricades," *New York Times*, 17 January 2007. Dowd's 2007 article reveals that, in the copy of the book Horne gave Rumsfeld, he had underlined the important passages referring to the immorality and futility of torture during the Algerian War for Rumsfeld to contemplate.

2   Spiro Kostof, *The City Assembled* (Boston: Bulfinch, 1992), 280.

3   On this topic, see Richard Rathbone and David M. Anderson, eds., *Africa's Urban Past* (Oxford: Currey, 2000).

4   Virginia Thompson, "'I Went Pale with Pleasure': The Body, Sexuality, and National Identity among French Travelers to Algiers in the Nineteenth Century," in *Algeria and France, 1800–2000: Identity, Memory, Nostalgia*, ed. Patricia M. E. Lorcin (Syracuse, NY: Syracuse University Press, 2006), 18–32; and Yaël Simpson Fletcher, "Irresistible Seductions: Gendered Representations of Colonial Algeria around 1930," in *Domesticating the Empire: Race, Gender, and Family Life in French and Dutch Colonialism*, ed. Julia Clancy-Smith and Frances Gouda (Charlottesville: University Press of Virginia, 1998), 193–210.

5   Tahar Ben Jelloun, "1962, les derniers jours de l'Algérie française," *Le monde diplomatique* 54, no. 642 (September 2007): 2.

6   Dennis Adams, *Double Feature* (New York: Kent Gallery, 2008), 5–7.

7   The importance of orality in constructing neighborhoods is hinted at in Arthur Pellegin's *Le Vieux Tunis: Les noms des rues de la ville arabe* (Tunis: Offprint from the *Bulletin économique et social de la Tunisie*, 1952).

8   Jacques Berque, *Structures sociales du Haut-Atlas,* 1st ed. (Paris: Presses Universitaires de France, 1955); see also Pierre Bourdieu's notion of *habitus* in *Practical Reason: On the Theory of Action* (Cambridge: Polity Press, 1998).

9   Dennis Adams, *The Architecture of Amnesia* (New York: Kent Fine Art, 1990), 86.

10 Joshua Hammer, "Save the Casbah," *Smithsonian* 38, no. 4 (July 2007): 36–37. This article demonstrates the difficulty inherent in demythologizing some of the most pernicious notions of Algeria, Algiers, and particularly the Casbah. Hammer reiterates the clichés about the Casbah, stating that it "conjured up both Arab exoticism and political turbulence" and summing up its history as "a refuge for pirates, freedom fighters, Islamic militants and petty thieves, all of whom found easy anonymity in its alleys and houses sequestered behind imposing stone walls."

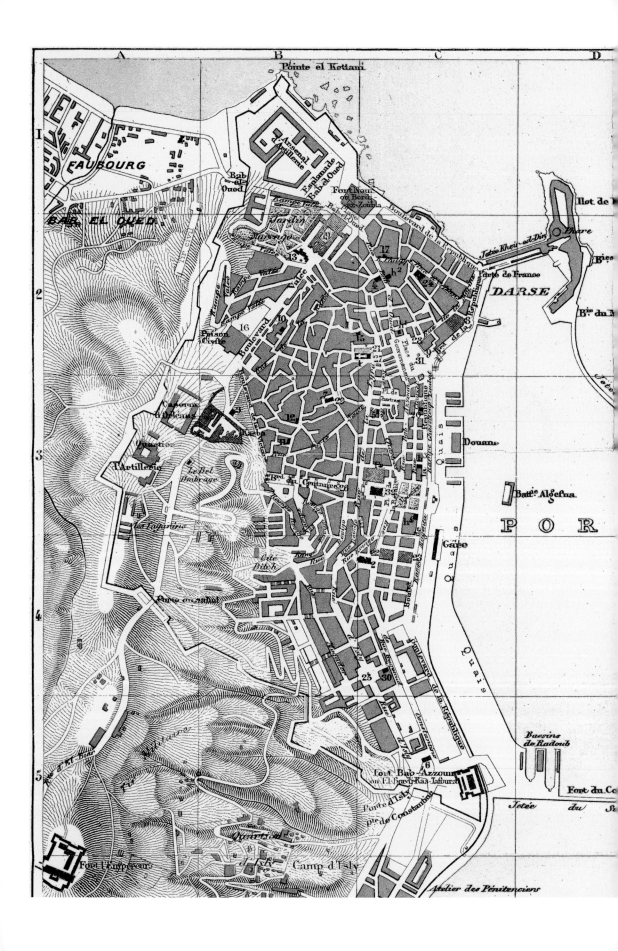

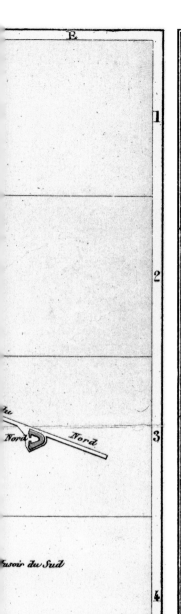

LÉGENDE:

1 Cathédrale St Philippe B.C.2
2 Église St Augustin C.4
3 id. Ste Croix B.3
4 id. N.D. des Victoires C.2
5 Temple protestant C.3
6 Chapelle Anglicane C.5
7 Synagogue B.3
8 Djama Kébir C.2
9 id. Djedid C.2
10 id. Sidi Ramdan B.2
11 id. Safir B.3
12 Zaouïa Mohammed ech-Chérif B.3
13 Zaouïa Abd-er-Rahman-et-T'çalbi B.2
14 Académie militaire C.3
15 Bibliothèque et Musée B.C.2
16 Prison B.2
17 Direction du Génie C.2
18 Hôpital civil B.C.2.8
19 Lycée B.2
20 Mairie C.3
21 Palais du Gouverneur B.C.2
22 id. de Justice C.4
23 Postes, Télégraphe et Trésor C.4
24 Préfecture C.2
25 Place Bugeaud (Ste du Maréchal) C.4
26 id. de la Lyre (Marché couvert) B.3
27 id. Malakoff C.2
28 id. Mahon (Marché aux fruits) C.2
29 id. Randon B.3
30 Société des Beaux-Arts C.4
31 Statue du Duc d'Orléans C.2
32 Théâtre National C.3

Principaux Hôtels

h¹ Hôtel de la Régence C.2
h² „ de Paris C.2
h³ „ de l'Oasis C.3
h⁴ „ de l'Europe C.3

MAP Louis Piesse, *Algérie et Tunisie: Collection des Guides-Joanne*, Paris: Librairie Hachette, 1888.

PEOPLES

1

EXOTICISM, ERASURES, AND ABSENCE

THE PEOPLING OF ALGIERS, 1830–1900

Julia Clancy-Smith

The violence of the French conquest of Algiers and rumors of atrocities against Muslims caused many city residents to flee during the summer of 1830 either to the countryside or to neighboring countries while the ruler, Hussein Dey, his family, and many Ottoman notables abandoned the country. As many as ten thousand left Algiers out of a total population of some 40,000; while some remained permanently in exile in Tunisia, Morocco, or parts of the Ottoman Empire, others returned only to find their homes, businesses, and streets occupied by the invaders.[1] The French expeditionary force numbered at least 64,000 men—one and a half times the size of the capital's population. The enormous army quartered in, and around, Algiers required vast quantities of food and supplies. One of the first tasks confronting Algeria's new masters was to re-populate the capital as well as attract immigrants, hopefully from France, to settle nearby in yet-to-be-constructed colonial villages. But herein lay the conundrum. Unlike many European regions at the time, such as Italy or the Mediterranean islands, France was not overpopulated—quite the opposite. And, aside from specific regions, such as the Auvergne, that traditionally exported their youth, the French, compared with other nations, were somewhat reluctant to leave home for distant lands.[2] Many of those arriving in Algiers from 1830 on were "uninvited guests"—spontaneous subsistence migrants from Sicily, Sardinia, Corsica, Malta, Spain, and the Balearic and Greek islands. Unregulated immigration from non-French nations must have dramatically increased soon after the invasion because, as early as April 1831, a law was passed "establishing penalties for ship captains who disembarked passengers not in possession of passports."[3]

What forces impelled tens of thousands of these people to cross the Mediterranean and fan out across French Algeria? And what did their successive implantations in Algiers mean for the capital city and ultimately the entire country, as well as for France and the French Empire? Overpopulation, the presence of latifundia on densely populated islands, such as Sicily, environmental degradation, and political upheaval were the major push factors causing the settlers to abandon their homelands in search of land and work in Africa. In colonial Algeria several types of official settlement programs existed: military land grants to ex-army officers; private experiments in colonization, often utopian in nature; and state-sponsored schemes. Yet, in the pre-1870 period, many of the newly arrived enjoyed neither French nationality nor any connection to France and thus had little hope of legally acquiring land.[4] For them rumors of wages two to four times higher than those offered in Malta or Sicily made Algeria a magnet for unskilled laborers.[5] Most of these "not-quite-Europeans" flocked to coastal cities, where they joined the ranks of the indigenous urban poor. As such, they posed problems of policing and heightened local antagonisms as well as intercommunal conflicts. They also brought with them very different traditions in terms of the construction, organization, and use of built space—for example, the distinctions between private and public space differed from one group to the next. Indeed, many were from island villages and thoroughly unfamiliar with urban life.

Migration to, and permanent settlement in, nineteenth-century Algiers constituted a major stimulus for political, cultural, and social transformations which endure even today. The influx of these settlers altered the uses of urban spaces: from the peopling of streets by Mediterranean women, novel forms of leisure and entertainment such as theater, gaming, and sea-bathing, to perceived increases in morally reprehensible acts, like public drunkenness, prostitution, and street fights.[6] While some urban practices changed beyond recognition, others continued in more or less the same manner; still others slipped in and out of customary usages and meanings. Tourism, which took off in the 1840s, also altered the urban landscape of Algiers, as did dramatic improvements in Mediterranean transportation. In short, the constant coming and going of diverse peoples from around the Mediterranean Basin to Algeria after 1830 introduced different practices of daily life, new hierarchies, and novel identities, while older forms of sociability were preserved.

From a political and ideological perspective, however, the peopling of colonial Algiers was fraught with contradictions and ironies, provoking Alexis de

Tocqueville's ire after his fact-finding mission to the colony. In his 1847 report to the French Parliament regarding conditions there, Tocqueville quipped something to the effect that France has hunted down the Arab population of Algeria to people the country with Sicilians, Maltese, and Spaniards. A report by a French official in 1842 illustrates the kind of welcome immigrants received when debarking in the capital city: "Possessed of a temperament where African blood dominates, degraded by misery, totally uneducated, and without any moral instruction, the Maltese arrive in our colonies with their native ignorance, their industrious spirit driven by need and stimulated by self-interest."[7]

Since the majority of Mediterranean settlers were unlettered, they rarely committed their lives and aspirations, joys and disappointments, to paper. Middle-class travelers, touring Algeria and Tunisia in ever-greater numbers after mid-century, frequently slighted these people in travel accounts, fixing instead on Islamic exotica or Roman ruins. For bourgeois literati, the "dregs" of European society transplanted to North Africa offered scant literary or artistic inspiration. Indeed, until late in the nineteenth century, Sicilians, Maltese, and other island peoples were considered by northern Europeans as "de race Africaine"—of African race. All of these elements conspired to silence the immigrants, whose voices are faintly heard through filters imposed by illiteracy and by colonial officials or European writers, who, when they did not ignore them, belittled the not-quite-Europeans. Moreover, in nontextual representations, the subsistence migrants are conspicuous by their relative absence as well. Whether in illustrations accompanying travel narratives, Orientalist art, or photography, they were partially or fully excised. By the end of the nineteenth century, however, Mediterranean folk were often satirized in highly stereotyped caricatures reproduced in popular postcards.[8] Of course, it was not only the poor who relocated to France's newest colony, which also attracted schemers, speculators, investors, and other bankers and pashas. And along with the mainly Catholic migrants came Catholic missionaries, who introduced private schools, hospitals, and orphanages. Efforts were made to convert Algerian Muslims—above all, the Berber-speaking Kabyles residing in mountain villages—to Christianity, but with limited success, apart from orphans or abandoned children. In the long run, modern education gradually erased many of the differences between immigrant groups, while giving voice to the Mediterranean flotsam who peopled North Africa, the foremost example being the writer Albert Camus (1913–60), who was born in Mondovi, Algeria.[9]

In this chapter I will argue that immigration to nineteenth-century Algiers poses problems for the historian that revolve around presence and absence. While indigenous Algerians, especially women, came to be amply depicted in colonial image and text, the growing Mediterranean community was signaled by a striking absence.[10] Juxtaposing textual discussions of the settlers with visual representations, the historian confronts a paradox—many of these peoples are not represented or are underrepresented. In other words, the island folk who flooded into the colony after 1830 looking for work and land might be characterized as the visual "present absents." How does one begin to think about these absences? What meanings are implicit in visual negation? Do they stem from an ideological project, an ideal image of French Algeria, deemed politically "appropriate" by the metropole or by those in power in Algiers?

To answer these questions, I will analyze key moments between 1830 and 1930. The first is the late Ottoman and early conquest period running from about 1829 to 1870. The second moment stretches from 1870 to the turn of the century, which witnessed a new wave of immigration to Algeria from mainland France as well as passage of the landmark 1889 naturalization law. The final moment covers the period from about 1900 to 1930, when French Algeria reached its apogee. However, among these three moments, the first is emphasized because it has been the least studied, and by concentrating our attention here, one can trace the elaboration of an implicit visual canon that determined which groups were represented and how, and which were minimized or erased. In addition, the scholarship devoted to the French conquest of Algiers continues to see that event as a prodigious break; in consequence, the historical narrative tends toward rupture. And, indeed, 1830 produced multiple ruptures, above all, in language and linguistic-based identities. For example, the Turkish language rapidly disappeared after 1830, and French, Maltese, Spanish, and Italian were superimposed upon indigenous Berber (Amazigh) and Arabic languages. Nevertheless, revisiting the notion of rupture allows us to detect the disappearance of certain groups, practices, identities, and their visual representations. Moreover, by triangulating text and image of both the native populace of Algiers, who were themselves extremely heterogeneous before the conquest, and the diverse newcomers, I argue for continuity as well as disjuncture—in unexpected realms.

In sum, the invasion and conquest meant that Algiers became a critical hub in Mediterranean-wide migratory currents that included other port cities or islands, such as Minorca, Tunis, La Valletta, Marseille, Toulon, Bastia, and so forth. The positioning of the capital in this system of displacements exerted an enormous impact upon the built environment, upon the creation and use of different kinds of urban spaces, and upon the very identity of the city and its inhabitants. By scaling walls and viewing "les murs d'Alger" from above, from within and without, older binary constructions that perceived only two groups—French and Algerian—are dismantled. In other words, this story chronicles the processes whereby "not-quite-Europeans" became "not-quite-Frenchmen and women," while Moors, Turks, Kulughlis, Berbers, Arabs, and sub-Saharan peoples were gradually transformed into *indigènes*, "indigenous, or native, people," a category structured by legal and social inequality.[11]

Let's open by asking what would a *flâneur*, or stroller, in the streets of Algiers just prior to the summer of 1830 have seen and whom would he or she have encountered? Our stroller would have noted that city streets, markets, residential neighborhoods, and the port were occupied by a diverse array of peoples, races, ethnic groups, and religions, a legacy of the past centuries that merits a brief historical digression. After Algiers was incorporated into the Ottoman Empire in the sixteenth century, the city became a major Mediterranean port whose positioning along the fluid borders between Christianity and Islam was expressed by its sobriquet: "The Bulwark of Islam." Turkish, Balkan, and Circassian ethnic elements were added through immigration into the largely Arab-Berber mix, which included both Muslims and Jews. In addition, privateering, or corsair, activity represented both economic operations and forms of political contestation in which all states adjacent to the Mediterranean actively participated. The trade in Muslim and Christian captives through the ransom racket was practiced by most maritime powers in the seventeenth and eighteenth centuries and further increased the ethnic plurality of ports such as Algiers, which may have boasted 50,000 inhabitants in its heyday. Renegades, including adventurer-sailors from Adriatic or Greek islands, the Balkans, and elsewhere, converted to Islam and melded with the local populace. The centuries-old practice of assimilating Christian renegades into the fabric of North African society was an important element in the Maghreb's intense involvement in the Mediterranean world. Many converts acted as cultural and diplomatic brokers—as multiple translators—between Europe, North Africa, and the Sublime Porte. Mediterranean social intermediaries, such as renegades, occupied liminal spaces between Islam and Christianity, between Ottoman and European states, thereby blurring and complicating categories considered stable and fixed. By the eighteenth century's close, however, the Mediterranean-wide corsair economy and culture were in eclipse as new kinds of powerful states arose on the sea's northern rim.

Eighteenth- and nineteenth-century European treatments of the precolonial population usually named seven "races": Moors, Jews, Arabs, Berbers, Negroes, Turks, and Kulughlis. Let's begin with the last category: a Turkish term, *kulughli* means literally "son of a slave" and designated the offspring of unions between Algerian Muslim Arab women and Turkish soldiers, who were largely recruited from Anatolia, the Balkans, or the Black Sea regions. In the Ottoman system as practiced in Algeria, the Kulughli theoretically was excluded from inheriting or holding military positions. Interestingly enough, the offspring of Christian Mediterranean women, taken captive, were regarded as Turks. However, Shuval argues that the military corps by about 1800 had come to include "indigenous" Algerians due to the inability to draft sufficient recruits from the Ottoman heartlands.[12] On the other hand, despite the admission of locals into the militia, ethnic-based distinctions between the civilian population and the warrior or military class appeared to have been maintained. The residential geography of the city reflected to a degree some of these differences, which were often constructed from a combination of elements—profession, religion, and ethnic origin, particularly language.

The city was divided into two main districts: the elite hill, or mountain (al-jabal), was home to the Turkish ruling caste, their households, servants, slaves, and clients. Considered semiprivate domestic space, the upper city was composed of about fifty small neighborhoods. The lower city (al-wati') stretched to the Mediterranean and sheltered a much more socially heterogeneous mix of peoples due in large measure to proximity to the port. Also found were major mosques, military barracks for the janissaries, and the Dar al-Sultan, or Janina Palace, built in the 1550s as the residence of the deys. The transversal artery connecting the central souks with Bab el-Oued and Bab Azoun was the largest thoroughfare in the city. Caravanserais provided accommodations and storage for traders from elsewhere in Algeria or from other parts of Africa or the Ottoman Empire. Taverns run by Algerian Jews or foreign Christians and cafés were also found here, particularly adjacent to the docks. The Jewish quarter, which sheltered about 5,000 Algerian Jews, was located in the lower city, although Jews, including large numbers of Italian traders from Leghorn, also resided elsewhere in precolonial Algiers. The "quarter of the Franks" housed roughly one hundred Europeans, mainly consular representatives-cum-merchants, who maintained close patronage ties with the rulers; the deys also rented out lovely villas set in the hills above Algiers to European diplomats.[13] Temporary laborers from the Sahara or the Kabylia, known as barraniya (outsiders), found shelter in the lower city, where they often worked as porters. African or Circassian slaves were mainly concentrated in middle-class or elite households, for whom they labored as domestic servants. Merchants from Anatolia, the Maghreb, sub-Saharan Africa, Europe, and the Mediterranean world traded in the lower city. Fishermen from Sicily and Sardinia harvesting tuna, coral, and sponge were seasonal visitors—and competitors—as well.

The Christian population of Algiers, composed largely of European traders, diplomatic representatives or consuls, and captives, dropped dramatically in the fourteen years separating 1830 from Lord Exmouth's 1816 expedition, which constituted a sort of rehearsal for the French conquest. In the spring and summer of 1816, a huge Anglo-Dutch naval force bombarded Algiers and put into other North African ports where treaties were imposed upon local rulers. Exmouth's ostensible objective was to liberate some 3,000 Christians held in Algiers, Tunis, and Tripoli.[14] Over one thousand captives from a wide range of European nations were released from slavery or servitude in Algiers alone. Christian slavery theoretically came to an end, as did the corsair economy, and relations between European powers and the Turkish military oligarchy in Algiers returned more or less to normal except for the matter of outstanding debts owed by France to Algeria.

On 1 January 1830, the British vice-consul stationed in Algiers, Alexandre Tulin, observed in his diplomatic logbook: "Nothing particular has occurred today." On 14 March he noted something rather different, even alarming: "By the arrival yesterday evening of a small Spanish vessel from Alicante, positive information has been received that the French are preparing an expedition against Algiers."[15] At the end of that month, British ships arrived in Algiers to transport the families of the Spanish, Danish, English, and American diplomatic representatives to safety in Malta or Minorca. The foreign exodus was triggered by Charles X's announcement of his decision to invade the country—despite domestic opposition—made in March 1830 to the Chamber of Deputies. The pretext for military adventure was a long-simmering crisis unleashed in 1827 when Hussein Dey allegedly struck the French consul, Pierre Deval, with a bejeweled fly whisk during an altercation over unpaid debts going back to the Napoleonic Wars.

The members of the French 1830 expedition, whether military or civilian, arrived with their own preconceived notions of, and prejudices about, not only Muslims, Turks, and Arabs, but also other ethnic, religious, and cultural groups. One detects echoes of the earlier Napoleonic occupation of Egypt in some northern European appraisals of southern Mediterranean folk in Algeria, particularly women of ordinary means.[16] Indeed, some of those involved in the invasion of Algeria had connections with the Egyptian campaign. In similar fashion, military draftsmen, artists, and, later, photographers perceived sites with eyes trained elsewhere—in other Mediterranean port cities, for example. In his two-volume *Alger: Voyage politique et descriptif*, the French writer Évariste Bavoux admitted that he "saw Naples" when he gazed upon Algiers for the first time in 1840: "Algiers is situated in a majestic gulf whose shape and bright colors bring to mind one of the most beautiful of nature's works: the gulf of Naples."[17] Thus, one question revolves around how older mental landscapes and ways of seeing were altered once large numbers of Europeans arrived in North Africa for the first time.

In violation of written agreements, the French army seized private, state, and religious buildings, looted homes, pillaged the treasury, burned the state archives, and expropriated or simply occupied vast portions of the country's arable land—so much for French promises of security for property and respect for native women that had been solemnly pledged to Algerine notables, whose fortunes plummeted as their traditional sources of wealth and status were destroyed. In 1832 the military began systematically demolishing Ottoman-Islamic Algiers by digging up Muslim cemeteries for road building and converting the Ketchaoua Mosque into a cathedral. The ancient core of the city was ripped open to make way for European structures and monumental spaces. When Alexis de Tocqueville visited in 1841, he noted with disapproval: "The entire lower town seems in a state of destruction and reconstruction. On all sides, one sees nothing but recent ruins, buildings going up; one hears nothing but the noise of the hammer."[18] Until the 1839 insurrection, the surrounding hills, however, were still densely populated by Algerians. After the uprising's defeat, these villages too lost their age-old inhabitants and were occupied largely by impoverished immigrants from southern Europe or Mediterranean islands. The Chamber of Deputies allocated huge sums of public monies to settle ex-soldiers and Catholic monks there as well as non-French migrant laborers—which eventually provoked a political uproar in Paris.

Some of the first settlers to arrive in search of land or work were from Spain's Balearic Islands. Indeed, soon after 1830, an entire Spanish village was re-created outside Bab el-Oued that conflated ethnic origin with a particular kind of trade—stone quarrying—and a specific space. The large numbers of Spanish islanders in Algiers sprang from the fact that the French expedition employed the port of Mahon on Minorca to supply the fleet and army, for medical evacuations, and as a source of casual labor—despite the Spanish government's interdiction upon emigration by its subjects without state permission. For the French in Algeria, the Balearic Islands held the same strategic importance in the Mediterranean as Malta did for the English. Indeed, of all the non-French groups to settle Algeria, the Spanish were the most numerous, with Sicilians and Italians second.[19]

In 1847, a military administrator, Captain Ernest Carette, inventoried the city's peoples. Of the slightly more than 100,000 inhabitants of Algiers and its suburbs, nearly one-quarter were categorized administratively as "indigène," understood in that period to encompass Muslims, Jews, and "Nègres." European nationals from over fourteen countries numbered 68,734 individuals; of these, fewer than half were French citizens, about 32,000. Finally, as much as 10 percent of the city's populace was characterized as "floating"—sailors, indigents, those without fixed domicile, refugees, criminals, etc.[20] In summary, the French invasion—and more importantly the decision to make Algeria a settler colony—transformed the city's orientation from networks of exchange privileging the Ottoman Empire to a north-south axis linking Algeria closely with France and the central or western Mediterranean. Less than two decades after France's occupation, Algiers had become a city of newly arrived minorities.

The erasure of the Mediterranean migrants despite, or because of, the fact that their presence became increasingly visible with each passing year, not only in the capital but also throughout the country, is most obvious in the representation of urban spaces invested with gradations of publicness: the central square, the port, side streets, and a major entryway to the city. These are the kinds of places where one would expect to find ethnic diversity under conditions of rapid in-migration.

The Swiss artist Adolphe Otth, who visited Algeria in the late 1830s, created a lithograph of a square bustling with activity (fig. 1.1). In the text accompanying his suite of lithographs published in 1839, Otth remarked that "the central square in Algiers has become a sort of meeting place for the entire population. Each morning, the market is frequented by Kabyles, Biskris, Kulughlis, Africans, Jews, Spanish, and French. German is spoken here in addition to Arabic, Kabyle, Spanish, French, etc."[21] In the 1840s the same square was similarly described by the French officer and exceptionally acute observer Carette: "above the sea, at the foot of the Moorish city, is a large space known as 'place du gouvernement.' A noisy meeting place, open to all religions, all passions, this bustling space is situated halfway between East and West."[22] In early visual sources, the recently arrived subsistence migrants from southern Europe and the Mediterranean islands are discretely tucked away—apart from soldiers, who are quite visible—while the Algerians, recognizable by their costumes, are foregrounded to emphasize the exotic and picturesque. A pattern was emerging.

Unlike many artists from this period, whose production was directly connected to military conquest, Otth was motivated by personal artistic and intellectual concerns, which confer upon his work a certain independent authority. Otth's interest in Algiers was probably sparked by representations of the city circulating in Europe that were inspired by the monumental panorama of Exmouth's expedition painted by the English artist Henry Aston Barker (1774–1856) and exhibited in London in 1818 and by the even more realistic panorama of the French conquest painted by Charles Langlois (1789–1870) and mounted in Paris for eighteen months in 1833 and 1834. One wonders if Otth himself

1.1   *The Palace of the Dey* (Janina Palace) *and the Market in Algiers*, Adolphe Otth, lithograph (Otth, *Esquisses africaines, dessinées pendant un voyage à Alger et lithographiées par Adolphe Otth* [Berne: J. F. Wagner, 1839], pl. 30)

had viewed the Paris panorama, since he studied drawing in the French capital for six months prior to visiting North Africa. The invasion greatly increased the circulation of textual and visual material on Algeria in Europe. To ascertain the veracity of these representations, Otth left his native Berne in 1837 and journeyed through Lyon, the Rhône Valley, and the Provence until he reached Toulon, where he embarked for Mahon. From Minorca, the ship made a stop in Bône (or Bougie), where the Swiss traveler witnessed the aftermath of the small port's virtual destruction by the French army. In any case, Otth has left us with important portrayals of the country's principal port, Algiers, in its transition from Turkish to French rule.

Under the Turks, Algiers had boasted quarantine facilities, customs houses, a state port authority, and European consular offices to verify ship manifests as well as passports and merchandise. Port facilities were expanded by French military engineers, often employing immigrant labor, and resulted in a spectacular increase in maritime traffic, both military and merchant, which heightened the cosmopolitan nature of the capital. Moreover, since roads in the interior were in poor condition or dangerous to traverse—only the army or those under military escort ventured into the hinterland around Algiers—much of the circulation between other Algerian towns captured by the French army and the capital city was by small boats rather than overland. Of course, as conditions improved, metropole officials, military personnel, travelers, traders, and immigrants debarked in Algiers from various parts of France, Europe, or the Mediterranean world in increasing numbers.

Otth's image of the port of Algiers (fig. 1.2) and its accompanying text have a number of intriguing aspects. He states that "the small boats in the harbor are sailed by Negroes, Moors, and Arabs." Who are these sailors, what do these descriptors mean? The sailors could have hailed from any number of ports, small and large, along the Algerian or North African coast. Moreover, dock work had

1.2   *The Port of Algiers Seen from the Docks*, Adolphe Otth, lithograph (Otth, *Esquisses africaines*, pl. 23)

traditionally been monopolized by certain ethnic groups, specifically the Biskris from the oases in the Constantine, although the Maltese and Sicilians would subsequently find employment as dockworkers. Also, Otth inserts sound into this image textually by recording the noises heard in a busy port: "the songs of European sailors and the raucous voices of indigenous sailors and porters which deafen the ear from dawn until dusk." An important question arises here: who is a European in the context of the period? Are Maltese, Sicilian, Greek, or Spanish sailors or dockworkers considered "European"? And who exactly was being collapsed into, or excluded from, this newly emerging category of "indigène"? Moreover, sound or noises, which purely visual evidence has difficulty translating, has a moral content inflected by culture, class, gender, and other variables. Unfamiliar noises and sounds at inappropriate times of day or night could signal moral transgressions to city inhabitants—or to newcomers—accustomed to other auditory repertoires. In short, the peopling of Algiers introduced new, unsettling sounds to the city's original inhabitants and the newcomers alike. These noises presumably would have reached Otth in his room at Hôtel du Nord, which overlooked the port but whose "European comforts made one forget that one was in Africa," which suggests that the hotel's interior, its curiously familiar spaces, clashed with the unfamiliar sounds emanating from the nearby port. In any case, sound is a kind of space, a morally resonant place, which historians of the city need to take into account.

Finally, one is struck by the female figures in this image. On the left is probably an Algerian Jewish woman, judging by her headdress. On the right, under the arcade, two Moorish women, once again judging by dress, are conversing. Coded as male space, docks were not generally places of female sociability because proximity to the Mediterranean rendered them dangerous. In the eyes of both Algerians and Europeans at the time, ports were culturally and sexually promiscuous and therefore locators of vice, although the extent to which these attitudes governed the use of that morally suspect space in the pre-1830 period is impossible to ascertain in terms of rupture or continuity. However, continuity between the Turkish and French eras can be detected in the arena of work since ethnicity and certain kinds of labor identified with specific city quarters were conflated.

Among the large fund of images devoted to old Algiers are two street scenes that are somewhat unusual since both show Europeans mingling with "native" city inhabitants in the course of daily life. Antoine-Léon Morel-Fatio's view of the souk emphasizes the French soldiers as they visit the various stalls but shows a woman, possibly an Algerian Jew from her head covering, passing through the market (fig. 1.3). Otth's view of a street published in 1839 discreetly depicts

1.3   *Market Scene,*
Antoine-Léon Morel-Fatio,
aquatint, 1810–71 (*Alger:*
Vues dessinées d'après nature/
par Morel-Fatio; et gravées à
l'aquatinte par Vögel [Paris:
Rittner et Goupil, c. 1840])

a European woman, dressed in a bonnet and accompanied by a French soldier, bargaining with an Algerian trader. In general, however, one rarely finds illustrations from this period of European women in Algiers, whose absence is not only intriguing but also significant.

In 1839, the year that Otth's image was published, population estimates for European civilians in Algiers revealed severe male-female imbalances—as is true of most immigrant societies in the earlier stages. For the French army, the matter was pressing; thus, the command arranged for "the importation of a substantial cohort of prostitutes, for whom every effort was undertaken to aid their arrival."[23] In addition, one of the first administrative acts of the French army was to regulate prostitution, according to Carette: "On the 12th of June [1831], the municipality of Algiers was given the legal right to control 'public women'; this measure complemented the decree issued on the 11th of August, 1830, establishing a medical dispensary. This measure so necessary for public health should have been taken earlier since the disorders (sexual) that this law aimed at ending had already made deplorable inroads."[24] In 1835, the governor of Algiers created villages in the suburbs around Algiers to provide food and supplies to the city. In some of these newly established villages, the French population was negligible, and due to chaos, disorganization, and the lack of competent personnel, tavern-keepers served as quartermasters or suppliers. In addition, legal marriages were rare for all early immigrant groups; at least one-third of the children born to French nationals were "enfants naturels," or illegitimate.[25] Could the paucity of images of European women in the historical record be partially explained by the textually well-documented presence of camp followers and the haphazard nature of efforts to settle and accommodate the "not-quite-Europeans" who flocked unchecked to the colony in this period? This striking visual absence becomes all the more significant because images of Algerian Muslim women in later-nineteenth-century sources increase precipitously.

This question brings us back once again to North Africa's changing relationship with both Europe and the Ottoman Empire as the nineteenth century wore on. Both Algeria and Tunisia served as dumping grounds for political undesirables and ne'er-do-wells—as a sort of "New World" for social classes unable to cope with the dislocations of nation-state building and industrial capitalism in western Europe. Indeed, the Mediterranean Sea functioned as an open-air, floating prison for criminals of all nationalities, who were often forced on board ships in one port city or another and dispatched without papers to neighboring ports. Otth seems to confirm this when he states that the streets of Algiers were perfectly safe—and this from an inhabitant of Berne, one of the sleepiest European cities at the time. Murders and robberies were not perpetrated by the natives but rather by the "nothing but undesirable Christians that the galleys and the prisons of Europe have vomited up upon this country since its conquest by the French." Once again, legislation enacted for the capital confirms what our artists say; because of the number of murders, the bearing of firearms was forbidden in the "arrondissement d'Alger" by the decree of 24 March 1831.[26] In any case, the criminalization of specific immigrant groups, which is a pattern in immigrant societies worldwide, may have led to their virtual exclusion from visual representation. Moreover, at certain critical junctures in metropole politics, for example, during the 1848 upheavals, the presence and status of non-French settlers in Algeria would become a burning issue.

Otth was not content to paint scenes of the port from his hotel room but found visual inspiration on the city's outskirts as well. In the Turkish period, the area around Bab Azoun attracted large numbers of rustics and urbanites alike on a daily basis since it was the principal entryway into the central souks. Like the markets, Bab Azoun constituted a space of sociability, being a favored

1.4   *Bab Azoun Gate*, Adolphe Otth, lithograph (Otth, *Esquisses africaines*, pl. 20)

haunt for urban dwellers to take walks, enjoy nature, and revel in magnificent sea vistas. Significantly for the issue of continuity in definition and use of space, Otth states that Bab Azoun was one of the most animated quarters in post-1830 Algiers. Situated at the juncture between countryside and city, it still attracted peasants and mountain tribesmen, who gathered there in large numbers before proceeding into the markets. In addition to exchanges of various kinds, this was a place for entertainment where storytellers, soothsayers, healers, and musicians abounded. Otth's depiction of Bab Azoun (fig. 1.4) with eight Algerians sitting or reclining in the foreground includes a woman clothed in the costume generally worn by non-elite Moorish women at the time. One wonders how to interpret this image. Were norms governing gender segregation in public not in force or not enforced? Was the woman an entertainer, soothsayer, or healer and thus outside the bounds normally restricting male-female interaction in public? Or were the men all close kin? Perhaps Otth inserted this figure into the tableau merely for exotic interest, although his inclusion of a detail heralding the modern seems to argue against improvisation or imagination and for documentary fidelity.

According to Otth, the carriages for hire seen just below the bedouin encampments in the upper-left corner belonged to, or were run by, Frenchmen and provided transportation from country villas surrounding Algiers, where notables and foreign diplomats continued to reside, to the city. While the neighborhood retained, at least for a time, much of its older, preconquest organization, social function, and essence, wheeled transport was a novelty. It is important that Otth chose not to excise the Europeans, who had introduced a visible emblem of modernity—the rental carriage. Finally, in characterizing Bab Azoun's diverse peoples, Otth employs the term "Arab" to refer to bedouins, pastoralists, or tent dwellers, which was more or less its connotation for urban Algerians at the time. The meaning of "Arab" would change dramatically in the course of the nineteenth century as a result of both European imperialism in the region and the Arabic literary renaissance spearheaded by educated Arab writers mainly in the Levant. This brings us to the taxonomies employed to sort, classify, and arrange in hierarchies of power the various peoples residing in Algiers during a period of extraordinary population flux.

In his travel notes from May 1841, Tocqueville, visiting Algiers for the first time, voices the tremendous visual impact that the city exerted upon the European visitor: "I have never seen anything like it. A prodigious mix of races, costumes, Arab, Kabyle, Moor, Negro, Mahonais, French. Each of these races, tossed together in a space much too tight to contain them, speaks its language, wears its attire, display different mores. This whole world moves about with an activity that seems feverish."[27] Among the "races tossed together" was a Polish refugee, the artist Robert Jungmann, who had fled to France just before the invasion of Algeria and subsequently served in the French army for four years before returning to his adopted home, Strasbourg, in 1836, where his work was printed. Although he did street scenes and panoramic views, such as *Vue des moulins à vents*, Jungmann's interest lay principally with portraits of native Algerians, who had long been classified into distinct categories by writers, such as Thomas Shaw, author of the 1738 *Travels or observations relating to several parts of Barbary and the Levant,* which Jungmann had consulted. According to the artist, the natives were divided up into "quite distinct races of men whose difference is due to physical characteristics, *moeurs,* and habits. These are the Moors, Berbers, Arabs, Negroes, Jews, Turks, and Kulughlis, or sons of Turkish fathers and Moorish women."[28] Jungmann portrayed a Kulughli wearing his winter costume (fig. 1.5). Claude-Antoine Rozet, working at the same time as Jungmann, also did a portrait of a "Kulughli, with a burnus [cloak] on his

1.5 *Kulughli in Winter Dress*, Robert Jungmann, colored lithograph (Jungmann, *Costumes, moeurs et usages des Algériens* [Strasbourg: J. Bernard, 1837], pl. 7)

shoulder."[29] All societies have complex systems of classification that shift constantly; significant for the Algerian case is how and why some categories were transformed or disappeared altogether under the impact of conquest and immigration. The Kulughli constituted a parallel construction to the non-French Mediterranean settlers in the period before the 1889 naturalization law because both occupied in-between positions and were products of various kinds of migratory influx to Algeria. The Turk and, with him, the Kulughli vanished rapidly from typologies and thus from visual representation; the same fate awaited the Moor, whose multiple definitions and meanings over time were solely a product of European invention.

The different types of Moors residing in Algiers depicted by Rozet (fig. 1.6) and Jungmann (fig. 1.7) are distinguished mainly by social class and profession, with costume serving as a critical marker. In his treatment of Algeria's races, Rozet admits that the "Moor" encompasses extremely heterogeneous elements; although few families have retained the purity of the original Moorish race by avoiding *misalliance*, Rozet argues that physically Moors are a distinct people nonetheless. While images of exoticized Moorish males persist in European painting, photography, and postcards, the Moorish woman—*la* Mauresque—

1.6 (Above)
A Rich Moor; Moorish Woman in City Dress, with a Sarmah on Her Head, Claude-Antoine Rozet, colored lithograph (Rozet, *Voyage dans la Régence d'Alger* [Paris: Arthus Bertrand, 1833], no plate number)

1.7 (Left)
Moorish Women outside Their Home, Robert Jungmann, colored lithograph (Jungmann, *Costumes, moeurs et usages*, pl. 13)

suffers the most spectacular shift as she is increasingly eroticized during the nineteenth century (see below). Along with Turks and Kulughlis, Moors were folded into a colonial construction without roots whatsoever in Algerian or North African culture or history. In 1831, the legal category "European" was admitted into colonial jurisprudence to impose order and construct a hierarchy of privilege and difference based upon access to French law.[30] The term "European" called forth a binary opposite, the *indigène*, which eventually effaced the older, more intricate taxonomies, such as those enunciated by Rozet and many European authors and painters, or the very real taxonomies extant in precolonial usage, such as Kulughli. *Indigène* evolved into a legal, as well as sociocultural, category signifying and enshrining dispossession, inequality, lack of civilization—indeed, lack of humanity—and encompassed Arabs, Kabyles, Moors, and the descendants of Turks, or Kulughlis. The designation "Moor" or "Mauresque" endured until the late nineteenth and early twentieth centuries, mainly as a sexually suggestive or explicit marketing label imposed by European photographers and painters upon Algerian women, whose images were reproduced in picture postcards by the tens of thousands. Most of these representations were studio portraits constructed in such a way as to give the sensation of a sly, illicit glance into the intimacy of the harem or the interior of the Muslim home.[31]

The title of Jungmann's image, *Moorish Women outside Their Home*, raises the issue of women and gender in public during rapid urban social change. Jungmann, who lifted material verbatim without attribution from Renaudot's pre-1830 *Alger: Tableau*, reported: "[Moorish] Girls can go out of the house only when escorted by their mothers; married women must be accompanied by other women when going out in public. Women of the upper class may go out only at night. Under the last dey, the women of Algiers enjoyed the privilege of having the doors to the city opened at night each time they wanted to go out to the countryside."[32] Whether this was true or not is open to question, although obviously, many earlier practices were swept away by the destruction and reconstruction of the capital, and the influx of female immigrants introduced new norms governing the use and gendering of urban spaces. What is not certain is whether the city's Muslim patriarchs, particularly from the Muslim and Jewish notable class, placed more restrictions after 1830 on women's access to public spaces because of the very fact of foreign occupation, accompanied by radically different gender practices. It seems that Jewish women, however, had traditionally been at more liberty to move around in spaces deemed public in the precolonial era.

Throughout the nineteenth century, Jews constituted an important segment of Algerian society, as their frequent depiction witnesses (figs. 1.8 and 1.9).

1.8   *A Jewish Man*, Vaccari,
lithograph (*Album africain:
Collection de 24 costumes
lithographiés au trait, d'après
nature* [Algiers: Chez l'auteur,
1831], 14)

1.9   *Jewish Women of
Algiers*, Robert Jungmann,
colored lithograph (Jung-
mann, *Costumes, moeurs et
usages*, pl. 10)

After 1830 the Jews remained more or less in the same quarter of Algiers, although they did not constitute a monolithic group by any means. In Laugier de Tassy's *Histoire du royaume d'Alger,* first published in 1725, he noted the number of Italian, Spanish, and French Jews trading and residing in Algiers, most of whom enjoyed the protection of foreign consuls. Moreover, these Jews could live anywhere in the city, although they preferred to reside in quarters where other European merchants did.[33] However, Algerian Arab Jews were subject to residential restrictions and rarely, if ever, intermarried with those from Europe. In accordance with Islamic law and local custom, their inferior sociolegal status vis-à-vis the Muslims was manifest in sumptuary laws governing clothing and in special taxes. Under the Turks, dress had served as one of the principal indicators of difference; clothing laws remained in force until 1834, when they were abolished by French decree. Nevertheless, since clothing was a fundamental element in collective identity, the Jews and many other groups persisted in their older practices for years after the decree. The major distinction gradually came to be European versus non-European clothing for the indigenous Algerian population as well as numerous Mediterranean groups whose dress was similar to "traditional" Algerian costumes. In 1870 the Crémieux laws were enacted, which conferred French nationality upon Algerian Jews by placing them in a legal category distinct from that of their fellow Muslims and thus imposing upon them a different social and political identity.

"Negro" was another category invariably found in European typologies of North Africa's indigenous "races," although "Negro" and "slave" should not be conflated. Prior to 1830, slavery in Algeria (and elsewhere in the Ottoman Empire) was not associated with any specific racial group or particular geographical region. Slaves came from various parts of Africa as well as from the Black Sea and Georgia. Until the 1816 Exmouth expedition, slaves might also be European captives taken in raids or during sea battles. The oases aside, slaves were mainly employed in households as domestic servants or as unskilled laborers for their masters. Black, or African, slavery was not abolished in colonial Algeria until 1848. Images of "Negroes" do not necessarily represent enslaved persons since these individuals could well have been manumitted. In any case, manumission often meant that slaves remained with their former masters' families. In Rozet's image entitled *A Negro Woman in City Dress* (fig. 1.10), the African woman covers her face, although in Jungmann's depiction (see fig. 1.7), we see a Moorish woman apparently accompanied by an African woman whose face is visible. Fisquet attempts to explain differences in female public comportment, opining: "Living among the Moors has caused the Africans to adopt their costumes. . . .

1.10   *Negro of Algiers in Work Clothes; a Negro Woman in City Dress*, Claude-Antoine Rozet, colored lithograph (Rozet, *Voyage dans la Régence d'Alger*, no plate number)

free [African] women dress exactly as Moorish women do, and cover their faces in the same manner, but without being as careful about covering up."[34]

Although a small community of freed persons, and then citizens, of African descent had resided in France for a long time, European writers and painters were struck by the presence of Africans in Algeria in the first decades after the conquest. People of color lost their shock value as the century wore on, probably because Europeans encountered more Africans as the French Empire moved across the Sahara. Later in the century, studio photographs of women and men of African origin were made and sold, but never in the same quantity as images of the highly eroticized "Arab woman." One photograph, dating from 1868 (and possibly by Claude-Joseph Portier), evokes Fisquet's argument about the African servant's laxness in completely covering her face while in public, although concealment was tied to social class (fig. 1.11). Popular postcards with caricatures of blacks (see below) were produced—as were satirical cartoons depicting other groups—but sub-Saharan Africans evolved into little more than

1.11 *Moorish Woman and Her Servant*, attributed to Claude-Joseph Portier, albumen photograph, 1868 (photograph album: *Views and Peoples of Algeria*, 1868, pl. 16; Getty Research Institute, 2002.R.9)

an ethnographic curiosity by the fin-de-siècle. In any case, race was a fluid category in North Africa due to extensive intermarriage, and it should also be recalled that Maltese and Sicilians were considered "de race Africaine" for much of the nineteenth century. If sub-Saharan Africans were often associated with domestic service in both the precolonial and colonial periods, another group of diverse peoples were defined by geographical origins as well as types of labor performed.

The term "Biskri" was inherited from the Turkish era and designated temporary workers from the desert who resided in Algiers and were under the supervision of a local master, or *amin*. Before the conquest, they enjoyed a mo-

1.12 *The Sea Gate*, Robert Jungmann, colored lithograph (Jungmann, *Costumes, moeurs et usages*, pl. 14)

nopoly over city bakeries, portage, and public works projects and were prized as "trusted servants."[35] During the 1830s, Rozet recorded the following scene: "along the quays of the port of Algiers the beehive of the Biskris buzzes with activity. You should see these Auvergants of Algeria, an energetic and hardworking race, carrying the heaviest of loads . . . running from port to city" (fig. 1.12).[36] The association that Rozet makes between the inhabitants of the French Auvergne and the Biskris is quite apt because in this period the Auvergne was a region of limited agricultural resources and thus exported its surplus workers to cities like Paris where they monopolized certain trades and professions. A decade later, Fisquet characterized the Biskris—the migrant workers from the oases—in similar fashion, yet also observed that a severe labor shortage had substantially raised wages, attracting many more manual laborers from all over.[37] After 1830, in addition to dock work and portage, the Biskris served as night guards in the city proper, particularly in predominantly Algerian neighborhoods. However, as the nineteenth century progressed, older customs and norms governing work eroded, and Biskris even labored on European-owned agricultural estates. Ethnically defined labor in the port persisted for decades after 1830, although the workers filling these roles later on hailed from a vastly different region—from Mediterranean islands and not islands in seas of sand. Although the French military had to rely upon the Biskris for unloading at the docks, they mistrusted them because of their information-gathering and rumor-mongering activities, which seemed to encourage numerous revolts against the occupiers as the French army penetrated into the distant reaches of the Sahara.[38] Ethnically defined military units had existed under the Turks but for reasons that differed from the social and economic forces that created temporary labor migration from the oases. As was the practice in many states at the time, the Turkish military had employed tribal auxiliaries or mercenaries, who were ethnically apart from the urban populace, as a shrewd political move; among these troops were, first and foremost, the Zouaoua.

The Berber-speaking Zouaoua tribes had long resided in the high Jurjura Range of the Kabylia in eastern Algeria. Fierce warriors, the Zouaoua (rendered as "Zouaves" in French military discourse) had been recruited for centuries as infantry for the deys of Algiers and beys of Tunis. Their ethnic difference made them particularly attractive to central governments, which were always concerned about military rebellions on the part of regular army units. The colonial army continued using them as recruits, raising the number of battalions to three by 1838. With the formation of the *tirailleurs algériens* composed of exclusively Algerian native corps, the Zouaves became purely French in recruitment and in composition, in a sense, nationalized. In 1860 a papal Zouave corps was formed in Rome, and soon thereafter an American unit was organized and fought in the Civil War, an interesting trajectory for an institution of Turkish-Berber origins. Each time that the Zouaves were adopted into another army, their costume was slightly altered, although its main characteristics remained to identify them. In Camus's autobiographical *Le premier homme* (*The First Man*), the protagonist's father enrolled in the colonial Zouaves in 1914 and was sent into the trenches in Europe wearing a straw hat and garbed in the typical neo-Oriental-styled bright blue and red uniform.[39] Jungmann's image of two Algerian Zouaves (fig. 1.13) from the 1830s is indeed precious since he documents the corps before it was converted into something else. Historically speaking, the Zouaves and the Kulughlis are similar in that they both were products of Algero-Ottoman history; "Zouave" denoted an ethnically bounded military contingent, while "Kulughli" designated mixed parentage, which in turn limited state (above all, military) employment and thus social privilege and status. As mentioned above, the Kulughlis disappeared altogether; the Zouaves underwent extensive internal change as well as being adapted to European and American military systems,

1.13 *Zouaves,* Robert Jungmann, colored lithograph (Jungmann, *Costumes, moeurs et usages,* pl. 17)

where they endured principally in name and in the form of an eccentric, colorful uniform. The carnage of the Great War put an end to the Zouaves and to Camus's father.

As forms of military organization were being exported from Algeria, militant missionaries arrived to tend to the army and the civilian settlers and to attempt to convert the Jews and Muslims. The early settlers often came to Algeria in lamentable condition. For example, in 1846, hundreds of destitute German families were dumped on the coast near Oran. They had not originally set out for Algeria but rather for South America via the North Sea port of Dunkerque. Unable to pay their passage to Brazil and a financial liability for Dunkerque's inhabitants, the hapless Germans were dispatched to western Algeria, where most eventually perished of malnutrition and disease.[40] The suppression of the Revolution of 1848 during Napoleon III's coup d'état meant that thousands of political undesirables were exiled from French cities, especially Paris, to Algeria, among them a number of women, including the Socialist activist and educator Pauline Roland. Regarded as needing strict institutional supervision, these women, who had been forcibly transported from France often without their families, were placed in convents that female Catholic orders were establishing in the new colony. The disorganized nature of the first decades of settlement led the military to welcome, or at least tolerate, missionaries, although many French officers were Saint-Simonians and hostile to the church and religion generally. Others feared that proselytizing would spark more rebellions among the Algerian Muslims.

The Catholic presence in Algeria signaled both a rupture and continuity because until the 1816 Exmouth expedition, members of male redemptionist orders had resided in Algiers to tend to the Christian captives, prevent their conversion to Islam, and try to obtain their ransom. However, females in religious orders were quite a novelty; the first female Catholic missionary order to arrive in North Africa was the Soeurs de Saint-Joseph de l'Apparition, founded by Émilie de Vialar in 1832. Their purpose was to civilize the "not-quite-Europeans" — the Mediterranean subsistence migrants and the "fallen women" who accompanied the army — as much as the native Algerians. Independently wealthy, Vialar was able to establish a significant missionary presence in Algiers by purchasing an enormous building suitable for a convent and social welfare activities in the upper city precisely because the French army had requisitioned so many residential structures belonging to the Algerian elite.[41] Other Catholic orders, such as the Jesuits, came in the 1840s, as did Protestant missionaries hoping to convert the "heathen" Muslims and Jews, although they had little success. The best-known group was the Société des Missionaires d'Afrique, known as the Pères Blancs and Soeurs Blanches because of their white habits; the order was founded by Charles-Martial Lavigerie (1825–92), who was named archbishop of Algiers in 1867 and was a very controversial figure in the annals of French colonialism.[42] The relationship between the church and the colonial state was always fraught and reflected ongoing struggles, frequently very bitter, in the metropole between militant secularists or republican anticlerical parties and the Catholic establishment.

Images of missionaries in Algeria are most commonly found as early-twentieth-century postcards since the orders used this medium to solicit funding by advertising their mission and good deeds. A prime example by the Soeurs Missionaires de Notre-Dame d'Afrique shows the *maison mère* of Lavigerie's White Sisters located at Birmandreïs in the suburbs of Algiers.[43] On the back is spiritual advertising for the order's postulate in Lille, including a map and its postal checking account number, encouraging both vocations and donations. Another missionary postcard-cum-religious promotion was published by the

1.14 *Missions d'Afrique, Saint-Charles, the Clinic,* photomechanical print, postcard (Getty Research Institute, 970031)

Missions d'Afrique, Saint Charles; it is typical in its depiction of Muslims or Africans and illustrates a classic missionary pose: the dispensing of medical assistance to needy, ailing natives (fig. 1.14). Frequently excised from these pious images with their stock scenes is the European presence—particularly that of the "poor whites," or non-French Mediterranean subsistence migrants, the present absents, who were often as violently anticlerical as their French counterparts.

By comparing textual with visual representation, one finds a quite different situation.[44] Generally, European writers echoed Otth's 1839 sentiments regarding the socially undesirable settlers taking root in the colony. Otth's contemporary Évariste Bavoux observed: "This new population of Africa carries the stamp of its origins; composed of the social outcasts of all countries, this population is incapable of keeping moral order on its own."[45] The French artist Théophile Gautier's 1845 *Voyage pittoresque en Algérie* offered this fairly typical description of multiethnic, multiracial port workers: "Maltese, Mahonais, Provençals, riff-raff from all over the world."[46] In the eyes of its bourgeois inhabitants and colonial officials, Algiers was becoming a magnet for peoples given over to vice and licentiousness. Worse still, the immigration of ne'er-do-wells from European cities, who had been corrupted by urban life, undermined the avowed colonial project—the implantation of sober, hardworking agricultural families in the countryside—which explains why Swiss and German peasants were eagerly solicited by French and colonial officials to people Algeria.

In contrast, French authorities in the metropole and in the colony strove from the 1840s on to exclude social undesirables, often defined as those from Mediterranean islands, especially the Maltese, who were under British protection. Maltese men were targeted since they were regarded as prone to violence and criminal behavior, but their women scarcely fared better in writings by northern Europeans. Undesirability was naturally gendered, and southern European or Mediterranean women were universally characterized as sexually loose, lazy, and slatternly. French colonial authorities attempted to erect a cordon sanitaire around the country and, above all, the capital to keep these people out; one instrument of exclusion was a barrier constructed of criminal legislation that spanned the Mediterranean. An 1843 law decreed that non-French nationals sentenced in Algeria for crimes committed there but incarcerated in French prisons were expressly forbidden to return to Algeria upon release, above all, to the capital city.[47] Nevertheless, excluding unwelcome immigrants was scarcely feasible since Algiers was a great port; sailors of all nationalities routinely jumped ship throughout the nineteenth century. And the land borders were extremely porous. Most importantly, laws such as the 1843 one contradicted the goal of peopling the colony.

In explaining visual excisions, we must look beyond the walls of Algiers to the metropole, where considerable opposition to colonialism had developed among statesmen and literati, such as the poet and parliamentary deputy Alphonse de Lamartine. Indeed, many in the Chamber of Deputies considered the colony a colossal failure and opposed releasing additional funds. However, not everyone felt this way about the "African Question." In 1846 the artist Théodore Chassériau was commissioned to go to Algeria for inspiration in conceiving his allegorical monumental murals for the Cour des Comptes in Paris. As Peter Benson Miller argues, Chassériau was not unconcerned with colonial politics. In 1846, he expressed support for the governor-general, Maréchal Bugeaud, arguing in favor of additional funds for Algeria. In Chassériau's view: "It is thus false to say that we haven't had any results. The results achieved are great on a fertile and savage land, and even if we pay for all this with sacrifices, at least we have real results." For Chassériau, and those like him, thriving colonial cities, such as

1.15 *Types of the Population of North Africa*, wood engraving (*Illustrated London News*, 14 January 1860, p. 33)

Philippeville, provided evidence of "results." Moreover, in Miller's words, "the vocabulary provided by excavation and reconstruction of Roman monuments [in Algeria was used] to justify national sacrifice and herald its results."[48] Here it can be posited that there was little visual room or representational space for depictions of the Mediterranean subsistence migrants in "consensus-building art" in France, given the politics of the period. Excision and propaganda were mutually enforcing processes.

The deliberate manipulation of text and image for propaganda purposes was, needless to say, not limited to France or the French Empire but represented one of the most widespread imperial and domestic strategies employed by European states at a time when public opinion mattered more and more to ruling elites. In January 1860, the *Illustrated London News* published an article accompanied by an image entitled *Types of the Population of North Africa* (fig. 1.15). Although unsigned, the article and illustration were clearly inspired by the war initiated by Spain against the Moroccan government on the flimsiest of pretexts. The text is quite disingenuous since it would lead the uninformed reader to suppose that

Great Britain had no imperial designs upon the independent Moroccan state when in fact Britain, Spain, and France were all battling for control of the country and its resources. The unnamed author stated:

> This portion of the African continent has been open to the invasion of conquerors ever since the earliest periods of history: the Phoenicians, Greeks, Romans, Vandals, and Goths, and even Arabs from Asia . . . so that the blood is mixed to a great extent by the various races occupying the country. The parts of the African coast west of Tunis are inhabited by numerous classes, each differing in character, manners, and habits, though all but the Jew profess the Islam faith. The principal of these classes are seven in number—viz., the Kabyles, Moors, Negroes, Arabs, Jews, Turks, and Koulouglis.

Since illustration and text cluster the people of North Africa—minus Tunisia—as an ensemble and introduce them to a general audience, the article's interest for us lies as much in the ways in which racial, ethnic, and gender differences and categories are transmitted to an English reading public as in the information about North African types. There are several critical things to note about the article. First, it posits that the only way mixtures of "blood" occurred historically was through military occupation and invasion, when in fact trade, travel, and conversions between religions had produced highly diverse populations. Second, the notion of degeneration caused by certain "racial" or ethnic fusions is prominent and reflects the growing fixation upon race as a constructed and exclusionary category deployed across the globe by European empires. Third, the only two "Europeans" in the illustration are a Spaniard and a Maltese, but they are virtually effaced visually, and the viewer perceives their presence only thanks to the textual reference. Finally, while the idea of seven ideal types of North Africans dates back to eighteenth-century European authors and was by no means exclusively a French notion, by the time that the *Illustrated London News* published these materials, three of the seven "classes"—the Moor, Turk, and Kulughli—either had disappeared completely from the social landscape or were in the process of being effaced.

In the years after 1870, a stroller or tourist exploring the place du Gouvernement for the first time would spatially confront the compressed history of migrations to Algeria. Joseph Maire, who spent two years in the capital, wrote in his 1884 *Souvenirs d'Alger*: "The shimmer of races and of costumes . . . white, yellow, black, and more nuanced colors pass before one's eyes . . . French, Algerians, English, Anglo-Maltese, Spanish from Murcia and Spanish from the Balearic Islands, Bedouins living in tents, urban Arabs, Jews . . . and all of the women belonging to these men."[49] Visiting Algiers in 1872 and again in 1885, the American writer and painter Frederick Arthur Bridgman noted: "Everybody is to be seen promenading in the charming place du Gouvernement, with its belt of trees. It is a kind of neutral ground which every one respects, and one can be entertained for days by simply studying the different types—Jews both rich and poor; sheiks and thalebs [teachers and students], whose turbans and garments are kissed by the passing Arabs; . . . an occasional woman from El-Aghouat [an Algerian oasis], with a child on her back, generally on a begging tour."[50] Of the sixty illustrations done by Bridgman for his 1885 account, only one showed Europeans. *Ball at the Governor's Palace* (p. 11) foregrounds several beautiful young European women in revealing evening gowns surrounded by Algerian men in turbans and traditional cloaks. A vague, generic European male in formal evening costume constitutes backdrop but reminds the viewer of what the ball was really about. The immigrants of various shades and degrees of Europeanness are visually absent from the book's illustrative material, although their presence is noted in the text. In the port of Algiers, Bridgman tells us that the "Frenchmen, Italians, Spaniards, Maltese, and Arabs crack their jokes and cook their supper under awnings and sails worthy of the reputation of dear old Venice."[51]

Of course, the diverse peoples who had come to call Algiers home, and who so amused writers and painters like Maire and Bridgman, could not be entirely concealed. A photo by Étienne and Antonin Neurdein from c. 1880 entitled *La Mosquée de la Pêcherie* (fig. 1.16) shows a more or less spontaneous street scene in which Europeans, Mediterraneans, and Algerians are mingled.[52] An Algerian boy holding a birdcage attracts the gaze of a toddler whose European mother clutches his hand as she walks quickly by. Furled umbrella, hat, and clerical garb mark a priest making his way among the pedestrians. An Arab notable in a white cloak and turban hurries by while several working-class European men, judging by hats and clothing, lounge about. In the extreme left of the photo, a bourgeois European man wearing a top hat and sporting a cane is barely perceptible. In the photo *Alger: Entrée de la rue de la Marine*, by Jean-Théophile Geiser (1848–1923), we also see Europeans and Algerians mingled in a "stock" street scene.[53] However, this quarter had a large Italian community and was even known as Petit Naples, in the same way that the Bab el-Oued neighborhood was called Petite Espagne, or Little Spain. Whether in the street scenes or in studio portraits, one seems to meet the Mediterranean immigrants either accidentally, in chance encounters, or in city quarters characterized by ethnic stereotyping and residential segregation.

The period from 1870 on was marked by two cataclysmic upheavals that directly affected Algiers: the 1871 Kabyle insurrections and the Franco-Prussian

1.16 *La Mosquée de la Pêcherie* [al-Jadid Mosque], Étienne Neurdein and Antonin Neurdein, albumen photograph, c. 1880 (Roger-Viollet Photo Agency, Paris)

War, followed by the Paris Commune (1870–71). It also witnessed the end of military rule over Algeria, a change that constituted a watershed in the country's history as well as in France's relationship with its African *départements*. These events in turn triggered both internal and external population movements. The French army's brutal suppression of the rebellions in the province of the Constantine caused the defeated and utterly destitute Berber Kabyles to crowd into the Casbah, which provided them a much-needed haven in the upper city. The loss of eastern France to Germany brought settlers from Alsace and Lorraine and Communard *transportés* to Algiers. In the two decades between 1881 and 1900, the European population rose from less than 200,000 to about 365,000, the consequence of birth, immigration, and, above all, changing legal definitions of French citizenship. The 1889 Naturalization Law automatically conferred citizenship upon the children of non-French nationals born in Algeria—in other words, the law begot the "French Algerians" or "Neo-French," as Pierre Nora put it.[54] If some Algerian Jews resisted the 1870 Crémieux Decree that forcibly

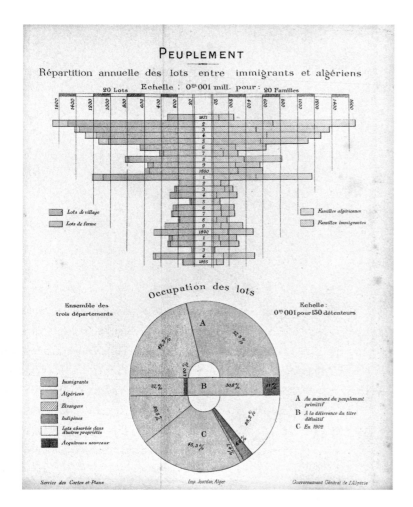

1.17 Population chart entitled "Peuplement" (Peopling), Henri Peyerimhoff de Fontenelle (Peyerimhoff de Fontenelle, *Enquête sur les résultats de la colonisation officielle de 1871 à 1895* [Algiers: Imprimerie Torrent, 1906])

naturalized them, the 1889 Naturalization Law engendered resistance as well. Some groups clung to their own cultures, languages, and identities, which were easier to preserve if the group occupied the lower rungs of the social pecking order and was uneducated. In *Le premier homme*, Camus observed that during the interwar era, "when his grandmother and other Spanish ladies of her generation gathered together to socialize, dressed in black with black mantillas on their heads, they spoke not even Spanish but rather the Mahonnais dialect."[55] In any case, a compressed encapsulation of these laws and their effects can be seen in the chart entitled "Peuplement" (fig. 1.17) in Peyerimhoff's *Enquête sur les résultats de la colonisation officielle de 1871 à 1895*, which he submitted to the governor-general of Algeria, Jonnart, and which was published in Algiers (but not Paris) in 1906. Thus, the erasures in the post-1870 era were as much legal as they were visual and representational.

By the end of the century, Mediterraneans and Algerians were caricatured in

Barbier Turc   Caïd (chef Arabe)   Mauresque (costume de Ville)   Cadi (Juge Arabe)   Napolitain   Mauresque (costume d'intérieur)   Cireur Arabe   Juive

1.18   Algerian types, colored photomechanical print, satiric postcard, c. 1900 (Getty Research Institute, 93.R.99)

satirical cartoon-like images published as postcards whose humor derived from portrayals of exaggerated "national" or "racial" characteristics. Ethnic typologies were informed by different uses of urban spaces and group comportment—what they ate, where they drank, how they dressed, what kinds of work they performed, what language they spoke, and, above all, how their womenfolk acted in public and private. In a signed card sent by Olive Molina from Algiers on 12 January 1905 (fig. 1.18) to an unnamed correspondent, he jokes: "So your nephew's brother has chosen one of these types for his wife!" Of the eight figures, only one is unambiguously Mediterranean—the Neapolitan sailor—although the Jewish woman appears to be wearing a dress that suggests hybrid European, and not North African, origins.

The popular Cagayous tales emerged from 1894 on and were published until after World War I. As Prochaska has argued, the jaunty, if ribald, hero of these tales is emblematic of the lower social strata of colonial society, composed mainly of down-and-out Mediterranean immigrants who are often satirized in postcards of the period, as depicted by the three women in the postcard titled "Egg Seller" (fig. 1.19). Cagayous emerged alongside of a specifically colonial

Types Algériens
Le marchand d'œufs

Le marchand. — *Assi, ti m'cassi la tite comm'ça ! c'i do sos la pice, j'ti dis.... si ti chiles pas alli-cos-en chi ta mison à la fin di compte !*

1.19 *Algerian Types: The Egg Seller*, colored photomechanical print, Assus, satiric postcard, c. 1900 (Getty Research Institute, 93.R.99)

type of novel and a sense of a distinct Algerian-European identity—different from French citizens of the metropole and from the colonized. "But the Algerians are absent; most colonial novels feature the better-off native French. By contrast, the Cagayous tales highlight the lower-class *pieds noirs*—generally Spanish, Italians, Maltese—the *petits blancs,* poor whites." Also significant is the fact that novels written by female authors in French about Algeria date from this period, as well as polemical tracts by French feminists deploring the cruel treatment of Arab Muslim women at the hands of colonial officials, settlers, and complicit "Arab" males.[56]

By the turn of the century, the "Arab woman," now conflated with *"la Mauresque,"* was on display—provocatively presented, covered or uncovered—to an ever-widening viewing public. During the nineteenth-century conquest of Algeria, a French general observed that "the Arabs elude us because they conceal their women from our gaze." Once brutal military pacification had rendered Algeria secure enough for Europeans to settle permanently and produce offspring, the status of Muslim women became increasingly significant for judging the culturally different, subordinate other. The dominant colonial discourse regarding an active, masculine, seditious Islam came to be accompanied by a parallel discourse about an unchanging, monolithic Islam that undergirded all family structures and sociosexual relations. In the imperial imagination, behind the high walls of the Muslim household, women suffered oppression due to Islamic laws and practices—not because of the inequities of the colonial system itself. As the colonial gaze fixed progressively upon Algerian women between 1870 and 1900, Muslim sexuality and marriage customs were deployed as reasons for denying the colonized legal rights and political representation.[57] The endless studio portraits of *la Mauresque* reveal a parallelism: the fetishization of the Algerian woman served to further distance the colonized from the rest of colonial society.

It is commonly argued that Orientalist art attempts the erasure of all traces of the colonizer. But what of those who fell between colonizer and colonized (and they were legion)?[58] In a sense, the Mediterranean poor who streamed into Algiers after 1830 were nineteenth-century versions of the older *renegados* who mediated between states and cultures during the earlier corsair centuries. Neither Orientalist nor colonial art came to terms with the fact that Algeria was a settler colony mainly populated by ordinary people. Pierre Nora observed in 1961 as the Algerian War still raged on: "In one way or another, all of those who came to settle in Algeria had left behind them in their country of origin failed lives."[59] And in the past decade, scholars of empire have emphasized the virulent association between representations of landscape and imperial conquest and mapping.

But what of human landscapes and colonialism? Several interconnected processes conspired to beget the visual absents in the social landscape of Algiers. First, as colonial society and culture developed, older social categories constructed historically by language, class, power, and ethnicity disappeared. This was the fate of the Turks, Biskris, and Kulughlis, whose identity had been made manifest by place of residence, employment, marriage partners, and costume. Second, the relative visual indifference—if not antipathy—to the subsistence migrants by artists and photographers was fed by several currents. By the middle of the nineteenth century, Algeria had become a tourist haven for bourgeois visitors from Europe, especially from France and England, many of whom—like Bridgman—came to paint and write in a strange and wondrous land. Indeed, as Deborah Cherry's work on the English feminists and female literati who flocked to Algiers in the 1850s has revealed, the demand in England for exotica meant that women's artistic production inspired by Algerian motifs found a ready market in London.[60] However, images of Europe's social outcasts would scarcely advance an artist's career. More importantly, sporadic, if enduring, opposition to the idea of French Algeria among influential individuals and political groups in France necessitated some erasure, a form of negative propaganda.

A parallel movement transpired in the physical reworking and peopling of the city itself. In a very short period of time, the upper city—the Casbah, once elite and residential space par excellence—became the haunt of the dispossessed and marginalized, who were increasingly consigned to the new, utterly alien category of *indigène*, the historical descendant of "Moor," a category that was also European in origin. In the lower city, demolitions had created empty spaces or crumbling structures where ancient Arabo-Turkish quarters and markets had once stood. Into these poured immigrant laborers who not only supplied the muscle needed to rebuild and refashion but also occupied city spaces once claimed by Algerians. Indeed, as Çelik has shown, the capital's chaotic expansion and haphazard growth throughout the nineteenth and into the twentieth century were in large measure due to steady currents of in-migration.[61]

It took much of the nineteenth century for the "not-quite-Europeans" to evolve into "not-quite-Frenchmen." Paradoxically, the 1889 Naturalization Law gradually created a distinct collective identity of French Algerians who saw themselves as different from the French of France as well as from Arabs and Berbers. This identity denied the legitimate presence of the native Algerians, who were consigned to a legal, social, and ethnographic reserve symbolized by the notion of *indigène* that informed discriminatory colonial jurisprudence, regulations, and practices. Population movements are always inherently political; the ironic tragedy of the peopling of Algeria was that it brought forth a bitter, protracted struggle in 1954 that ultimately resulted in the general exodus or expulsion of nearly one million European Algerians by 1962, forcibly repatriated to a mother country that many regarded as a foreign and unfamiliar land.

NOTES

1 Marc Barioli, *La vie quotidienne des Français en Algérie, 1830–1914* (Paris: Hachette, 1967), 12–13; and also Pierre Nora, *Les Français d'Algérie* (Paris: René Julliard, 1961).

2 Leslie Page Moch, *Moving Europeans: Migration in Western Europe since 1650,* 2d ed. (Bloomington: Indiana University Press, 2003).

3 Capitaine [Ernest] Carette, *Algérie,* in *L'univers pittoresque: Histoire et description de tous les peuples, de leurs religions, moeurs, coutumes, industrie, &* (Paris: Firmin Didot, 1850).

4 Michael Heffernan, "French Colonial Migration," in *The Cambridge Survey of World Migration,* ed. Robin Cohen (Cambridge: Cambridge University Press, 1995), 33–38.

5 Gérard Crespo, *Les Italiens en Algérie, 1830–1960: Histoire et sociologie d'une migration* (Calvisson: Éditions Jacques Gandini, 1994), 91–92.

6 Julia Clancy-Smith, "Gender in the City: The Medina of Tunis, 1850–1881," in *Africa's Urban Past,* ed. David Anderson and Richard Rathbone (Oxford: Currey, 2000), 189–204; Julia Clancy-Smith, "Europe and Its Social Marginals in 19th-Century Mediterranean North Africa," in *Outside In: On the Margins of the Modern Middle East,* ed. Eugene Rogan (London: I. B. Tauris, 2002), 149–82; and Julia Clancy-Smith, "Algerian 'Expatriates' in Colonial Tunisia," in *Identity, Memory, and Nostalgia: France and Algeria, 1800–2000,* ed. Patricia Lorcin (New York: Syracuse University Press, 2005), 3–17. On prostitution specifically, see Christelle Taraud, *La prostitution coloniale: Algérie, Tunisie, Maroc (1830–1962)* (Paris: Payot, 2003).

7 Marc Donato, *L'émigration des Maltais en Algérie au XIXème siècle* (Montpellier: Collection Africa Nostra, 1985), 172–73.

8 David Prochaska, *Making Algeria French: Colonialism in Bône, 1870–1920* (Cambridge: Cambridge University Press, 1990); and Patricia M. E. Lorcin, *Imperial Identities: Stereotyping, Prejudice and Race in Colonial Algeria* (London: I. B. Tauris, 1995).

9 Alain Calmes, *Le roman colonial en Algérie avant 1914* (Paris: L'Harmattan, 1984); and Jean Déjeux, *La littérature algérienne contemporaine* (Paris: Presses Universitaires de France, 1975).

10 The extensive Association Connaissance de l'Histoire de l'Afrique Contemporaine collection at the Getty Research Institute, with its large photograph and, above all, picture postcard holdings, further confirms the argument regarding the "present absents" in French North Africa.

11 This is a story that was partially excised from the historical narrative of colonial North Africa after about 1960 or so, although immigration to both Tunisia and Algeria in the nineteenth and twentieth centuries on the part of non-French nationals—mainly Sicilians, Maltese, and Spanish—generated a huge colonial literature, often alarmist and racist, on the movements of Mediterranean peoples into the region; for examples,

see Paul Melon, *Problèmes algériens et tunisiens: Ce que disent les chiffres* (Paris: Challamel, 1903). In the midst of the Algerian revolution, when the future of the colony for Europeans was increasingly in doubt, Jeannine Bordas's *Le peuplement algérien: Essai démographique* (Oran: Fonque, 1958) appeared. Scholarship began to address the issues raised by immigration and settlement in the past decades, challenging the older paradigm; earlier examples are Guy Tudury, *La prodigieuse histoire des Mahonnais en Algérie* (Nîmes: C. Lacour, 1992); and Juan Vilar, *Los Espagnoles en la Argelia Francesa (1830-1914)* (Murcia: Universidad de Murcia, 1989). Currently, immigration is attracting wide scholarly interest: for example, Jennifer Elson Sessions, "Making Colonial France: Culture, National Identity, and the Colonization of Algeria, 1830–1851" (PhD diss., University of Pennsylvania, 2005).

12 Tal Shuval, *La ville d'Alger vers la fin du XVIIIème siècle: Population et cadre urbain* (Paris: Éditions du Centre National de Recherche Scientifique, 1998).

13 Zeynep Çelik, *Urban Forms and Colonial Confrontations: Algiers under French Rule* (Berkeley and Los Angeles: University of California Press, 1997); and Jean-Louis Cohen, Nabila Oulebsir, and Youcef Kanoun, eds., *Alger: Paysage urbain et architectures, 1800-2000* (Paris: Éditions de l'Imprimeur, 2003).

14 Daniel Panzac, *Les corsaires barbaresques: La fin d'une épopée, 1800-1820* (Paris: Éditions du Centre National de Recherche Scientifique, 1999), 97-103; and Claude-Antoine Rozet, *Algérie* (Paris: Firmin Didot, 1850), 26-27.

15 Excerpt from British consul's Logbook, Public Record Office, London, Foreign Office series, Algeria, 113/5, 1829-30.

16 The most recent work on the Egyptian campaign is Philip G. Dwyer, *Napoleon: The Path to Power, 1769-1799* (New Haven, CT: Yale University Press, 2008).

17 Évariste Bavoux, *Alger: Voyage politique et descriptif dans le nord de l'Afrique*, 2 vols. (Paris: Chez Brockhaus et Avenarius, 1841), 2:129.

18 Alexis de Tocqueville, "Notes on the Voyage to Algeria in 1841," in *Writings on Empire and Slavery*, ed. and trans. Jennifer Pitts (Baltimore, MD: Johns Hopkins University Press, 2001), 36-37.

19 Tudury, *La prodigieuse histoire des Mahonnais en Algérie;* and Crespo, *Italiens en Algérie.*

20 Carette, *Algérie,* 39-41.

21 Adolphe Otth, *Esquisses africaines, dessinées pendant un voyage à Alger et lithographiées par Adolphe Otth* (Berne: J. F. Wagner, 1839), pl. xxx.

22 Carette, *Algérie,* 38.

23 Charles-André Julien, *Histoire de l'Algérie contemporaine*, vol. 1, *La conquête et les débuts de la colonisation (1827-1871)* (Paris: Presses Universitaires de France, 1979), 120, 158; Taraud, *Prostitution coloniale;* and Julia Clancy-Smith, "The Colonial Gaze: Sex and Gender in the Discourses of French North Africa," in *Franco-Arab Encounters*, ed. L. Carl Brown and Matthew Gordon (Beirut: American University of Beirut Press, 1996), 201-28.

24 Carette, *Algérie,* 276. The major work of the period addressing these issues was Edouard Adolphe Duchesne's *De la prostitution dans la ville d'Alger depuis la conquête* (Paris: J. B. Baillière, 1853).

25 Julien, *Histoire,* 1:120, 158.

26 Carette, *Algérie,* 275.

27 Tocqueville, "Notes on the Voyage to Algeria," 36.

28 Rozet, *Algérie,* 8–14, quotation from 8; other authors repeat the list based upon eighteenth-century travel writing, for example, P. Clausolles, *L'Algérie pittoresque . . .* (Toulouse: J. B. Paya, 1843).

29 Claude-Antoine Rozet, *Voyage dans la Régence d'Alger; ou, Description du pays occupé par l'armée française en Afrique: contenant des observations sur la géographie physique, lagéologie, la météorologie, l'historie naturelle . . . ,* 3 vols. plus atlas (Paris: Arthus Bertrand, 1833), vol. 3, pl. 25.

30 Jean-Robert Henry, introduction to *French and Algerian Identities from Colonial Times to the Present: A Century of Interaction,* ed. Alec G. Hargreaves and Michael J. Heffernan (Lewiston, NY: Edwin Mellen Press, 1993), 1–18; and Jean-Robert Henry, "La norme et l'imaginaire: Construction de l'altérité juridique en droit colonial algérien," *Procès* 18 (1987–88): 13–27.

31 Clancy-Smith, "Colonial Gaze."

32 R. Jungmann, *Costumes, moeurs et usages des Algériens* (Strasbourg: J. Bernard, 1837), 17, plagiarizing the second edition of Renaudot, *Alger: Tableau du royaume, de la ville et de ses environs, état de son commerce, de ses forces de terre et de mer, description des moeurs et des usages du pays; précédés d'une introduction historique sur les différentes expéditions d'Alger, depuis Charles-Quint jusqu'a nos jours* (Paris: P. Mongie ainé, 1830), 67. The second, third, and fourth editions of Renaudot's work were all published in 1830, suggesting that the French military issued it as a manual for the army of occupation in Algeria. This hypothesis is strengthened by the fact that a German edition was also published in 1830, the French army having German-speaking units in it.

33 Laugier de Tassy, *Histoire du royaume d'Alger,* 2d ed. (Paris: Chez Piltan, 1830), 87.

34 Honoré-Jean-Pierre Fisquet, *Histoire de l'Algérie depuis les temps anciens jusqu'à nos jours* (Paris: A la Direction, 1842), 382–83.

35 Ibid., 403.

36 Rozet, *Algérie,* 38.

37 Fisquet, *Histoire,* 400–413.

38 Julia Clancy-Smith, *Rebel and Saint: Muslim Notables, Populist Protest, Colonial Encounters (Algeria and Tunisia, 1800-1904)* (Berkeley and Los Angeles: University of California Press, 1994), 97–103.

39 Albert Camus, *Le premier homme* (Paris: Gallimard, 1994).

40 Alexis de Tocqueville, *Oeuvres complètes,* vol. 3, *Écrits et discours politiques* (Paris: Gallimard, 1991), 375–76.

41 See Sarah Ann Curtis, "Emilie de Vialar and the Religious Conquest of Algeria," *French Historical Studies* 29, no. 2 (2006): 261–92; she is working on a monograph on the Soeurs de Saint-Joseph. See also Agnès Cavasino, *Émilie de Vialar, fondatrice* (Dourgne: L'Abbaye Sainte-Scholastique, 1987).

42 Karima Direche-Slimani, *Chrétiens de Kabylie, 1873–1954: Une action missionaire dans l'Algérie coloniale* (Paris: Éditions Bouchene, 2004).

43 Postcard, *Soeurs missionnaires de Notre Dame d'Afrique* (photomechanical print, Getty Research Institute, 970031).

44 The study by Louis de Baudicour (1815–81), *La colonisation de l'Algérie: Ses éléments* (Paris: J. Lecoffre, 1856), in the Getty Research Institute collection, demonstrates the dangers of working only with published materials as opposed to the archival record; this is a structurally similar problem to that of interpreting images without text or context. Baudicour examined the various peoples who had settled in Algeria. Of all the groups, he extolled the virtuous Maltese for being hardworking, industrious, and devout Catholics whose leisure time, he claimed, was spent in church. Archival and other documentation reveals quite another picture: that of a group marginalized and criminalized to the extent that specific laws were enacted to exclude them from the colony.

45 Bavoux, *Alger*, 2:166.

46 Théophile Gautier, *Voyage pittoresque en Algérie*, ed. Madeleine Cottin (Geneva: Droz, 1973), 132.

47 Aix-en-Provence, Centre d'Archives d'Outre Mer, Algeria, F 80 586, 17 September 1846.

48 Peter Benson Miller, "By the Sword and the Plow: Théodore Chassériau's Cour des Comptes Murals and Algeria," *Art Bulletin* 86, no. 4 (December 2004): 690–718, quotations from 695–96 (Chassériau) and 696 (Miller).

49 Joseph Maire, *Souvenirs d'Alger* (Paris: Challamel, 1884), 7–8.

50 Frederick Arthur Bridgman, *Winters in Algeria* (New York: Harper and Brothers, 1890), 71–72.

51 Ibid., 4.

52 Malek Alloula, *Alger: Photographiée au XIXe siècle* (Paris: Marval, 2001), 83.

53 Cited in David Prochaska, "History as Literature, Literature as History: Cagayous of Algiers," *American Historical Review* 101, no. 3 (June 1996): 680, fig. 5.

54 Nora, *Les Français d'Algérie*, 82–83.

55 Camus, *Le premier homme*, 88.

56 Prochaska, "History as Literature," 675; see also his "L'Algérie imaginaire: Jalons pour une histoire de l'iconographie coloniale," *Gradhiva* 7 (Winter 1989): 29–38. On women's writings from, and on, the Maghreb, see Jean Déjeux, *La littérature féminine de langue française au Maghreb* (Paris: Karthala, 1994), 6–12; and Patricia Lorcin, "Teaching Women and Gender in France d'Outre-Mer: Problems and Strategies," *French Historical Studies* 27, no. 2 (Spring 2004): 293–310.

57 Clancy-Smith, "Colonial Gaze."

58 Homi K. Bhabha, "Culture's In-Between," in *Questions of Cultural Identity*, ed. Stuart Hall and Paul Du Gay (London: Sage Publications, 1996), 53–60.

59 Nora, *Les Français d'Algérie*, 81.

60 Deborah Cherry, "Earth into World, Land into Landscape: The Worlding of Algeria in Nineteenth-Century British Feminism," in *Orientalism's Interlocutors: Painting, Architecture, Photography*, ed. Jill Beaulieu and Mary Roberts (Durham, NC: Duke University Press, 2002), 103–30.

61 Çelik, *Urban Forms and Colonial Confrontations*, 71.

2

MEDINA AND MODERNITY

THE EMERGENCE OF MUSLIM CIVIL SOCIETY
IN ALGIERS BETWEEN THE TWO WORLD WARS

Omar Carlier

"Civic community is the realm of difference intermediate between the family and the State. . . . the creation of civic community belongs to the modern world which alone has permitted every element of the idea to receive its due," wrote Hegel in his *Philosophy of Right*.[1] Even if the philosopher was simply referring to the sphere of social "wants" assumed by that intermediate realm—and supervised by the police and the law—the potential field of action was enormous. Twenty years later, Tocqueville, in his role as historian, reformulated the theory of relations between civil society and the political. Having taken leave of Europe for the New World, he predicted the ineluctable advance of democracy and emphasized the exceptional disposition of members of American society—from whom native and black Americans were then excluded—to form associations without waiting for a tutelary government to care for their needs. In France, the Third Republic's law of 1901 provided a "universal" legal framework for citizens to associate freely, without authorization or registration, provided that public order remained undisturbed.

In their own way, the European settlers of another land, Algeria, asked the same of the triumphant Republic that rid them of the military yoke of the Second Empire in 1870 after the settlers had seized and sequestered native landholdings and transformed indigenous property into simple merchandise.[2] To compensate for the isolation and constraints of life in the *bled* (countryside), settlements throughout the colony developed associations.[3]

In 1892, however, just as the "radical" Republic, for which Algeria constituted the main base of its colonial empire—the justification for its "civilizing mission"—was honing policies to thwart dissident settler activity, the former prime minister Jules Ferry, symbol of the new Republic, was confronted with unexpected petitioners. Neither aborigines off the reservation nor slaves, neither renegade warlords, priests, nor paid servants of the colonial order, these men shared Ferry's philosophy, some his French nationality, while challenging the use of the symbolic term "Algerian" to include Europeans in the colony. Pioneers of the indigenous movement aiming at creating forms of civil society, the "Young Algerians"[4] were intent on reducing the previous generation of Muslim Algerian leaders' "natural right" to represent their community and had decided to take advantage of the new public rights and freedoms. Should they fear for their religion, Islam, which had been under attack from 1830 on? Those closest to religious reformism, the followers of Cairo's Shaykh ʿAbduh, then rector of the al-Azhar Mosque-University in Egypt, were hopeful.[5] Indeed, France's "disestablishment" laws of 1901 and 1905 separated church and state, which appeared to foreshadow the future liberation of Muslim institutions from French colonial interference and control.

Without rejecting the past, this small vanguard group was seeking a way out of the colonial dilemma, to give direction to their existence by defining a framework for social action. They believed in progress, in rationalism, in modern politics. They also believed in education and culture. The timing of the law of 1901 was particularly fortuitous. While still under attack from the right-wing colonial lobby, the young Muslim modernist reformers enjoyed the support of those in Paris in favor of "native rights." The state was open to diverse social initiatives, including ethnic and religious, hoping to gain power from the emergence of indigenous civil society in Algeria.

Algiers was not the only site displaying new social and civic undertakings. The first Algerian "Muslim" newspaper came into being in Bône, the first reformed mosque in Constantine, the first soccer club in Mascara. Nonetheless, Algiers was the heart and crucible, the country's topographic and topological center. The overwhelming majority of the Muslim population of the capital continued to cling—or be restricted—to the old site, the Casbah. In 1901, the vital center remained in the upper city within the limits of ancient walls no longer standing. It had seemed earlier that the Casbah was condemned to survive solely as a remnant of the past.[6] However, during the first third of the twentieth century, cultural initiatives, novel in their very nature and manner of functioning, burst upon the scene from the medina (the historic city) and its periphery. These initiatives grew steadily, bearing witness to a new social dynamic that not only stretched the framework of daily life but also reshaped the desire for different ways of coming together. New reasons and strategies for collective action led to the emergence of associations. The 1901 law assumed forms and established roots; the society wrote its own agendas. In this essay I will examine how the encounter between the old medina and the young associations would, in the period between the two world wars, give birth in the country's capital to the foundations of Algerian civil society, one capable of calling into question the order established a century earlier and of upholding the historic passage from colonial state to national state, albeit at the risk of becoming its victim.

THE MEDINA: INVENTOR AND TEACHER

Transformations in the social life of the medina did not wait for the Great War, which did, however, generate and accelerate change. The foundations of the associations that proved critical to the formation of civil society were laid at the beginning of the century; then, during the two decades between the world wars, the enterprise became more diverse, dense, and widespread. The culture of the printed page and schooling, in conjunction with the law of 1919, which extended some political rights to Algerian Muslim males and was dictated to the Europeans settlers, provided the medina with the means to transform itself during the 1920s.[7] Reaction to the social and moral crisis brought about simultaneously by the world economic depression of 1929 and the local celebrations of the centenary of the 1830 conquest accelerated the proliferation of associations.

The Medina Innovates and Initiates

Two types of educational and patriotic associations, in the spirit of the Young Algerian movement, marked the Muslim city with their imprint: the gymnastics society and the cultural circle. The first known association, with the heady name of the Avant-garde, came into existence even before the 1901 law. It was a gymnastics society formed jointly with Europeans in 1895.[8] Its headquarters were located on the Rampe Vallée, just a stone's throw from the old ramparts, on the Bab el-Oued side. As late as 1911, the prefect of Algiers called it "the only Franco-Arab association in the district of Algiers"; it managed to survive until the 1930s under a more countrified name, Vie au Grand Air (Healthy Life). The Avant-garde was not exclusively "indigenous"; according to the language of the time, the expression was meant to indicate an organization composed essentially of indigenous members and officers of Muslim faith.[9] Significantly, the sports counselor of the Avant-garde was a "native": Omar Ben Mahmoud ('Umar ibn Mahmud) was probably the first sports trainer in the history of Algeria. Less surprising is the fact that he worked for the gas company; a number of the leaders and members of the association were also employed there. The Muslims on the governing board were essentially merchants or public employees, several among them from the national education service. The majority of the officeholders and dues-paying members were, of course, European. In contrast to other more or less liberal European associations, the Avant-garde admitted a few Arabs or Kabyles as token members. Despite its inherent paternalism, the Avant-garde, perhaps for the first time, formed a new constituency that transcended the colonial world's great divide that distinguished and opposed Europeans and natives, citizens and subjects, Christians, Muslims, and Jews.

Another association, the Rashidiya (Rachidiya)—founded in 1902 and registered in the *Journal officiel* in 1910[10]—was doubtless the first in Algeria to be organized principally, if not exclusively, by Muslims.[11] In the Casbah, its president, Sarrouy, is still remembered with respect. He was the director of the indigenous school on rue Montpensier, also situated along the old walls but on the opposite side near the Rovigo bend. The Rashidiya was founded by former students of the Algiers schools for native children; a few years later it extended its boundaries by opening sections in other cities and diversifying its role. It was both an educational and a benevolent society, running libraries, teaching evening classes for adults, and providing financial assistance to students in difficulty. Its goals, however, were essentially intellectual and cultural. Beginning in 1907, with the participation of a few European supporters, it organized a regular cycle of lectures by distinguished members of the native elite. Among its sponsors figured the mayor of Algiers, Charles de Galland, and William Marçais, a renowned Arabic scholar and director of the Algiers madrasa (religious college for Muslim students), who would finish his career at the Collège de France. According to his description, the purpose of the Rashidiya was to ensure that "this bourgeoisie, which has become so French through education, reach the highest level of culture" and instill in its members' "knowledge of Muslim society, its past and its present development."[12] In turn sponsorship council and school fund, charitable organization and reading room, this cultural endeavor preceded the Association of Reformed Ulema (Muslim religious scholars) by thirty years, albeit with a decidedly French profile. With the objective to advance Muslim society, it was probably modeled on the cultural association in Tunis, the Khalduniya, named after the famous fourteenth-century North African statesman and philosopher, Ibn Khaldun.

Beginning in 1908, the Rashidiya faced competition from another association, the Tawfikiya, a "literary and social education" alliance whose goal was to "propagate the advantages of French education and civilization among the indigenous Muslims of Algeria."[13] Article 2 of its statutes, revised on 2 March 1911, gave as its goal: "to unite those among the indigenous population who desire to be educated and develop their scientific and social capacities." The modification of the statutes was not random but derived from changes on the leadership council. Chaired at its inception by Omar Djezaïri, a journalist at the newspaper *L'akhbar* (The News), published in Algiers, and galvanized by a new generation of young Muslim university students—future doctors and lawyers—the Tawfikiya was soon taken over by the most ambitious of the young Algerians, Dr. Bentami, who brought along a number of members of the now-rival Rashidiya.

Two other types of associations complete the picture of social and cultural organization in Algiers prior to World War I: religious groups and musical associations. The Association Culturelle Musulmane d'Alger, founded in 1908, was of the first type.[14] It might have been seen as an early positive response to the French disestablishment law of 1905—had the colonial regime not been determined to manipulate the law in order to maintain the mosques under their control. Unlike the membership of the Rashidiya, merchants and the new elite of the liberal professions—not teachers—predominated, bringing together the capital city's leading personalities. The association proposed to "underwrite the expenses [related to the] maintenance and exercise of the religion"[15] and at the same time provide charity to the needy, especially on Muslim holidays. Its headquarters were located in the home of one of its most notable members, the merchant Ben Merabet, on rue de la Lyre, the main business street of the heights that was also the main thoroughfare of the Jewish quarter.[16]

Intercommunity proximity was further extended by the arrival of another type of association, the musical society. Founded in 1912 and destined to have a long life, the goal of the Mutribiya (deriving from the Arabic root "to sing, chant, play music, please, enchant, and delight") was to "save the art of Arabic music from oblivion, to make it known through periodic concerts and free music classes."[17] Its first president, Edmon Yafil, a musician and musicologist from an old Algiers Jewish family, created and edited, with the help of his friend Seror, the first collection of Andalusian (medieval Muslim Spanish or Iberian) music. The society's first headquarters were in the home of Edmon Yafil on rue Bab el-Oued at the foot of the Casbah. At the start, it was a primarily Jewish organization in that its governing body was composed of thirteen Jews and only two Muslims. The Mutribiya does nevertheless qualify as an indigenous association in the real sense of the term since its members, like its president, were descendants of the old Algiers society of Judeo-Andalusian origin. It registered as an organization and set about immediately to introduce new ways of transmitting musical knowledge through periodic classes held at fixed times for children who were regularly enrolled; the classes were taught by designated teachers in a locale reserved for that purpose. Another musical society, created in 1913, attempted to promote Andalusian music with a membership that was "Franco-Arab" and excluded the Jewish community, but it was short-lived.

Although strictly a professional group and not an Algiers association, the Amicale des Interprètes Judiciaries de Kabylie (Association of Judicial Interpreters for the Kabylia) was founded in Algiers on 4 November 1913. With two Muslim members on its first governing board, its seat was registered at the Brasserie de l'Étoile in the capital, a good distance from the old neighborhoods; most of its members worked and lived elsewhere in the country.[18] It was not an Algiers association, even less one of the Casbah.

On both the spatial and social planes, the pioneer indigenous associations founded in Algiers before World War I, whether Muslim or Jewish, shared a strong bond with the medina. Their headquarters could be found in the upper Casbah or along its periphery. The majority of the membership resided in the old city or maintained activities there, and several among them—usually the presidents—descended from long-standing Algiers families. Obviously, the narrow and irregular streets of the heights were not convenient for activities requiring large spaces, but the membership of these new organizations had no need or desire for such spaces, with the possible exception of the sports association. The social and cultural and leisurely activities that developed after the war—among them soccer, movies, as well as political activism and trade union activity—would introduce substantial changes.

As the formation of the associations show, the old Casbah was capable of innovation. Nevertheless, its innovation occurred, not in isolation, but in tune with the active and inventive spirit of the Nahda (Arab awakening movement), which had arrived from Egypt and the Arab Near East. Ten years earlier, in 1903, on a brief visit to Algiers, Shaykh ʿAbduh regretted that the Nahda was not better represented in Algeria.[19] It was about to begin.

The Medina: Matrix of Civil Society?

Within the perimeters of old Algiers, associations took off following World War I. They multiplied, widened their scope, increased their membership, and started networking beyond the medina. As in the preceding generation, it all began with sports. A veritable craze for cycling, boxing, and soccer developed among the Muslim male population, in particular, the lower classes.[20] The Club Sportif Algérois (Algiers Sports Club), the first really autochthonous sports club, became official on 1 March 1919; it was run by a group of students and young employees representative of the new Algerian elite. It was located on the rue Marengo, a few steps from the Thaalibiya, the official madrasa. When, on 14 June 1923, it merged, probably for financial reasons, with the Alger Université Club (Algiers University Club) to form the Club Sportif Algérois Universitaire (Algiers University Sports Club), it lost its "indigenous" character. In the meantime, a newcomer, with Muslim leadership, arrived on the scene: the Muludiya Club d'Alger (MCA), which captured a similar audience.[21] Like other contemporary Algerian clubs active in Oran and Constantine, its rallying symbols, clearly stated in the bylaws, were community and religious identity. Founded on the *mulid* (the day the Prophet's birth is commemorated), the club's young members were, symbolically, the children of Muhammad and represented the future of the Muslim community. On the strength of this calling, the MCA was destined to have a long life.[22] Created on 31 July 1921 by a group of students and business employees, the club was linked intrinsically to the old town. Its president resided there, as did most of the governing board. Although its first official seat was in the place Mahon in the lower city, which was dominated by Europeans, the surrounding neighborhood (the Marine quarter) was largely inhabited by Algerians until its renovation in 1937.

Moved many times, the headquarters finally climbed the hill in 1945, settling on the place de Chartres, just above the old Bab Azoun–Bab el-Oued intersection, close to the residential area of the Muslim masses. Just a few short steps from the place du Gouvernement, it remained within the old site. It took less than ten minutes to descend from the Casbah to that rallying point, whereas it required more than double the time to go on foot to the Champ de Manoeuvres, the industrial area to the southeast, to actually practice a sport, and even longer to reach Saint-Eugène, northwest on the bourgeois *corniche,* to discover a real stadium built for the European population. The *yauled* (young Algerian Muslim boys) began playing soccer in the Casbah with rag balls; they continued with cheap balls on small plots of ground near the old wall. The more courageous among them, or the more talented, managed to sign up for scheduled matches.

The sports map of Algiers was to become more complex as the city's network of associations grew stronger. The MCA's success was emulated, giving rise to competitors and rivals. Soccer's influence spread to the outlying neighborhoods and suburbs.[23] Belcourt, the popular working-class neighborhood where Albert Camus's family lived, was the first among the quarters developed outside the Ottoman walls to take up the challenge. The Union Sportive Musulmane (Muslim Sports Union) was founded in January 1929, on rue de Lyon, by a group whose background was decidedly more modest than that of the MCA faithful.[24]

The president may have been an accountant, but the secretary was a plumber and the treasurer a stock clerk. Rivalry in sports did not take place only between Belcourt and the rest of Algiers. The creation of the Union Sportive Musulmane d'Alger (USMA) in July 1937 by a group of young men from the Casbah's rank and file was to divide the sons of the *jabal* (literally "mountain," used to designate the city's heights) into two sports clans; like family feuds, their matches were a throwback to their juvenile neighborhood bouts. Lacking a real locale, the USMA registered its seat at the Café des Sports, rue Bruce, just above the divide between the upper and lower Casbah. So it was that the two clubs—one grassroots, the other old school—were to face each other on either side of the rue Bab el-Oued at equal distance from the place du Gouvernement.

Sports may have set the tone, but music was not far behind. While the MCA attracted the young sports enthusiasts of the Casbah, Andalusian classical music also developed a remarkable following. The Mutribiya opened the way to many other musical groups; classical music was recomposed and underwent a renewal. As in the past, the club linked the art of song and the art of living; it consolidated its training activities and sought to revive Zirieb's tradition (Zirieb was an Iraqi musician associated with the birth of this type of music in Muslim Spain), all within the new cultural dimensions of the city. On the same pattern as the MCA, the music society developed a following and became the object of infighting; it finally broke up, with the splinter group, the Andalousia, forming in January 1929.[25] Almost exclusively Jewish, the Andalousia set up in the rue du Divan, its goal being to "propagate Arab musical art through the periodic organization of concerts and festivals," to which would be added "excursions and tourist activities of all sorts." One year later, El Djezairia would form, with an exclusively Muslim base.[26] It found shelter at the Nadi Taraqi (Taraqi Club), where a fiery preacher, Shaykh al-ʿUqbi, had recently made his mark. Only the Mutribiya stayed on course: Yafil passed the presidential crown to his successor, Mahieddine Bachterzi, whose name suggests that he hailed from the old Turkish elite, and the association became, fully, a Judeo-Muslim society.[27] The governing council remained open to the two communities, although it was only in January 1924 that total equality was attained with the election of seven Muslims and seven Jews. From 1926 to 1939, the number of Muslim members was never less than a third.

Until the war for independence, Jews and Muslims were to practice their art together in brotherly harmony, pursuing a common passion for a mixed musical tradition, which they continually reasserted. No longer satisfied to play for family festivities or to provide entertainment during Ramadan, their concerts were scheduled on the European model, without regard for the religious calendar or chance family events. The society turned away from its traditional musical masters by taking a name indicative of its role as a collective undertaking that could outlive its leading lights. As a school and model, the Mutribiya guaranteed the permanence of its art and contributed, even more than in 1912, to the creation of a new social actor, the public, with an extended outlook that had recently converted to records and the gramophone, at least in the cafés.

The Casbah was the natural site for this small-scale enterprise. Andalusian music was the privilege of the ancient site, the inspired creation of old neighbors: the mosque and the synagogue. In the years 1919–39, many members continued to reside in the old city, even among the Jewish community, gravitating between the place Randon and the rue de la Lyre. Those who had moved to the rue d'Isly or Saint-Eugène would return to the medina to mix with friends and former neighbors and share in the celestial art.

Two new artistic endeavors would soon be vying with music and sports for public performance: one on stage, the other in the cafés. Out of the Mutribiya came a type of popular theater in spoken Arabic, developed by the duo formed in 1924 of Allalou and Bachterzi, respectively assistant secretary and president of the music society. Unlike European theater, it did not take place in a given space. Within two years time, Allalou, who had begun his career as a comic actor, was adapting sketches from Molière and the Arabian Nights in the Algiers dialect. He quickly found an audience in the city, where classical Arab theater from Lebanon and Egypt via Tunis had failed. Joined by a comedian, Rachid Ksentini, Allalou and Bachterzi formed a theater company, attracting an enthusiastic young crowd. Bachterzi, son of a *fanardji* (a lamp lighter), filled a number of functions and roles: musician, singer, actor, impresario, veritable cultural entrepreneur.[28] He was the Casbah's protean man, even after he moved to Saint-Eugène. He crystallized better than anyone the creativity of the old city as it adapted to modern times. While still the backbone of the Mutribiya, he went on tour with his orchestra and his troop throughout Algeria performing plays, and as far as London and Paris playing music. All this activity would survive the ordeals of 1930, the loss of jobs and buying power of Algerians and the tightening of controls on the part of a colonial regime menaced by the religious and nationalist upsurge of the indigenous population. Laughter played a cathartic role for a people facing increasingly difficult political and economic times.

Out of the crisis came another musical genre, *sha'bi* (*chaabi*; "of the people"), that would gradually leave its mark on the old city. *Sha'bi* is derived from the *madh* (*medh*), a religious chant of Moroccan origin practiced throughout the Maghreb. *Sha'bi* developed outside the orthodox Andalusian tradition, with a subtle layering that might well have been understood as the unadulterated product of first-generation residents of Algiers. It was a simplified linguistic and musical mode that expressed the emotions and the expectations of a generation beset by poverty and humiliation.[29] It was nurtured by an explicit dialogue of recognition between artists with no classical training and a public less refined than Zirieb's fans, but it stood out for its beautiful lyrics that combined the sacred and the profane. In the 1930s, El Anka and M'rizek were the pillars of this novel musical expression. Both were from Kabyle families newly arrived in the capital; they quickly became leading figures of the Casbah, inventing what might be called the Algiers blues. No association was created in their name; no locale supported their art by developing teaching methods, as had the Mutribiya. They found favor in the cafés and developed a following throughout the country; they gave form to a genre that remains alive today. The Café Malakoff, located behind the place du Gouvernement, became El Anka's appointed locale. He later succeeded his emulator, El-Hadj M'rizek, as its proprietor.

A third, more discrete type of association also found its niche in the old city. Based on ethnic or regional solidarity more or less explicitly defined, this type encompassed both benevolent and literary societies. On 14 February 1929, the Entente announced that its membership, practically exclusively from the Mzab region in southern Algeria, was setting up a library and organizing lectures in Arabic and French.[30] The next day, the Association Amicable d'Entraide et d'Éducation Sociale Musulmane (Muslim Association for Social Welfare and Education) announced its intention to aid the poor, contribute to the education of the indigenous population, and improve the lot of Kabyle women.[31] It brought together a number of Kabyle leaders from Algiers, including the reformer Shaykh Ibnou Zekri. Two months later, the Union des Laghouatis Algérois (Union of Algiers Residents from the Oasis of Laghout) would take on responsibility for their compatriots who "are drifters, out of work, without means or shelter."[32]

With Es Salam (Peace), a fourth type of association was established in Greater Algiers in the 1930s.[33] Both benevolent and educational, this type of association reformed teaching of the Quran in line with the methods developed in 1912 in Constantine by Shaykh ʿAbd al-Hamid Ben Badis, an Islamic reformist, and formalized in 1925. Es Salam was founded in February 1929, with its headquarters in rue des Abderames—one of the streets often depicted in Orientalist imagery. Its goal was "to foster the education of indigent Muslim children" passed over by the colonial school system. The Rashidiya and the Tawfikiya had a similar goal but within the secular, bilingual framework of an elitist cultural circle (of the Young Algerian type), led by an educated French-speaking directorate. Es Salam was in no way their emulator. Its first governing board was composed of business people, merchants, and artisans born in the Casbah and still living there. One of its presidents, Yahia Lakehal, a confectioner on the rue Randon, descended from an old Casbah family, but none of the teachers and students who had set the tone for the first literary circles were among the membership. Toward the end of 1932, shortly after the purchase of a building on the rue Porte Neuve meant to house a madrasa, the number of members declined. Was it administrative pressure, internal divisions, or a takeover by reformists of another stripe? No records survive.

The famous Shabiba (Young People's Association), another association whose goal was to teach Islam to children outside the established Quran schools and which was directly connected to the Ulema (Muslim reformist) movement, took up the challenge on the other side of the old city, near the Rampe Vallée.[34] Its most prestigious teacher was a brilliant, young intellectual, Mohamed Laïd of Ain Beida in eastern Algeria, who had studied at the Zaytuna Mosque-University in Tunis. He was considered the first modern Algerian poet in the Arabic language. The excitement produced by the Neo-Wahhabi sermons of Shaykh al-ʿUqbi thrust the Shabiba and its school into the limelight. Its "reformist" ideas were anathema to French colonial authorities. For example, in the spring of 1934, Chama Boufedji, a young teacher of Islahi (Muslim Reformist) leanings, was suspended from her teaching position, an event that created a stir throughout the city. The prefecture had, over the previous year, been tightening its control of religious schools and the mosques.

The dynamics were such that even those associations that were careful to avoid politics could not help but stir up political confrontations by the very fact of moving Algerian Muslim society onto modern foundations, a fact that perturbed proponents of the status quo.[35] No longer able to regenerate, the old city was on the offensive.

THE MEDINA UP IN ARMS: ASSOCIATION AND POLITICS

Three other types of associations aimed at collective action among the Muslim population of Algiers, first and foremost in the Casbah during the period preceding World War II: religious associations, trade unions, and political parties. The 1920s might be seen as a preparatory period with the old city as its laboratory. The medina provided the foundation for these movements, but it was soon made aware of its limits, a possible indication that its historic creativity was coming to an end.

The Casbah and the Za'im *(Political Leader)*

For politically aware Algerians of the 1930s, Emir Khaled, 'Abd al-Qadir's grandson, was not a distant memory ('Abd al-Qadir was the legendary Algerian resistance leader of the 1830s and 1840s). Certainly, his death in Damascus on 9 January 1936 did not go unnoticed. Mohamed Salah Benjelloul, a medical doctor and powerful political leader who argued for the rights of Algerians, and Ben Badis rendered homage to him.[36] The Communist Party went further, using his name to launch several cultural circles. The younger generation commemorated Emir Khaled's death, albeit with an aura of nostalgia. The figure of 'Abd al-Qadir's grandson left its mark: he established a link to a bygone era and personified the *za'im,* waiting to be reincarnated.[37] In actual fact, Khaled had appeared and disappeared with the speed of a meteor. At the top of the political ladder, he was elected successively city councilor, general councilor, and financial delegate in June 1919. Four years later, submitting to administrative pressure, he quit the political arena and went into exile. He had been the principal spokesman for his compatriots during four long years. It was he who, for the first time, defied the colonial order within its own framework and according to its own methods of rule, turning it against itself. The title of his newspaper, *Ikdam* (Progress), was both a program and a symbol; it became the standard-bearer of Muslim Algeria, the spearhead of the new spirit of enterprise.

'Abd al-Qadir's grandson was not just a Casbah personality. He had a lovely home in the Allée des Muriers in Belcourt in addition to his Casbah residence. His stature was greater than a mere general councilor of Algiers, even if he was also the financial delegate. In 1923 he symbolized, by himself, the new political unity of Muslim Algeria. He had national standing, but he was also the hero of Algiers and of the Casbah, even of the "three Casbahs."[38] The old city was his fief, the upper Casbah his sanctuary. "May God protect Emir Khaled," the youngsters of the *jabal* would cry as night fell, in defiance of the adversaries of their idol. His attempt to create a political party failed, however. The Fraternité Algérienne formulated on paper in 1922 had no bite. Those who followed Khaled under that banner—an agricultural engineer, a few young lawyers, some students, sons of prominent families—were not ready to confront the colonial administration. What was possible in Paris for immigrant workers, within the Union Intercoloniale or in the ranks of the Communist Party, was not possible in Algiers.

What the medina lost politically in terms of initiative and even self-esteem, it was able to recover with sports, theater, and music. As the concrete expression of a collective identity, these sociocultural initiatives constituted the civic training ground for (proto)-national sentiment. From then on, the religious and political movements would come into the open, better armed as a result of the double shock of the 1930s—the centenary celebration and the Great Depression.

The Ulema and the Literary Circle: Reconquering the Center

In 1927, three years before the centenary extravaganza and four years after Khaled's forced departure from the city, a new cultural circle, the Nadi Taraqi, was set up in the old city.[39] It revived the type of association previously exemplified by the Rashidiya, but with a more religious bent. It did not immediately shake up the world of associations culturally or politically, although it did provide the Muslim city with a focal point between the heights and the sea. Situated at the ancient Bab Azoun–Bab el-Oued intersection overlooking the place du Gouvernement, its location was a stroke of genius, even if the purchase of this site was due to the opportunism of one of its main financial backers, Abbas Turqui, also a supporter of the Ulema. The headquarters of Nadi Taraqi became the focus of the city and gave meaning to it. Larger than the largest Algerian café, the size of its meeting hall made it possible for dozens of members to gather around large tables for general assemblies and for hundreds of spectators to attend lectures or special events. From the stage, the governing body or the lecturer had a dominant position, and solemnity was enforced on significant occasions. The Muslim Congress held its first deliberations there in July 1936. On the third floor of the building the association provided its leaders with a privileged balcony overlooking the place du Gouvernement, the city's communications hub, commercial center, and main meeting place. Better still, it was the perfect rostrum for addressing crowds on major occasions, as, for example, after the political victory of the Popular Front in France in 1936. Across the way, near the sea, were the two largest mosques of the city, al-Jadid and al-Kebir. On Fridays, hundreds of faithful would wend their way to the square, forming a willing public for a speech.

The Nadi Taraqi did not immediately operate as a catalyst, not even in reaction to the centenary celebrations, but its development was of singular importance. In the early days, it was a functional space in which Muslim elites could socialize. With its program of lectures, it seemed to bring the Rashidiya back to life. The names of the first and subsequent governing bodies, however, are nowhere to be found. The owners or silent partners were necessarily property owners and merchants located in the old city, but their actual identities remain unknown due to a lack of sources. In any event, they soon welcomed an out-sider, Shaykh Tayyib al-ʿUqbi, who had arrived at the end of 1927 to preach the Salafi ideology in Algiers with militant fervor, calling for Islam's return to the purity of its beginnings. In three years time, the shaykh became both catalyst and catharsis. More than his theological or juridical erudition, or the prestige accrued by his long stay in Mecca as a teacher, his exceptional talent as an ora-tor and his position as a crusading imam, independent of official Muslim clerics under the thumb of colonial officials, best explain his increasing influence over sectors of the old city.

Two circumstances favored his rise to power. The failure of Emir Khaled in 1923 had left a political vacuum that no new force had filled: neither the Muslim elected officials who had come together in a federation in 1927 nor the Communist Party, composed of Europeans and atheists and hunted down by the authorities that same year. There were many talented people, from Dr. Ben-tami to the pharmaceutical student Ferhat Abbas, among secular, French-speaking Algerians, but their approach to political representation and the colo-nial situation was too elitist and their reactions were excessively European. In addition, an intellectual and moral vacuum, or at the least a generational gap, was felt among Islahi reformists. The two reformist newspapers of Algiers pre-dating 1914 had no successors, nor had the two respected teachers at the official madrasa, Ibnou Zekri and Bensmaïa. None of the leaders of the older Muslim lineages were capable of opposing al-ʿUqbi's brand of Islamic reformism, with its rational critique of the reasons for the country's subjugation to the Euro-peans, as well that of the Muslim world. Intellectual authority and moral au-thority were up for the grabs. Tayyib al-ʿUqbi arrived at a momentous juncture in the history of civil society and the life of associations; in a certain sense, the educational circle had been waiting for him. The shaykh assumed the oratorical functions that had been lacking, moving his critical discourse from the political terrain to the religious.[40]

The shock of the centenary celebrations accelerated and strengthened the process that consolidated the shaykh's takeover, making it possible for the movement he represented to reach Algiers, where it attracted a large following. More than ever, the chant of the Quran would mobilize proponents of a return to Islamic law, inspire partisans of militant discourse, imbue the young with a new combative spirit of the faith, and provide hope to proletarian workers, especially among the city's longshoremen.

In this climate, the Association des Oulémas Musulmans Algériens (AOMA; Association of Muslim Algerian Ulemas), registered as an association on 5 May

1931, discovered a ready audience. Even though the movement and its publications had started in Constantine, its official seat was located in the center of Algiers, among the most densely concentrated Muslim urban population, near the ancient Janina, previously the Ottoman government palace.[41] AOMA was devoted to religious reformism but was discretely organized along the lines of a political party that called for social and moral renewal. By 1932, the reformist ulema outranked their religious competitors, that is, the leaders of the sufi brotherhoods, who then broke away, losing the exceptional podium offered by the circle. The following year, the AOMA was targeted by the so-called Michel circular, a colonial administrative decision declaring that sermons in the mosques were to be under surveillance, in particular, those delivered by al-ʿUqbi at the great Maliki Mosque (al-Kebir Mosque). Far from being discouraged by this, the movement took off and grew in force. Although its local leader, in conformity with the bylaws, forbade his followers from engaging in political activity, the association became the principal focus of opposition to the colonial power, expressing the hopes of the Casbah far more than the opportunistic native elected officials did.[42] Its influence advanced well beyond the framework envisaged by al-ʿUqbi, in ways that he would soon disavow, thus running the risk of being disavowed himself.

At the end of 1935 in Constantine, Ben Badis launched the idea of a Muslim Congress aimed at gradually emancipating the Algerian people in an alliance with, and even within, the French Republic. Paradoxically, he received the immediate backing of the Communist Party and, somewhat less surprising, of the Popular Front in France. Ben Badis, the reformist religious scholar who had already formed a sort of duo with Dr. Benjelloul, became the guarantor, the moral emblem, of an astonishing troika.[43] Sustained by the dynamics of the Popular Front since February 1934, bolstered if not manipulated by the Communist Party and its trade union affiliate the Confédération Générale du Travail Unifiée (CGTU; General Confederation of Unified Workers), Ben Badis's proposal found an immediate echo in the Casbah, where al-ʿUqbi was decidedly unprepared for it. The education circle was favorable to the idea and became the rallying point of Greater Muslim Algiers, and later of Algerian Algeria, the head and the seat of the first mass movement in the country's history. Until the summer of 1937, the AOMA remained the principal spearhead of the movement even if the Communist Party was the mainspring. The Muslim Congress was convened at the education circle's headquarters; it was from its balcony that Ben Badis and Benjelloul addressed the crowd; it was there that all the delegations converged, and from there that marching orders for the entire country emanated.

Then came the political party's hour, the last type of association of the period. In short order, the idea of independence was enunciated publicly. Until the end of 1935, only the Communist Party and the CGTU had evoked the idea of liberation. They included a small ethnically mixed minority with a few Arabs (although an "Arab workers congress" was held in 1930 in Algiers). They also tried to launch a revolutionary nationalist organization similar to the Étoile Nord-Africaine (North African Star, the party of Messali Hadj) in Paris. In both cases, their main support came from the Casbah. Si Boualem (pseudonym of Sid Ahmed Belarbi), the top Communist Party Arab leader, was from Belcourt, whereas the young leaders of the al-Umma Party were mostly from the Casbah or nearby; among the latter was the main trio of Mestoul, Mezghenna, and Hadj Smaïn, who, in the spring of 1934, founded the first section of the Étoile Nord-Africaine in Algiers. A small nucleus of young rail workers, several of whom were from old Casbah families, was its mainstay. As for the better-known personalities, they jockeyed for positions, a clientele, and funding. The so-called independents were clearly agents of the colonial administration. The others, for the most part members of the Fédération des Élus (Federation of the Elected), thought of themselves as their countrymen's spokesmen—never forgetting their own interests, however—and even tried introducing the idea of *"résistance-dialogue,"* to use an expression coined by Algerian historian Aek Djeghloul in his *Eléments d'histoire culturelle algérienne* (Algiers: Enterprise Nationale du Livre, 1984).

While not an empty shell, the Fédération des Élus vanished regularly, reappearing only at election time. On the other hand, the Communist Party and its satellite organizations—the CGTU, Jeunesse Communiste (Communist Youth), Amsterdam Pleyel, Secours Rouge (Red Assistance), Friends of the USSR—were militant organizations active on a daily basis. Algerians began joining up in 1935. By the end of 1936, the high point of the Popular Front, there were several thousand in their ranks. The Casbah was obviously not insensitive to this movement, which was more popular than revolutionary, but could not contain it. However, as a site, the Casbah did enjoy a ringside seat, since all the demonstrations and processions crisscrossed the place du Gouvernement at its feet, and it was one of the principal contributors to those events. Dockworkers constituted the Arab proletarian base of the Algerian Communist Party created in October 1936. Many of the dockworkers lived in crowded conditions in the overpopulated Casbah and the Marine quarter, where they had come into contact with Socialist or Communist ideology.

At the same time, the Étoile Nord-Africaine, the nationalist party born in Paris, managed to cross the sea and make a breakthrough in Algiers. Barely off the boat, on 2 August 1936, its leader Messali, who was practically unknown in Algiers, took advantage of the triumph of the Muslim Congress, shoving its leaders aside on the very day and on the very spot where they were reporting to the Muslim crowd assembled at the municipal stadium. The radical nationalist organization was hence alone in profiting from the vicissitudes of the Popular Front. Banned in January 1937, the Étoile Nord-Africaine resurfaced in March under another name, the Parti du Peuple Algérien (Party of the Algerian People), and attracted a following all through Algiers the following summer. In June 1936, as in June 1937, the two largest chapters of the nationalist party were to be found in the Marine quarter and the Casbah.[44] They shared ground with the associations of rail workers, the only professional group whose members still lived in the old city.

With the circle and the club, the association and the party, the medina was equipped with the modern tools of collective action. On its native ground and along its edges, it had mobilized and organized, laid down guidelines, and re-created a territory that the actors along its periphery would broaden and intensify. The Casbah had found its political fulcrum, sense of purpose, and hope for the future, hence regaining its meaning among the Muslim population of Algiers. Yet, in the end, it was unable to fully function as a command center.

CONCLUSION

In post–World War I Algiers, in the old Muslim city below the Turkish dey's ancient fortress on the hill, along the waterfront, and adjacent to the place du Gouvernement, a dynamic new collective sociopolitical undertaking, whose extent and impact upon succeeding generations could not have been imagined, began. Associations sprang from the Third Republic's law of 1901, defined and elaborated upon in such a way as to give form to fundamental public rights, which represented novel social and cultural practices derived from European history. These practices were initiated in Algiers in the middle and the end of the 1930s. They were then experimented with and popularized by the urban residents of major cities from Tlemcen to Oran, from Annaba to Constantine, and were gradually appropriated and reinvented by Algerian society in small towns.

For most members, the act of joining was already perceived as the prelude to the process of becoming a citizen. In 1902 in the capital, at a stone's throw from the ancient wall, two modest associations, the Rashidiya and the Avant-garde, symbolized the timid beginnings of momentous changes. On the eve of World

War I, there were six associations fundamental to the emergence of civil society. Half a century later, more than one hundred associations could be counted in greater Algiers alone; they had for some time been spilling over the boundaries of the old city, still home to the majority of Muslim residents of Algiers.

Many members were influenced by French republican ideals but reiterated their deep attachment to the religion of their forebears. They had been inspired by the Young Algerian spirit of defiance to the colonial order and were in political alignment with Paris and its local representative, including the prudent, but liberal, governor-general of Algeria, Charles Jonnart. They were also attracted to various political and religious ideologies and movements coming from Egypt and the eastern Arab world, particularly several strands of Islamic reform. These novel ideologies, institutions, and practices that came to Algiers from different directions—from Paris, the notion of the Republic, and from Cairo, the idea of the *Nahda* (Awakening) and *Islah* (Islamic renewal)—provoked a profound shift in collective attitudes and identities.

The issue of what it meant to be Algerian was asserted as well as interrogated and interiorized by certain sectors of indigenous society at a time when sociocultural forms were being borrowed from the Republic through the creation of associations and organizations that in fact rendered Algeria an integral part of France to a degree never experienced in the previous century of colonial domination. One philosophical trend or variation of this larger movement was epitomized by Shaykh Ben Badis, who called for the existence of an Algerian nation reclaiming its own past, in some way parallel and compatible with the linkage to metropolitan France—based on the theory of two nationalities, one religious and one political.

An indigenous civil society was born. The Casbah remained essentially, if not exclusively, "native" in its built and human components, Muslim and Jewish; it served as the birthplace for civil society, provided it with a public platform. The old medina, conservatory of the past and alembic of the new, Turco-Andalusian heir infused with new blood, embarked on a constructive path with the colonizer, both imitative and distinctive, espousing and differentiating the consensual and the conflictive. While averse to ethnic fusion, for reasons of colonial prejudice or religious proscription—at least for women—the new Casbah generations were sensitive to cultural crossbreeding accomplished by direct or indirect contact with a "creole" world re-created daily with the Europeans in a shared and disputed space on the old site. The words and goods exchanged daily contributed to the subtle and irreversible mixing of different languages, food, and dress. Starting from the middle Casbah, within and along the diamond-shaped meeting ground of four old streets (Randon–Marengo, Lyre–Bruce) with their concentration of markets, crafts, and liberal professions, the burgeoning life of associations moved outward in the direction of the Marine quarter and its major mosques by way of the place de Chartres and the place du Cardinal Lavigerie, using as relays the swarm of small voluble trades and chattering cafés. The milieu of associations set the tone, led the search for new social configurations, and readjusted the spaces of the city and the mentality of its inhabitants.

Associations also found space and created branches on the outskirts of the old site. The Shabiba, for example, followed the traces of the old wall from the boulevard de la Victoire to the Rampe Vallée, where earlier the Avant-garde had had its quarters. Just as significantly for its demonstrations and cultural events, it engaged the large Bab el-Oued movie house and the Algiers Opera, and for sports events it extended into stadiums in the outlying districts. Exploited by the Ulema association, the Shabiba united with the Cercle du Progrès, but finally joined the national movement at the time of the Popular Front, in the wake of the humiliating commemoration of the centennial. Dominating the place du Gouvernement from its balcony, the Nadi Taraqi reestablished a form of physical and symbolic centrality for the Muslim population in pursuit of the nationalist ideal. Spurred on by dynamic associations, in transition from the civic to the political, the place du Gouvernement became a space to reconquer: an ancient territory reclaimed and gradually transformed into a theater for demonstrations under the auspices of an Algerian-Muslim culture open to modernity.

Translated from the French by Elaine Mokhtefi.

NOTES

1 G. W. F. Hegel, *Philosophy of Right*, trans. S. W. Dyde (Mineola, NY: Dover Publications, 2005), 96. Hegel adds, "As the family was the first, so the corporation, grounded upon civic society, constitutes the second ethical root or basis of the state." If the family is the first substructure of the state, the social realm is the second: "The family contains the elements of the subjective particularity and objective universality in substantive unity. Then, in the civic community, these elements are in the first instance dissociated and become on the one side a particularity of want and satisfaction, which is turned back into itself, and on the other side abstract legal universality" (131).

2 Charles-André Julien, *Histoire de l'Algérie*, vol. 1, *La conquête et les débuts de la colonisation (1827–1871)* (Paris: Presses Universitaires de France, 1965).

3 Karima Benhassine, "Vie associative en milieu colonial et nostalgie du terroir," in *Constantine, une ville, des héritages* (Constantine: Media Plus, 2004), 95–111. For the birth of an indigenous settler culture, see the pioneering work of David Prochaska, *Making Algeria French: Colonialism in Bône, 1870–1920* (Cambridge: Cambridge University Press, 1990).

4 Charles-Robert Ageron, "Le mouvement jeune algérien de 1900 à 1923," in *Études maghrébines, mélanges Charles-André Julien* (Paris: Presses Universitaires de France, 1965), 217–43.

5 Shaykh Muhammad ʿAbduh (1849–1905) was an Egyptian Muslim scholar and religious leader who visited Tunis and Algiers in 1903 and became the symbol of Islamic reformism in the late-nineteenth and early-twentieth centuries; ʿAbduh came to represent the moderate cultural wing of Islamic reform, in contrast to the revolutionary political wing epitomized by the Iranian anti-imperialist Jamal al-Din al-Afghani, who opposed British colonialism in India and Egypt as well as the corrupt local Muslim leaders who collaborated with the British.

6 "Casbah" is the metonymic term by which the Europeans have forever called this upper section of the old city. Strictly speaking, the Casbah is the fortress built on the Algiers heights, the place where one of the last deys of the Regency resided so as to better protect himself from the unruly militia units in the army.

7 The so-called Jonnart Law of February 1919, named after Charles Jonnart, the governor-general of Algeria after World War I, increased the size of the indigenous electoral body and improved the representation of the indigenous Muslim population in the various deliberative assemblies. It was passed in recognition of the Muslim Algerian contribution to the war effort. Some 206,000 Algerians, either Arab or Kabyle, served under the French flag during the Great War; 26,000 lost their lives and 72,000 were wounded. In addition, the colonial regime requisitioned some 89,000 male workers for the factories in France, and another 30,000 Algerians volunteered to

work in the metropole. Astonishingly, during the war years, one-third of the Algerian male Muslim population between the ages of twenty and forty served France in one way or another, and this was the principal impetus for the 1919 law.

8   According to a notice of the police headquarters in the Fourth District of the City of Algiers, dated 3 May 1907, the society was created on 14 July 1895. It was registered at the Algiers Prefecture on 24 March 1904 and recorded in the *Journal officiel* on 1 January 1905; it received the approval of the War Ministry on 5 August 1910. See Archives of the Wilaya of Algiers (AWA), file 1221.94.

9   Other so-called Franco-Muslim or Franco-indigenous associations also came into being prior to 1914 in other cities of Algeria, some devoted to sports, some not. Branches of the gymnastic society were also established in Tlemcen and Mostaganem, cities in western Algeria, as well as Guelma and Annaba, in eastern Algeria.

10   AWA, file 1394.

11   It was soon followed by the Cercle des Jeunes Algériens (Circle of Young Algerians), founded in 1904 along the same lines and with the same social composition.

12   *Bulletin du Comité de l'Afrique Française*, no. 1 (1909).

13   Registered at the Algiers Prefecture on 7 November 1908 and in the *Journal officiel* on 21 November 1908, AWA.

14   Registered in the *Journal officiel* on 2 August 1908, AWA.

15   This type of funding for social welfare activities originated in precolonial times when it had been under the aegis of the Islamic endowments, or *habûs,* the equivalent in Muslim law of the French *main-morte,* which in the Arab East was called *waqf.*

16   The Jewish quarter in Algiers did not resemble the enclosed quarter, or *mallah,* in which urban Moroccan Jews lived; it is uncertain whether the Moroccan form of sociospatial religious and residential organization ever existed in Algeria.

17   AWA, file 126/420.

18   *Journal officiel,* 22 September 1914, AWA.

19   Shaykh ʿAbduh, the rector of al-Azhar Mosque-University in Cairo, spent only a few days in Algiers in 1903 and, as a stranger to Algeria, was unable to grasp the elements of change and appreciate their political significance.

20   Youcef Fatès, "Sport et politique en Algérie, de la période coloniale à nos jours" (PhD diss., Université de Paris I, 2003).

21   AWA, file 1218/857.

22   Of the clubs that still survived, the Muludiya was the oldest in Algiers, if not in Algeria; the Galia, organized in Mascara in 1912, was the first of the Muslim soccer clubs.

23   While it was only at the end of World War II that a Muslim sports club came into existence in a middle-class community like Saint-Eugène, where many of the Algiers Muslim elite then resided, or in a working-class neighborhood like Clos Salembier, the extension of the "sport of sports" from the old center to a working-class outlying district began well before—as the case of Belcourt proves.

24 Albert Camus (1913–60) spent most of his childhood on rue de Lyon.

25 Registered at the Algiers Prefecture on 28 January 1929 and recorded in the *Journal officiel* on 9 February 1929, AWA.

26 Registered on 18 February 1930 and recorded in the *Journal officiel* on 4 March 1930. Article 2 of its statutes was the same, word for word, as a clause in the bylaws of the Andalousia.

27 Yafil had certainly recognized the promising talent of this young tenor who had begun his career as *muezzin* at the Grand Mosque.

28 Bachterzi's father descended from an old Algiers family of Turkish origin. He was known throughout the Casbah for his spice shop and as the person in charge of lighting the streetlamps.

29 The full effects of the 1929 crisis were not felt until 1931 in Algeria. Every community experienced its negative impact, but Muslims were the most deeply and adversely affected because of their generally precarious socioeconomic conditions. The old city and beyond suffered increasingly from the massive influx of impoverished peasants, who sought refuge in the already-crowded medina. Adding to their misery was the blow to morale engendered by the humiliating centenary celebrations.

30 *Journal officiel*, 13 March 1929, registered on 14 February 1929, AWA.

31 *Journal officiel*, 25 February 1929, registered on 15 February 1929, AWA.

32 *Journal officiel*, 23 April 1929, registered on 15 April 1929, AWA.

33 *Journal officiel*, 12 February 1929, registered on 31 January 1929, AWA.

34 James McDougall, "The Shabiba Islamiyya of Algiers: Education, Authority, and Colonial Control, 1921–1957," *Comparative Studies of South Asia, Africa, and the Middle East* 24, no. 1 (2004): 149–57.

35 Every association had an article which dissociated itself from politics in its statutes.

36 Gilbert Meynier and Ahmed Koulaksis, *L'émir Khaled, premier za'im? Identité algérienne et colonialisme français* (Paris: L'Harmattan, 1987), 279.

37 Charles-Robert Ageron came close to presenting him in this way, underscoring very correctly "that he was above all, from 1919 to 1923, the incarnation, in the eyes of Muslim Algeria, of the awakening of Islam and accentuated the protests of the Young Algerians against the colonial regime." See Charles-Robert Ageron, *Histoire de l'Algérie contemporaine* (Paris: Presses Universitaires de France, 1979), 2:292.

38 At the time of the centenary, three social entities drawing upon a wide base could be distinguished in and around the Casbah, representing in fact "three Casbahs." The top elites, distinguished by their social status if not always by their income, made up the first; they continued to intermarry with the old Turkish and Andalusian families of Algiers. Their counterparts lived in the former province of Algiers, which included the cities of Blida, Cherchell, and Dellys, as well as the former Turkish province known as the Titteri, whose main cities were Medea and Miliana. This elite maintained stately homes, rarely renting to outsiders, but would leave the old site willingly for other city districts, such as Kouba or Saint-Eugène. Second came the working classes, who

were crowded into deteriorating housing units that sheltered ever-more-impoverished renters and transient laborers in the most squalid corners of the Casbah and the Marine quarter—dockworkers, unskilled workers from the interior, and those who scrambled to make a living in petty trade and outmoded crafts. The third stratum comprised small shopkeepers and salaried workers in the private sector (bookkeepers, bank and insurance employees) and in the public services (postal employees, railway and other transport employees). These people enjoyed better living conditions in traditional homes or in newer buildings on modern streets—for example, on rue Marengo and in recently constructed housing blocks on boulevard de Verdun at the northern edge of the Casbah.

39 It was also known by its French name, Cercle du Progrès, or even Cercle de l'Éducation. I have not been able to find its statutes, either in the AWA or in the overseas archives in Aix-en-Provence. Concerning this Circle, see Ali Merad, *Le réformisme musulman en Algérie de 1925 à 1940: Essai d'histoire religieuse et sociale* (Paris: Mouton, 1967), 96–98; and especially McDougall, "The Shabiba Islamiyya of Algiers," 151–52.

40 Tayyib al-ʿUqbi hailed from an ancient and illustrious North African family whose name was associated with the first Arab Muslim conquerors of North Africa in the seventh century CE. He satisfied the expectations of the educated, who had been open for some time to the ideas and discourse of reformist Islam, and of the pious bourgeoisie, who had been troubled by the deterioration of morals since World War I.

41 Knowledge about the Islahi ideology has been profoundly improved with the publication of James McDougall's *History and the Culture of Nationalism in Algeria* (Cambridge: Cambridge University Press, 2006).

42 See the articles by Joseph Desparmet, beginning in 1933, in the *Bulletin du Comité de l'Afrique Française*, for example, his "Naissance d'une histoire 'nationale' de l'Algérie," July 1933, 387–92.

43 Mohamed Salah Benjelloul, trained as a doctor, entered politics in the 1930s. At first his political positions regarding the rights of native Algerians vis-à-vis the colonial government appeared to presage a significant radicalization of the Young Algerian movement. As a redoubtable orator, he was for a while the most powerful leader of the "Élu" movement and promoted the idea of assimilation to France—which the right-wing European settlers opposed vehemently. When the Popular Front came to power in France in 1936, Benjelloul led a Muslim delegation to Paris to present a number of demands for political representation for Muslim Algerians as well as for education, health, and other unmet social needs. He was considered both a leading social figure and a man of the people. For two years, he was the political leader of eastern Algeria, if not the actual successor to Emir Khaled on the national level.

44 They numbered about two hundred, and militants began referring to them as "those from the Second," meaning the Second Ward, that is, the Casbah.

PART 11

IMAGES

3

THE PROMISE AND POWER
OF NEW TECHNOLOGIES

NINETEENTH-CENTURY ALGIERS

Frances Terpak

From this gate which faces it, from the Admiralty mole, I picture the old Algiers as some prints still show it, bathing its bare feet in the sea. These monumental quays, these buildings, behind which the Mosque of the Fisheries is buried, these hideous warehouses, these wine-vaults, these black vessels,— my eye suppresses them and puts only greens and whites in their place:—the narrow strip of land, connecting the islet on the mole with the town, reveals beyond it another glimpse of the sea; where the rock stopped, the earth was very green. Some houses by the water's side, but few. To reach the sea, a ravine. A path leading to the sea drops down from some white houses, leaning over the edge of this ravine. . . . I imagine it by night and, as it leads to the fountain, I see women following it. The fountain is near the sea where feluccas come and go.

Alas! Alas! White-gleaming Algiers is no more.

—André Gide, *Amyntas*, trans. David Villiers, 1958

This passage from the journal of André Gide, who first visited Algeria in 1893, shows how France's greatest colonial possession had lost much of its exotic charm by the end of the century. But Gide—like many educated Europeans— suppressed the modern urban growth resulting from several decades of French occupation to remember an earlier version of Algiers that had been embedded in the nineteenth-century psyche through prints and photographs. Gide's poetic

3.1 *The New Mosque [al-Jadid Mosque] and the Great Mosque [al-Kebir Mosque] in Algeria*, Adolphe Otth, lithograph (Otth, *Esquisses africaines, dessinées pendant un voyage à Alger et lithographiées par Adolphe Otth* [Berne: J. F. Wagner, 1839], pl. 17)

metaphor of Algiers "bathing its bare feet in the sea" recalls the lithograph by Adolphe Otth representing the old port of Algiers when only the barren cliffs separated the shore from the city above, with the towering great mosque situated at its edge (fig. 3.1).

Printed in 1839, Otth's lithographs, which form a suite of thirty prints with title page and text, were published in his hometown of Berne, Switzerland. Lavish because of their large size and use of yellow ocher color, Otth's lithographs furnished some of the most picturesque early views of Algiers, including the palace of the dey before the French army corps of engineers razed the structure (see fig. 1.1). In this print, where the newly created square spreads out in front of the palace, a lively market is represented with local vendors shaded under pitched tents, protected from the sun, which bleaches the famous cascade of white houses forming the Casbah above. Here, as in Otth's other prints, there are a few Europeans discreetly posed among an animated crowd of Kabyles, Moors, Biskris, Kulughlis, blacks, and Jews who reflect Otth's choice of title: *Esquisses africaines*. In the accompanying text, Otth notes that he chose this scene as the closing print in his suite in order to impress upon a prospective traveler—fatigued by the monotony of European cities—how Algiers represents a rich cultural fabric filled with new experiences.[1] At the same time, Otth remarks how he deplores the destruction of one of the city's most beautiful mosques, the al-Sayyida Mosque, and a considerable number of Moorish houses undertaken to create this square known as the "place du gouvernement." Otth is conflicted by the loss of these monuments, whose existence should have been guaranteed by the French terms of occupation,[2] and yet he recognizes the utility the square provides for commerce and military functions. Otth's dilemma of wishing to preserve the traditional, but also wanting the convenience of Western advances, underscores issues of modernity that continue to reverberate in our own era.

An equally poignant dilemma resides in the medium of the print and its later follower the photograph, since both captured the transient state of a colonial entity, preserving in some sense the indigenous culture while serving as powerful communication tools that promoted colonization by fueling tourism, business, and immigration because of their widespread dissemination. The most obvious political agendas were those of artists attached to the invading *armée française en Afrique* in 1830. But the watercolors and sketches produced by these artists, headed notably by Alexandre Genet (fig. 3.2), were primarily intended for a select audience: to enrich the royal *galerie des Batailles* at Versailles and serve as a record for the combatants.[3] Yet besides the official representations of the siege and occupation, there was another, much larger body of mass-produced images created to answer Europe's enormous desire to learn about this newly opened land. Among these works, some of the earliest were produced by members of the French military—such as Captain Claude-Antoine Rozet—who on their own initiatives published illustrated accounts of their sojourns in Algiers.

Perhaps Rozet's training as a geologist influenced the tenor of his three-volume work, *Voyage dans la Régence d'Alger*, published in 1833, which represents one of the most nuanced accounts of Algiers before its makeover by the French. The thirty lithographs in the accompanying atlas are based on sketches made by Rozet and by another officer, M. de Prébois, that present the city first from the sea and then depict various views of the suburb Bab el-Oued, the city gate of this name, a café, an unnamed street, the interior of a house, and other views of the surrounding landscape and its monuments (fig. 3.3). Rozet's atlas establishes a repertoire of images depicting the city that are repeated and expanded upon in such contemporary works as *Voyage pittoresque dans la Régence*

3.2 *View of Algiers from Bab el-Oued,* Alexandre Genet, watercolor (Service Historique de la Défense, Château de Vincennes, Paris, SH/D145)

d'Alger exécuté en 1833 et lithographié par E. Lessore et W. Wyld. Dedicated to the painter Horace Vernet, with whom Lessore and Wyld traveled, these plates, far more descriptive of daily life than Rozet's compendium, show such urban details as close-up views of street merchants, the interior of a mosque, a wealthy family seated for a meal in their dining room, a teacher and his pupils studying in the shade of a small two-story street alcove, and craftsmen dyeing cloth (fig. 3.4). Both sets of prints, although created by different professionals for different purposes—to illustrate a description by a scientist and a travel account by two artists—typify the colonial image of Algiers disseminated in the 1830s: a city captured from mythic pirates, whose pacified state lends itself to habitation, exploration, and exploitation.

This attitude is most succinctly summed up, not by a Frenchman, but by R. Jungmann, a little-known Polish refugee artist and author, whose poignant text on the French colonization of Algiers seems to be reflected in his evocative lithograph of Algiers, in which the city is cast in shadow and lighted only in its lower parts, as though France's presence in Africa will bring it out of darkness (fig. 3.5): "All that has been exposed in the course of this work proves that the

3.3 *Bab el-Oued Gate and Fountain, inside the Walls,* Claude-Antoine Rozet, lithograph (Rozet, *Voyage dans la Régence d'Alger* [Paris: Arthus Bertrand, 1833], no plate number)

regency of Algiers indeed presents the advantages for the establishment of a colony. The colony formed here by the Romans with much success validates my conclusions. All of humanity is interested in seeing Africa become civilized. Africa cannot be destroyed without causing much wrong to the rest of the globe . . . because otherwise we would be deprived of our portion of products that Africa ought to furnish us."[4]

The potential wealth of Algeria was long evident to western Europe: it had been the bread basket for the Roman Empire[5] and again, between 1793 and 1798, had supplied shipments of grain and other foodstuffs to Napoleon's armies in Egypt and Italy, the unpaid bill for which caused a dispute between the dey of Algiers and the French consul that ultimately let to the invasion by the French in 1830.[6] From the sixteenth century, when Algiers came under Ottoman rule, its contact with the West, beyond limited trade, was confined to the establishments of a few European consuls residing in the city. As the seat of the largest Ottoman navy in the western Mediterranean, Algiers built its wealth from corsair activity and unfairly gained a reputation for attacking and plundering European trading ships and selling the Christians onboard as slaves or holding them for ransom, activities that Mediterranean powers engaged in at the time.[7]

Before the French invasion of 1830, the most popular printed image of Algiers among Europeans was one taken from the sea, showing the expanse of the city

3.4 *(Left)* *Dyer*, E. Lessore and W. Wyld, lithograph (*Voyage pittoresque dans la Régence d'Alger exécuté en 1833 et lithographié par E. Lessore and W. Wyld* [Paris: C. Motte, 1835], pl. 23)

3.5 *(Below)* *View of Algiers*, Robert Jungmann, lithograph (Jungmann, *Costumes, moeurs et usages des Algériens* [Strasbourg: J. Bernard, 1837], pl. 34)

cascading down to the harbor, with the breakwater jutting out on the right.[8] Although early travelers published descriptive accounts of the city,[9] the lack of a visual representation "intra muros" must have only been emphasized by the multiple panoramas that dramatized the English bombardment of Algiers by Lord Exmouth in 1816, after which the dey of Algiers freed several hundreds of Christian slaves and agreed to other concessions. Because Algiers had competed with other maritime states trading in the western Mediterranean for several centuries, Lord Exmouth's triumph proclaimed far-reaching results that one panorama promoter boastfully advertised as "illustrative of the most interesting events of that victorious enterprise glorious in itself, and so important in its consequences to the interests of Great Britain, and the maritime world at large."[10]

From all accounts of the many panorama versions of Lord Exmouth's bombardment, Algiers was depicted from the sea as though the viewer were in one of the English boats. The most spectacular Algiers panorama was the one painted in 1818 by Henry Aston Barker, who erected the first panorama theater in 1792, in London's Leicester Square. Round in shape, the panorama theater held a 360-degree canvas, with a viewing platform in the center that created the illusion of transporting the spectator to the middle of the event.[11] With his canvas measuring 10,000 square feet, Barker positioned his bombardment of Algiers as though the spectator were in the middle of the harbor at 9 p.m. on 27 August 1816, just as the British flotilla, consisting of the *Queen Charlotte* and fifty-four other gun, mortar, and rocket boats, barges, and yawls, had set on fire most of the Algerian contingent of between forty and fifty vessels: "It was by their fire all the ships in the port with the exception of the outer frigate were in flames, which extended rapidly over the whole arsenal, store-houses, and gun boats— exhibiting a spectacle of awful grandeur and interest no pen can describe. . . . At this moment a violent thunder-storm began, accompanied with lightning, which swept along the ships in vivid streams; whilst the pealing of the thunder far exceeded in loudness the 'cannon's deafening roar.' The combined effect of the thunder, the lightning, the noise of the loud-mouthed cannon, and the arsenal and the ships, now in flames, was at once terrific, overwhelming, and sublime."[12] Already famous for earlier naval battles that he had painted, Barker re-created the bombardment of Algiers not only with stunning drama but with assured accuracy, since he had consulted with several of the fleet officers and Mr. Salamè, who accompanied Lord Exmouth on the *Queen Charlotte* as interpreter.[13] Barker's monumental canvas does not survive, but its published program includes a diagram of the composition (fig. 3.6).

Lord Exmouth's bombardment of Algiers might be described as a box office hit among the panorama theaters of England, and even to some extent on the

3.6　Schematic drawing of Henry Aston Barker's panorama, etching (James Jennings, *Description of Lord Exmouth's Attack upon Algiers Painted by Henry Aston Barker: Now Exhibiting in His Panorama, Leicester Square, written by James Jennings* [London: Jas. Adlard and Sons, 1818])

Continent. Information gleaned from handbills and advertisements in contemporary British newspapers reveals that several large-scale panoramas were exhibited throughout the country.[14] Between 1816 and 1817, William Turner exhibited a panorama of the bombardment of Algiers in the New Panorama Theater in Birmingham. Messrs. Marshall advertised "The Grand Historical Peristrephic Panorama of the City of Algiers" as being exhibited in Dublin, Edinburgh, Glasgow, Manchester, Norwich, Sunderland, and York between 1819 and 1827 (fig. 3.7). Mr. Barker and Co. (who seems to be unrelated to Henry Aston Barker) had a "Grand Peristrephic or Moving Panorama of the Bombardment of Algiers" that he installed in the Great Room of the Swan Tavern in Exeter in 1827. J. B. Laidlaw commissioned Clarkson Stanfield and David Roberts to paint a panorama of the bombardment, which was taken on a European tour and exhibited, among other places, in Rotterdam, Amsterdam, and Cologne. Curiously, in 1831 Monsieur Daguire and Co. staged a panorama of Algiers also at the Swan Tavern in Exeter.[15] As late as 1852, George Danson and Sons mounted a panorama of "Algiers and Its Bombardment in 1816" at the Belle-Vue Gardens, and John Williams Wilson exhibited "The Storming of Algiers" before emigrating to Australia in 1855.

While no large-scale panoramas of Lord Exmouth's victory seem to have reached France, the visual reporting there was conveyed through a hand-colored

ONE WEEK LONGER.
IN THE
Large Assembly-Room, Blake-Street,
THE MAGNIFICENT PANORAMA OF
LORD EXMOUTH'S SPLENDID VICTORY OVER THE
ALGERINES;
Accompanied by a full MILITARY BAND.

, Day Exhibitions at TWELVE and Two o'Clock.—Evening Exhibitions, Doors to open at Half-past SIX, to commence at SEVEN. Second ditto, to commence at EIGHT, when the Room will be most BRILLIANTLY ILLUMINATED.—Books, descriptive of the Battle, with original Letters, and Algerine Cruelties, to be had at the Room, price 6d.

The WHOLE PROCEEDS OF WEDNESDAY EVENING will be APPROPRIATED to the BENEFIT of the YOUNG GIRL who was injured by the accident on Friday Evening last.

MESSRS. MARSHALL, impressed with the deepest sorrow for the accident which occurred on Friday Evening last, beg leave to state that the Gallery has been inspected by an Architect and proper Workmen, who have signified their approbation of it; the Public may therefore now visit it with perfect safety and pleasure. They have been prevailed upon at the solicitation of numerous Friends, to remain ONE WEEK LONGER; it will therefore be necessary for all who wish to be gratified with a sight of this MAGNIFICENT SPECTACLE, to embrace the only opportunity they may ever have of enjoying such an intellectual treat, consisting of the Grand PERISTREPHIC PANORAMA of the

BOMBARDMENT OF
ALGIERS
AND THE
Abolition of Christian Slavery; also the City as it appeared before the Battle, and all the Vessels engaged in that glorious Enterprise, and the

City of ALGIERS in Ruins,
AS IT APPEARED AFTER THE BATTLE,
With the British Boats bringing away the Christian Slaves from bondage, to liberty, happiness and home.

This tremendous event, so interesting to every feeling heart, (in which our gallant Tars bore so conspicuous a part, and none more so than the son of the Very Rev. the Dean of York, who was severely wounded,) is represented upon upwards of 16,000 square feet of Canvas, in a superior style of brilliancy and effect, the Vessels being on the largest scale ever delineated upon Canvas, Painted under the direction of Captain Sir JAMES BRISBANE, K. B. from Drawings made on the spot by eminent Naval Officers.

Order of the Subjects in this Panorama, & appropriate Musical Accompaniments.

SUBJECTS.	MUSIC.
I. The City, Harbour and Bay of Algiers, previous to the Bombardment, with their immense Fortifications and Batteries	Overture and Turkish Air.
II. The approach of the Queen Charlotte, Admiral Lord Exmouth conspicuous on the Quarter Deck	See the Conquering Hero.
III. The remainder of the British Fleet entering the Bay to take their stations	Hearts of Oak.
IV. The Bombardment of the City, with the British Fleet anchored close on the shore—the Flotilla of Gun, Mortar and Rocket Boats, in the act of throwing Congreve Rockets into the City; and the perilous situation of the Leander	Grand Battle Piece.
V. Continuation of the Attack—daring position of the Admiral's Ship—the Algerine Frigate in flames—the Emperor's Fort and the Citadel throwing down Shot and Shells on the Fleet, from their elevated situations	Naval Battle Piece.
VI. The British Fire-ship exploding under the Octagon Light-house of the Mole—the City also illuminated from the flames of the Algerine Fleet, Dock Yards, Store-houses, &c. which decided the action, and compelled the Dey to submit to all the demands of the British	Rule Britannia.
VII. The City, Batteries, &c. in Ruins, as they appeared after the Battle	Britons strike home.
VIII. The Christian Slaves released from bondage, borne away in Boats, shouting and throwing their caps in the air for joy	The Galley Slave.
The Dey of Algiers and his Ministers viewing the destruction of the City, &c.	Finale—God save the King.

Admission,—Front Seats, 2s. Second Seats, 1s. 6d. Back Seats, 1s. Children, in the Front Seats, at Half Price.

PRINTED BY J. WOLSTENHOLME, GAZETTE-OFFICE, YORK.

3.7 *Bombardment of Algiers*, letterpress, handbill of Marshall's panorama, 1819–27 (Collection of David Robertson, London)

"vue d'optique" published by Chereau, the leading printer of these fashionable types of prints, measuring approximately ten by sixteen inches; it was meant to be seen through a convex lens built into a viewing box, or zograscope. Compressed and telescopically seen, the city of Algiers in this print forms the backdrop to the naval siege described in the accompanying text as having resulted in the freeing of the Christian slaves and the abolition of Christian slavery in the Regency of Algiers.[16] Not surprisingly, just after the French conquest of Algiers in 1830, two popular entertainments featuring that city opened in Paris: a "Cos-

morama" by the abbé Gazzera in the Passage Vivienne and Mazarra's "Musée Cosmopolite" on the rue de Provence.[17] However, both these entertainments simply represented a cityscape of Algiers from the sea. As one reviewer of Mazarra's panorama stated, "All we know at present is an exterior view of the city, but we hope we will not have to wait too long for interior views, since the area is now being explored by the painters Gudin, Langlois, Tanneur, Isabey, and Berville."[18] In other words, Algiers was known only summarily, so that when Victor Hugo declared in 1829 that the Orient preoccupied his thoughts and imagination, Algiers did not contribute to shaping his illustrious verse forms in *Les Orientales* because the collective visual impression of the city was too scanty.[19]

All of this changed abruptly on 17 February 1833, when Charles Langlois opened his panorama entitled "La prise d'Alger" at no. 40 rue Saint-Martin in the Marais. For the next twenty-two months, until the panorama closed at the end of November 1834, the inhabitants of Paris virtually walked into Algiers and gained an inside look at the city as though they were standing on the balcony of the dey in the Casbah. As one critic noted, experiencing the Algiers panorama was like traveling to North Africa and only paying the cost of an omnibus across Paris.[20]

Similar to the first panorama theaters in London, Langlois's circular structure measured thirty-five meters in diameter and twelve meters high (fig. 3.8). However, according to contemporary accounts, Langlois had refined the trompe l'oeil effect by installing frosted glass in the skylights that diminished the shadows on the canvas and by placing actual built structures between the viewing platform and the canvas so that the boundary between illusion and reality was blurred.[21]

Today, it is difficult to describe what it was like to view the Algiers panorama in 1833–34, since neither the painting nor the theater survives. Nonetheless, in her study of Langlois's panorama, Marie-Paule Petit presents an insightful overview of the colossal image through an exhaustive review of the contemporary literature on the panorama and the numerous existing preparatory sketches made by the artist.[22] To heighten the otherworldly experience, upon entering the theater the spectator first walked through a re-creation of one of the principal courtyards of the Casbah and an exquisitely detailed room in an Algerian palace before mounting the stairs to the viewing platform.[23] Having reached the platform, the spectator to the Algiers panorama had the sensation of standing on the dey's balcony high up in the Casbah overlooking the city, with its white and uniformly squarish houses interspersed with terraces descending below to the bay, which stretched out in front. In one direction of the circular viewing plat-

3.8   Cross section of panorama theater, Jean-Charles Langlois, watercolor, 1830–32 (Musée Carnavalet, Paris)

form was the "Fort l'Empereur" and in the other the "Fort des Anglais" under attack from three nearby French gunboats. Gunfire continued across the bay, erupting from a line of French boats and frigates headed by "la Provence" commanded by Admiral Duperré.[24] In another direction, opposite the bay, stretched a distant view of the snow-capped Atlas Mountains. According to one critic, experiencing the panorama was not an illusion but was like really being in Algiers, walking among the cannons on the lookouts: "The great whitened block of the city, the transparent waters of the sea, the distant haze, the countryside with its richness of color and vigor, arrested our view."[25]

Since the panorama was painted to represent the highpoint of the French invasion on 4 July 1830, just moments after the explosion of the Fort l'Empereur, the spectator experienced this decisive event as the premier inhabitant of the

3.9   *Al-Jadid Mosque and the Battery of Hussein Dey,* Jean-Charles Langlois, oil on paper, 1830–32
(Musée des Beaux-Arts, Caen, MJ 86-482)

Casbah, Hussein Dey, would have seen it. Oddly comparable to reporting in our
own time on current world affairs, the Algiers panorama represents the CNN of
its time, placing the viewer right inside the opponents' territory, just as Western
journalists were reporting from the Palestine Hotel during the 2003 bombardment of Baghdad. Eusèbe de Salle, who was a translator in the French army
during the 1830 siege of Algiers, said that, upon seeing the panorama, all the
sensations he experienced during the battle returned. For Salle, the panorama
underlined how Algiers embodied the "most beautiful conquest of the army,
a city hailed to form the kernel of the richest and largest French colony."[26] In
essence, the panorama represented a visual conquest that re-created the glorious
triumph for a broad spectrum of the public.

To make the preparatory sketches for the panorama (as seen, e.g., in figs. 3.9
and 3.10), Langlois visited Algiers twice in 1830 and again in 1832. Although
Langlois himself was an army officer who held the rank of "Chef de Batail-

3.10 *Algiers in 1830*, Jean-Charles Langlois, oil on paper, 1830 (Musée des Beaux-Arts, Caen, 7J 86-506)

lon au corps royal d'état major," he paid his own expenses to accompany the French army to Algiers in order to sketch and study the city. Clearly, Langlois was a visionary, for when he embarked with the French army for North Africa, construction of the panorama theater in the Marais had only begun in February of that year.[27] Langlois's sole recorded comment about the Algiers panorama refers to representing France's "ancienne gloire," but he must have expected that the subject would draw large crowds.[28] Having been on display for a little under two years with a regular ticket price of 2.50 francs, the panorama of Algiers grossed over 68,000 francs and attracted some 27,000 spectators, coming not just from the capital but from the provinces and abroad.[29] But it was not just the novelty of this "new" city that augmented ticket sales; it was also the way the panoramic image was "scientifically" rendered, as noted by several critics.[30] Using both a camera obscura and a camera lucida while working in Algiers, Langlois produced a pseudophotographic style (several years before the invention of photography) that did not go unnoticed.[31] Unlike other contemporary artists who may have been reticent to disclose that they were using optical devices in their work,[32] Langlois did not hide the fact and may actually have used it as a means to promote the Algiers panorama, which drew fewer visitors than his first and preceding panorama representing the "Bataille de Navarin."[33] Though the Algiers panorama reached a smaller audience than probably anticipated, it may have played a critical role in persuading French opinion to colonize the Regency of Algiers, as this issue was under parliamentary debate in May 1834.[34] It should be noted that colonization had not been the intent of the 1830 intervention, which was ostensibly undertaken to redress an insult to the French consul and abolish piracy (which, however, was no longer a threat at the time). The spike in visits to the panorama during this month correlates with a small notice on 5 May 1834 in the *Journal des artistes* that connects the panorama to the debates in the Chamber of Deputies: "The important discussion in the Chamber of Deputies on the question of knowing if France will retain or abandon this colony adds much interest to the painting in which M. Langlois has so aptly rendered the city of Algiers and its rich surroundings. Thus, one should hurry to go and contemplate these things, at least in a painted form, although the platform for the spectators is too small."[35]

Tantalizingly real, Langlois's re-creation of Algiers undoubtedly helped to win favor for the institution of a military colonial government in the city, which was ultimately concluded by the ordinance of 22 July 1834. At the Algiers panorama, popular opinion may have been further swayed by the attendant guides, who were the actual conquerors of Africa, described by a contemporary reviewer as perfectly complementing the illusion since these veterans explained the smallest details of the memorable expedition that were represented in the painting.[36]

While Langlois's panorama brought Algiers to Paris for the public to visit and study, I would argue that the illusion of seeing the city firsthand was continued into the midcentury by the newly invented medium of photography, which was considered by leading critics of this period not only authoritative in detail but—like a panorama—complete in the view presented.[37] Although massively different in scale than the panorama, the photograph can be understood as the visual descendant of the panorama theater: they both rely on the mechanical device of the camera obscura to capture the image, and both were considered by their critics to create a more concrete reality than other forms of artistic expression. Since its invention in 1839 and through all of its subsequent processes, photography has retained an unmatched reputation as the medium that can convey the viewer to another place or another time because of its truthfulness.[38]

In spite of the numerous (and now mainly lost) daguerreotypes and, later, prints and salted-paper and albumen photographs that were taken of Algiers

3.11 *Entrance to the Casbah of Algiers*, Félix-Jacques-Antoine Moulin, albumen print (photograph album: *Algérie photographiée*, 1856/57, no. 25; Service Historique de la Marine, Château de Vincennes, Paris)

and filtered back to western Europe in the 1840s and 1850s, it was the extensive photographic record of the Regency created by Félix-Jacques-Antoine Moulin that formed the most substantive reportage for the visually literate public. Moulin was a Parisian photographer who spent eighteen months in Algeria during 1856–57, producing several hundred negatives, from which he printed 300 photographs bound (50 to a volume) in six volumes that were sold in his studio and other locales in the capital (fig. 3.11).[39] For its time, Moulin's dense photographic reportage was unusual and caught the attention of the press. In the weekly *L'illustration*, a two-page essay on Moulin's work (fig. 3.12), featuring six wood engravings after his photographs, noted that although Algeria had been a French possession for twenty-seven years, it was scarcely known from earlier descriptions: "The physiognomy [of Algeria] . . . is still only imperfectly

3.12 Woodcut after photograph by Félix-Jacques-Antoine Moulin (reproduced in G. Julien, "L'Algérie photographiée," *L'illustration* 31 [1858]: 200)

apparent to our eyes. We certainly possess numerous details, but we lack the ensemble, which eludes us. Just a few months ago, the entire living portrait of Algeria remained to be created, and this work was naturally reserved for photography, so able to capture raw nature and reproduce it with the most minute exactitude."[40]

By not only complementing but also greatly adding to the early visual portrayal of Algeria, Moulin's extensive coverage was regarded as providing the definitive picture. And while his original photographs reached a broad audience, the frequent reproduction of them in a printed medium, such as the wood engraving in Charles Lahure, *Histoire contemporaine de la France*, published in 1864 (p. 235), reached an even larger literate public. Though Moulin's motives for photographing Algeria remain vague, his work clearly represents a "collection of photographs that necessarily serve the political and military interests" of the Second Empire.[41] Indeed, Napoleon III accepted the dedication of this work, as a midcentury journalist noted in *L'illustration*, because Moulin's work "is especially destined to popularize Algeria, where France has already made such great sacrifices, and where she is in the process of founding a new empire."[42]

In the 1830s it was the virtual presence of Algiers in the form of a panorama that helped to buttress support to retain the Regency as a colony; but by the 1850s it was the photographic coverage that helped the French public assimi-

3.13   *Place du Gouvernement*, Jean-Baptiste-Antoine Alary, albumen print (photograph album: *Views of Algiers*, c. 1857; Getty Research Institute, 92.R.85*)

late Algiers into its visual consciousness and adjust its thinking to a new world order. By bringing the image of Algiers and the outlying regions—more and more of which was coming under military domination—home to the metropole, photography helped the French public consider Algeria as "la nouvelle France."[43] Because of its new and startling immediacy, photography broke down provincial thinking and expanded the outlook of a curious nation. This midcentury thirst for a "virtual" experience of Algiers extended even to visitors and inhabitants of that city: an 1857 photograph of the place du Gouvernement (see fig. 3.13) shows a camera obscura building positioned next to the balustrade (on the left side of the photograph) to capture a view of the port and city's edge for those spectators willing to pay for a virtual image of what they could see firsthand.[44] With the camera obscura's lens positioned out toward the water, this

3.14 *Sidi Ferruch*, Moulin, albumen print, 1856/57 (photograph album: *Tunis-Algerien*, 1861; Getty Research Institute, 95.R.106)

view—unlike a photograph or a painted monumental panorama—would have also captured in full glistening color the busy marine traffic in the port and the ever-changing pattern of the sea on its viewing screen.

A prime audience for images of the Regency of Algiers, as captured in the new medium of photography, would have been the veterans of the military expeditions themselves. Whether for or against colonization, veterans of the 1830 intervention—of which the number must have been sizable since the expeditionary forces constituted some 64,000 individuals—would have returned home with vivid firsthand accounts of this newly conquered land and its foreign culture.[45] Certain prints and photographs produced even decades after the French invasion represent locations around the city that hold little visual interest except for their importance in the unfolding and retelling of the French victory. Two obvious examples are Moulin's photograph of the barren shore at Sidi Ferruch, captioned as depicting the landing site of the invading French army (fig. 3.14),[46] and the photographs taken by Moulin and also by Jean-Baptiste-Antoine Alary—one of the earliest proprietors of a photographic studio in Algiers—that show the fountain near the Porte Neuve, where the victorious army entered the

3.15 *Porte Neuve*, Alary, albumen print, late 1850s (photograph album: *Belgique, Angleterre, Suisse et Algérie*, fol. 1r; Getty Research Institute, 95.R.100)

city (fig. 3.15).[47] Although the actual city gate by which the army entered was destroyed in the French rebuilding of the city walls, the nearby Arab fountain became the historic marker for this event. That Alary and Moulin included a view of the Porte Neuve when each exhibited at the Société Française de Photographie in 1857 and 1859, respectively, seems hardly a coincidence.[48] It is also significant that both these photographs were taken in the 1850s—some twenty-five years after the actual event—to commemorate its occurrence. Indeed, there is no doubt about the intent of the image, since the printed caption accompanying the Moulin photograph states: "It is the Porte Neuve (Bab el Djedid), called also the Gate of Victory, through which the French made their entry into Algiers, after having captured it on 5 July 1830."

A print from the same negative as Alary's 1850s photograph of the Porte Neuve survives as a *carte-de-visite*,[49] or small-format photograph that was invented at the end of the 1850s and flourished in the 1860s as a popular visual medium, revealing that, for at least another decade, the image continued to sustain and illustrate the oral history of the French intervention.

If the existing 1850s photographs of Algiers are representative of what actually was taken at the time, then the frequency of an architectural detail of the Casbah—depicting the exterior of the portico where the famous fly whisk inci-

3.16 *Casbah Portico*, Charles Marville, salted-paper print, 1850s (photograph album: *Belgique, Angleterre, Suisse et Algérie*; Getty Research Institute, 95.R.100)

dent unfolded and often captioned as the "coup d'éventail"—takes on symbolic meaning as visual justification for the French intervention. Not only are there unusually many photographs of this portico, given the rarity of 1850s photographs, but there are several almost identically framed photographs of this portico taken by four quite different photographers: Alary, a resident photographer in Algiers; Charles Marville, a Paris photographer who either visited Algiers himself or sold the work of another photographer who visited that city (fig. 3.16);[50] an anonymous photographer who may have been attached to the military;[51] and Gustave de Beaucorps, an amateur photographer who sojourned there in 1859.[52]

The insult to the French consul in 1827 when the dey allegedly hit him with a fly whisk became a cause célèbre in contemporary accounts and later nineteenth-century histories that explained France's march against Algiers as avenging French honor.[53] This veiled excuse for the 1830 intervention continued well into the Second Empire and formed the foundation for further territorial expansion in the name of *"la mission civilisatrice."*[54]

The repeated portrayal by different photographers of the Casbah portico where the fly whisk incident occurred indicates that this image took on broad national symbolism, according to Max Weber's definition of "nationalism" as being "based upon sentiments of prestige, which often extend deep down to the petty bourgeois masses of political structures rich in the historical attainment of power-positions. The attachment to all this political prestige may fuse with a specific belief in responsibility towards succeeding generations."[55] Although photographs memorializing the 1830 intervention mirrored the official rhetoric on the topic, it must be kept in mind that they were largely produced by independent commercial photographers, who either subscribed to the current thinking on nationalism or had specifically selected these subjects with a profit motive in mind (or both). By visually repeating landmarks evoking the 1830 intervention, these photographs served—on a much more popular level—the same function as certain high-art battle paintings that, as Todd Porterfield has shown, were employed by the Restoration and July Monarchy to rationalize and celebrate the French intervention in the Middle East and North Africa.[56] There was no direct governmental sponsorship for photography in North Africa as there was for painting, but because of photography's commercial underpinnings and its status as a reproductive medium, it contributed nonetheless to the imperialist outlook of the Second Empire.

The extent of the photographic portrayal of Algiers from 1839, when the medium was invented, to the end of the Second Empire, when French attention was temporarily shifted away from Algeria because of the Franco-Prussian War, can only be surmised due to the fragmentary state of the remaining body of work. However, even from this imperfect picture, Algiers emerges as a subject frequently captured in the photographic lens of amateurs and professionals alike. Perhaps the nineteenth-century image of Algiers that most closely aligns with the outpouring of literary descriptions during and after the French conquest is one taken by Louis Ducos du Hauron—one of the foremost inventors of color photography[57]—because it contrasts the intense azure blue of the Mediterranean with the white of the city's buildings (fig. 3.17). Although this is the only one of Ducos du Hauron's color photographs of Algiers that is known, he probably took many since he lived in the city between 1884 and 1896. Planting his camera just outside Bab Azoun, he must have had a fast shutter speed to catch a small boat, whose distant white sails mirror the white urban buildup of the place de la Republique stacked up in the foreground. In spite of its fuzzy

3.17 *View of the Harbor, Algiers,* Louis Ducos du Hauron, trichrome photograph, c. 1870s (Biblio-thèque Nationale de France)

quality, Ducos du Hauron's photograph—because of its powerful, almost abstract streaks of color—strikingly portrays the legendary character of Algiers.

But the photographic career of Algiers actually begins half a century earlier with the city's inclusion in one of the seminal publications to use photographic illustrations. First appearing in 1841 and later expanded and republished, Noël-Marie-Paymal Lerebours's *Excursions Daguerriennes,* which features sixty prints pulled from daguerreotypes, was available for sale "by all the principal booksellers, opticians, and print sellers in France and foreign parts."[58] In other words, it was widely available for sale and—even for those who may not have been able to afford it—was readily accessible to browsers in local shops. In Lerebours's *Excursions,* a view of the al-Jadid Mosque in Algiers (fig. 3.18) heads the series of European and Middle Eastern sites.

Dramatically lighted, the mosque in Lerebours's etching and aquatint stands massively on the left of the composition, contrasting with the jumbled piles of an active building site represented in the shadowy details on the right. The tightly framed composition seemingly spotlighting the mosque reveals—on closer inspection—the dominant French presence explained in the accompanying text: "Algiers is today a French city, as our travelers and soldiers have recast it and changed its physiognomy."[59]

Lerebours's much-published world tour, as captured in the dark chamber of the new and mysterious daguerreotype, must have inspired the subsequent

3.18 *The New Mosque* [al-Jadid Mosque], Noël-Marie-Paymal Lerebours, lithograph after a daguerreotype (Lerebours, *Excursions Daguerriennes* [Paris: Rittner et Goupil, 1841], pl. 1; J. Paul Getty Museum, 84.XB.1187.1)

series of twenty-two lithographs devoted entirely to Algeria that were printed from daguerreotypes taken by an anonymous photographer and an equally unknown daguerreotypist named Bettinger. For the most part, each view concentrates on a picturesque aspect of Algiers or, as in the print of the place Mahon (fig. 3.19), a French presence that integrates harmoniously with the Algerian culture. Printed by the leading French lithographic studio of Lemercier and the smaller establishment of Decan, the series was for sale both in the French capital, at the publisher Wild located near the place de la Bourse, and in Algiers at the publisher Dubois Frères and Marest.[60] More romantic than photographic, the now-lost daguerreotype plates in this series had been heavily reworked by lithographic artists who also enlivened the scenes with people, since the daguerreotype camera could not capture figures in motion.

Only two other lithographs from daguerreotypes of Algiers survive, but these are strikingly different in scale and technique from Bettinger's series of

3.19 *Place Mahon*, Bettinger, lithograph after a daguerreotype, 1847 (photograph album: *Views of Algeria*, pl. 15; Getty Research Institute, 94.R.3)

twenty-two. Representing sweeping panoramic views of the harbor of Algiers (fig. 3.20),[61] they retain a photographic realism that transports the viewer into the picture. The large lithographs (measuring 39 by 121 cm each) were printed in Paris by Auguste Bry, on the rue du Bac, from daguerreotypes credited to a certain F. Geay, whose photographic career is otherwise unrecorded.

Besides multiple prints pulled from daguerreotypes, tourists visiting Algiers could purchase original and unique daguerreotypes of the city by 1848, when two daguerreotypists are recorded as established there: Monsieur Louis from Orleans and Delemotte, an officer attached to the État-Major.[62] While no daguerreotypes by the former are known, three of Delemotte's signed quarter-plate daguerreotypes taken in 1850, when he was in partnership with Alary, survive. Depicting Algerian sites outside Algiers, these three daguerreotypes attest to the activity of the Delemotte/Alary studio.[63] If the process for transferring a daguerreotype to a printed image had been more successful, photographic illustrations printed from daguerreotypes would have undoubtedly been used instead of the engraved drawings that accompanied the government-sponsored publication undertaken by the Commission d'Exploration Scientifique d'Algérie. In various reports made by Colonel Bory de St. Vincent, head of the commission, daguerreotypes are noted, although there is no mention of who is taking the images or their subject.[64] In a glowing report written on 20 December 1842 concerning the work of Amable Ravoisié, who was the architect responsible for the commission's report entitled "Beaux arts, architecture, sculpture, inscriptions et vues," Ravoisié's activity with a daguerreotype camera is noted along with the implication that either Ravoisié or the author of the report placed more credence in the daguerreotypes than Ravoisié's own drawings: "M. Ravoisié has submitted for our examination some fifty daguerreotype plates which represent both general and specific views taken in various parts of Algeria. Some of these plates will be very useful to complement or rectify the drawings [accompanying his study]."[65]

During the four years that Ravoisié spent studying the ancient monuments of Algeria, there were actually two daguerreotype cameras and well over one hundred plates at his disposal.[66] What is most surprising is that the Commission d'Exploration Scientifique de l'Algérie received its first daguerreotype camera in a shipment sent on 4 December 1839, just months after the invention of the instrument had been announced to the public. Besides the fifty daguerreotypes taken by Ravoisié and sent to Paris at the end of 1842 to accompany his study, he may have also been the maker of other daguerreotypes of unspecified subjects that were documented in a report of 25 April 1842 and that were to be sent along with "art objects, including sculpture and antique inscriptions, medals, drawings, plans and views," to the Musée du Jardin du Roi.[67] Despite this scant information on the early history of the daguerreotype in Algeria, it is apparent that the instrument came to Algiers early and was used by various practitioners, including government-sponsored photographers and well-to-do travelers.

Precious and unique, daguerreotypes reached only a limited audience. However, as multiple paper photographs printed from negatives became the dominant photographic process in the early 1850s, Alary, the primary commercial photographer in Algiers in this period, was mastering the new technique and persuaded the elite artistic community of Paris to focus on his stunning photographic panorama of Algiers. In 1856 Alary submitted six photographs printed from collodion negatives to the second annual exhibition organized by the newly founded Société Française de Photographie in Paris. The Exhibition Commission, comprising some of the most illustrious photographers, artists, and intellectuals of the time, included Count Olympe Aguado, Hippolyte Bayard, Eugène Delacroix, Léon de Laborde, Vicount Vigier, Auguste-Adolphe Bertsch,

3.20 *Panorama of Algiers Taken from the Lighthouse*, Théodore Müller after a daguerreotype by F. Geay, hand-colored lithograph, c. 1845–50 (printed by August Bry, Paris; Getty Research Institute, 2007.PR.101**)

and Gustave Le Gray.[68] From 15 December 1857 to 15 February 1858, Alary's photographs of Algiers hung alongside the work of such renowned practitioners as Gustave Le Gray and Charles Nègre in a gallery at 35 boulevard des Capucines. Completely unknown today and presumably lost, his panorama garnered exceptional praise:

> The great panorama of Algiers by Monsieur Alary is one of the most important and successful works in this genre: the picture, about two meters wide, comprises [a view of] the entire port of Algeria in impressive proportions. The difficulty of such work does not usually permit one to be overly demanding in artistic results that are not generally applied to panoramas in any case. Nevertheless, we must say that the nine parts that make up this work are not only perfectly aligned and in perspective but also quite well matched in tonal values. In addition, the different views that accompany the panorama give testimony to the great skill of this master.[69]

In the same year at the Exposition des Arts Industriels in Brussels, Nègre, Édouard Baldus, and Félix Nadar captured the top prizes in the photographic section, while Alary won a lesser medal for his views of Algeria.[70] In the following year in London, Alary exhibited a panorama of Algiers, along with one view

of the city and four views of Algeria, at the Photographic Society Exhibition
held at the South Kensington Museum.[71]

Undeniably, Alary's photographs represent the best photographic work produced by a resident Algiers studio not just for its time but for the rest of the
Second Empire. No other Algiers studio during the Second Empire would have
its works juried at the prestigious exhibitions of the Société Française de Photographie or at other European venues. Nonetheless, Algiers—as recorded by
the deep, almost purplish tones of albumen prints—continued to capture the attention of artistic circles to the end of the 1850s because the city attracted some
of the most remarkable elite amateur photographers of the period. The prob-
able reasons for the popularity of Algiers are summarized by historian Michael
Brett, who states that "as a tourist resort, reassuringly French and excitingly
Islamic, Algeria generated a travel literature in which it appeared, literally and
metaphorically, as an oasis, exotically picturesque."[72] For the traveler with a
camera, Algeria offered another incentive. Besides being tantalizing different,
the people of Algiers seem not to have been afraid of being captured in the lens,
as one English traveler, who sojourned there in 1858, noted: "They pass along
without paying the least attention to my aperture; and if I happen to direct the
lens toward a body of them, they are not in the slightest degree discomposed,
and I have been able to obtain pictures free from the stiffness generally apparent
in the photographs of groups of individuals where the figures appear to have

3.21 *Rue de la Porte Neuve*, Edward King Tenison, salted-paper print, 1856 (J. Paul Getty Museum, 84.XP.368.24)

been arranged for the purpose. These Arabs are perfect models."[73] While the series of letters that this anonymous English traveler sent to the *Photographic News* document his encounter with Algeria, his photographs, which do not survive, suggest that the existing photographic portrayal of Algiers by a handful of midcentury travelers should be understood as representative of a much broader, but now lost, visual phenomenon.

In the early 1850s, an unknown traveler, possibly Firmin-Eugène Ledien, a student of Gustave Le Gray, captured a mystic view of the al-Jadid Mosque, although attention to its domed rooftop is detracted by two Christian crosses jutting into the skyline.[74] Also dating from this period are the only two known photographs of Algiers by the Irish aristocrat Edward King Tenison. Initialed and captioned by Tenison, the photographs portray the Porte Pescade and the rue de la Porte Neuve (fig. 3.21).[75] Paul Jeuffrain, a cloth manufacturer from Louviers and member of the Société Française de Photographie since 1855, donated ten views of Algiers and Constantine to the society from a trip he made in 1856.[76] Each of Jeuffrain's five photographs of Algiers represents an unexpected glimpse into the changing city, where two cultures clash (fig. 3.22).[77] The following year marks the visit of another French photographer, Camille Silvy, who ventured to Algiers two years before he opened his London studio (1859–68) famous for exquisite *carte-de-visite* portraits. From the photographs

3.22 Detail of a photograph taken from Jeuffrain's hotel in Algiers, Paul Jeuffrain, salted-paper print, 1856 (Société Française de Photographie, Paris, dossier 0464)

that Silvy took, it is clear that he was familiar with the history of the French diplomatic relations with and conquest of Algiers since two of his views were described as "casbah pavillon du soufflet" and "porte neuve ou porte de la victoire." The rarity of Silvy's Algerian photographs suggests that he did not market them in his London studio or that they did not attract a ready market in the British capital.[78] In 1858 Emmanuel de Noailles offered a series of photographs to the Société Française de Photographie, of which only a single image, showing the ramparts of Algiers, survives.[79] Another Frenchman, Gustave de Beaucorps, visited Algeria in 1858 and 1859 while on an extensive trip to the Middle East and Ottoman Empire. An accomplished amateur photographer, Beaucorps must have been familiar with the published and exhibited professional photographic depictions of Algiers, since his own views repeat details of the Islamic city already recorded by Moulin or Alary, including a five-part panorama of the harbor.[80]

Some of the most stunning views of Algiers were taken by a native of Mannheim, Jakob August Lorent, who can be considered one of the most technologically proficient amateurs working with waxed-paper negatives, or calotypes. He produced eight large-format photographs of Algiers in 1859 that attempt to capture the Islamic character of the city.[81] In contrast to Lorent's selected view of Algiers, Paul Marès, a medical doctor from Montpellier, turned his attention to the broad vistas of the city that revealed how the European presence was gradually taking over certain districts below the Casbah.[82]

Besides these well-off, pleasure-seeking travelers, Algiers also attracted another sort of photographer: those who looked at the picturesque with a profit motive in mind. Some only passed through the city; others are recorded just once; but some photographers remain established in Algiers for several years. The earliest is an unnamed entrepreneur who apparently tried to capitalize on the novelty of his instrument by using it to make some money on the side. This daguerreotypist placed the following advertisement in the journal *L'akhbar* (it appeared nine times between 1 January and 9 March 1843): "Daguerreotype portraits taken in just seconds (15 francs) on the terrace of Madame Arnaud's house, rue des Consuls, 55." Several years later, in 1851, when the daguerreotype was being supplanted in Europe by paper and glass negatives, the painter Charles-Théodore Frère is credited in *L'atlas* (no. 346, 22 August 1851) with having exhibited a daguerreotype portrait of "Mlle. R." taken in Algiers. Another itinerant photographer placed a single notice in the same newspaper (*L'atlas*, 16 May 1851):

Daguerreotype Portraits
M. Durrieu will render your daguerreotype portrait perfectly.
He uses all the necessary colors, including gold and silver as well as diamond hues, so that they become the very likeness of natural tones. Having operated successfully in the major cities of Portugal and Spain, and having established a loyal clientele in Algiers, he plans to depart for the interior of Africa and asks those who still wish to honor him with their patronage to take advantage of the last few days that remain before his departure.[83]

Although Durrieu claims that he had a list of loyal clients, clearly his studio, situated on rue Tanger next to the Gambini bazaar in the Bab Azoun district, must have been short-lived. Whatever Durrieu's reasons for leaving the colony, the long list of other commercial photographers recorded in Algiers can be equated with the host of speculators who descended upon the city "to make a fortune either in wines and liquor, hotels, restaurants, cafés, and buying and selling land without improving it."[84]

Though sketchy and certainly incomplete, the following overview gives a sense of the photographic competition prevalent in the 1860s. Jean-Baptiste-Antoine Alary operated the main photographic studio in Algiers during the 1850s. Although he went into partnership in 1854/55 with the widow Julie Geiser, who had had her own studio since 1852, Alary exhibited photographs solely under his own name in European expositions during the late 1850s.[85] The "Alary & Geiser" studio, as it was advertised in the 1860s, was located at 2, rue Neuve Mahon. In 1867, Jean-Théophile Geiser, Julie's son, took over the operation and stayed at this location at least until 1869 while opening a second studio at 7, rue Bab Azoun, at the corner where it meets the stairs of the "passage de Chartres."[86] His closest competitor at this time was C. Klary, located at no. 1 Galerie Malakoff.[87]

In 1862, when Sebastien Bottin's *Annuaire et almanach du commerce* lists photographers in Algiers for the first time, there were, besides Alary and Geiser, five other photographic studios advertising: Boyer Frères (5, rue Jenina), Ferdinand, Maler, Moutier, and Mulon. In January 1863, A. Clavier advertises in the *Courrier de l'Algérie* that he does "photographie moscovite" and, in addition to portraits, can supply "vues des monuments de Moscou et de St. Petersburg, types russes."[88] From May to June 1863, J. Trésorier, situated at 3, rue Sainte, advertises in *L'akhbar* that he has just arrived from America, where he had worked for ten years. At the end of 1863, he places a long advertisement in the *Courrier de l'Algérie* in which he describes his work as "photographie américaine" and mentions he can supply "Types algeriens, vues algeriennes et américaines."[89] Only a few advertisements printed in *L'akhbar* in December 1863 witness what seems to be the short-lived existence of the Studio Émile (successor to Maurin), located at 12, rue Napoléon. Its disappearance may be attributed to the business savvy of his neighbor Claude-Joseph Portier, who probably spent more in advertising than all the other studios combined in Algiers. Portier's studio was located at 7, rue Napoléon for almost two decades, and his advertisements credit him as a member of the Société Française de Photographie and a student of Belloc and announce that he can provide "photographie nouvelle" in the form of portraits, *cartes-de-visite,* views, and stereoscopes, in addition to photographic equipment and chemicals.[90] The numerous photographic studios and steep competition among them at this time may explain why the Polish photographer Maximilien established himself outside the city on the rue du Diable in Blidah. Appearing in just three issues of *L'akhbar* (11, 18, and 25 January 1867), Maximilien's advertisements, featuring the very unusual earthquake photographs of Mouzaïaville and El-Afroun, suggest, perhaps, his attempt to find a niche market in a less competitive locale outside the capital. Charles Leinack's advertisements (*L'akhbar*, 26 February to 12 March 1865) signaling his specialty in taking photographs of horses at his studio in the Villa-Rioux in the suburb of Mustapha also suggest an attempt to create a new market.

The mid-1860s seem to have witnessed the greatest number of photographic studios in Algiers,[91] but in 1869 there were still six studios listed in Bottin's *Annuaire*—Bertrand, Boyer Frères, Clavier, Geiser, Mulon, and Portier. In addition, J. Weil, located on place Bresson, placed a single ad in *L'akhbar*, 28 April 1865, and Mouttet, located at 2, rue du Laurier, also advertised only once in the same newspaper, on 30 December 1869.[92] From the studio advertisements printed and stamped on the backs of *cartes-de-visite*, seven other photographers were active in Algiers in the second half of the nineteenth century. Feliss Rozier, whose studio was at 6, rue Maugrebins, created the most distinctive examples of *cartes-de-visite*: he often pasted his small photographs of ethnic types on pink stock and signed each card individually with rose-colored ink, ending with an elaborate flourish under his name. A certain Righan used a stamp to record his name and only that of Algiers without a street location on his *cartes-de-visite*, which showed veiled women dressed in flowing white robes. Famin et Cie also depicted ethnic types; Famin lists his location as 8, rue Bab Azoun, but it is difficult to discern from the style of the image whether he preceded or followed A. Clavier, the photographer originating from Moscow, who advertised his studio at this address for most of the 1860s. Based on the fin-de-siècle-style lettering printed on the *cartes-de-visite* of Alexandre Leroux, 14, rue Bab Azoun, and L. Nesme, 22, rue Bab Azoun, it would seem that this thoroughfare continued to attract enterprising photographers until the end of the century.[93] The studio Photographie Saharienne, located at 1, rue Tourville, is distinctive for its geometric carpet on which its subjects are posed, while the studio of Charles Leinack, established at 44, rue Napoléon, places its unveiled Algerian women in an utterly plain setting.[94] If the traveler to Algiers in the late 1860s was not satisfied with the images offered by these studios, he could choose from the selection of photographs for sale at the bookstore of Madame Philippe Tissier, which was the exclusive repository in Algiers for Moulin's photographs and also offered a "dépôt de toutes photographies, représentant les types, vues, monuments, ruines, etc., des trois provinces de l'Algérie."[95]

Besides the traveling and local European audience who were interested in

3.23 Album cover and slipcase, anonymous; box: carved cedar wood; cover: carved wood, tooled and painted leather, brass backings and hinges (photograph album: *Algeria/Tunisia*, 1881; Getty Research Institute, 2001.R.20)

photographs of Algiers as a record of their presence there, an extraordinary example of photography's use to showcase the autochthonous cultures of Algeria (and, to a lesser degree, Tunisia) to the exclusion of a Western presence is recorded by a unique album.[96] The album is protected by an ornate walnut box, carved with a design evoking the familiar *tugra* (seal) of Ottoman sultans (fig. 3.23). Nonetheless, the signature is a playful conflation of two legendary sixteenth-century pirates—Kheireddine and Aroudj. A more abstract reference to the *tugra* design, which gives the title of the album as *Al-Jazair/Tunis* (Algeria/Tunisia), decorates the leather and brass front cover. The title page bears an inscription from the Quran in Arabic and gives the date as 1881—curiously not using the *hijra* calendar. The photographs (fig. 3.24) are carefully selected, emphasizing North African culture while deleting the European interventions; furthermore, all captions are in Algerian dialectical Arabic or Judeo-Hebrew. As an ensemble, the album seems to relay a story about an Algiers uncontaminated by colonial occupation. The compiler and purpose of this album may

3.24 *Ouled Nail Woman*, anonymous, albumen print (photograph album: *Algeria/Tunisia*, 1881, p. 39; Getty Research Institute, 2001.R.20)

never be discovered, but considering the album's expensive artistic presentation and orchestrated content, I am tempted to speculate that it was created as a gift for a high Maghrebi official, perhaps from a French authority. Given that the date of the album coincides with the annexation of Tunisia, this suggestion may not be far-fetched.

If this album stands as a silent witness of how photography was employed to showcase the very cultures colonialism was transforming, it was really the medium's other role as an agent of change that made the greatest impact. During the 1850s and 1860s, when some of the most sweeping changes occurred to Algiers, the photographic studios were there not only recording the transformations to the city but directly contributing to the new urban fabric. The dramatic disappearance of precolonial Algiers under French domination is difficult to grasp from our historical perspective, but Charles Desprez, who moved there in 1853 and published *Alger naguère et maintenant* in 1868, recorded his frustration:

[Algiers] this dazzling quarry, this trapezoid of white marble, this fantastic accumulation of undefinable things that astonish the traveler and delight the artist . . . there are no longer any stepped terraces, no longer an ensemble, no longer a harmony. Houses of all form and height appear, here, there . . . pumpkin-colored, chestnut-colored, the shade of dead leaves, dull, dirty, even black, at the mercy of the proprietors, with their pointed roofs surmounted with rusty pipes, smoking chimneys, or photographic huts. Is this Algeria? Is this the Orient? It might as well be Melun, Charenton![97]

The photographic huts disfiguring the skyline were those very structures with skylights or glass walls, built to maximize light, that photographers constructed on rooftops as their ateliers. Indeed, one such photographic hut appears to be captured in the spontaneous photograph that Paul Jeuffrain took from his hotel window in 1858 (see fig. 3.22). Hardly passive, the photographic industry in Algiers contributed to the material culture of the city and its perception in Europe, as relayed through visual culture. On the simplest level, photography functioned as a conveyor of current events and culture.[98] But as a commodity in the imperial endeavor, photography acted as a double agent: one that promoted change and one that preserved the eroding mantle of Orientalism.

For the vast majority of the inhabitants of the metropole, who could not travel to Algiers, a "musée de l'Algérie" had been established under the guidance of the Ministry of War in the early 1850s on the rue Grenelle-Saint-Germain; it displayed items that had been exhibited at the Crystal Palace and other items that arrived regularly. Sometime before the Universal Exposition in 1855, this collection, along with the "Musée Algérien" on the rue de Bourgogne, was folded into the Exposition Permanente de l'Algérie et des Colonies, which was installed in the seven bays of the south gallery of the Palais de l'Industrie (fig. 3.25).[99] Like an imperial "Wunderkammer," the vast quantity of materials was classified into four sections: vegetal, mineral, animal, and indigenous industries and ethnography.[100] More than didactic in character, the exhibition functioned as a propaganda tool, as the published catalogue openly states: "Was not this exposition an argument with no counter which could not be overcome by any who still doubted the riches and resources of our marvelous African colony, which all the world envies and for which, for the most part, we seem to have so little regard?"[101] In the ethnographic section, next to sixteen marble busts and statues of Algerian "types" carved by sculptor Charles Cordier,[102] were displayed the photographic albums by Moulin, which, according to the catalogue, were considered to be "the most complete representation of picturesque Algeria."[103] Clearly assembled there not only to familiarize the metropole with the colony but also to provide a visual justification for the intervention in Algeria, Moulin's photographs showcased the very culture they were destined to change. Com-

3.25 *Permanent Exposition of Algeria and the Colonies*, woodcut (*L'illustration* 26 [1855]: 56)

parable to the abundance of goods shown at the Algerian exposition or to the ephemeral displays fashioned for the great expositions, Moulin's albums represented a visual encyclopedia of the colony.

At the Universal Exposition held in Paris in 1867, bits and pieces of Algeria were reconstituted into an organized arrangement next to the Seine to advertise the colony's potential as a significant player in the expanding world economy (fig. 3.26).[104] While the products in the Algerian display of 1867 won several medals, the ensemble as a whole also supported the national interest in promoting the importance of Algeria as a colony. Whether in their capacity of illustrating the colony or representing the stylish displays of Algerian products,

3.26 Algerian display at the Exposition Universelle, Paris, albumen print, 1867 (Getty Research Institute, 2003.R.12)

photographs functioned as powerful "consumer goods, charged with meaning,"[105] that helped to market the colony and expand local horizons. Like the displays at expositions, photographs of Algiers provided an immediacy that made the unfamiliar more comprehensible.

Living in a media-saturated world as we do today, it is difficult to comprehend how photography, in the decades following its invention, was perceived almost as a wonder of nature that intensified society's encounter with the world at large. Charles Desprez, a French painter and writer, helps us to understand the mid-nineteenth-century viewpoint in an article entitled "La photographie à Alger," published in the journal *L'akhbar* (7 May 1865). To delineate the visual power of photography, Desprez compares it to painting: "The only difference between them—which, to tell the truth, is an enormous difference—is the gift to create: the power to transform in one word the imagination; this heavenly daughter, this pure ray that descended from divine intelligence."[106] Even for Desprez, a painter by profession, photography was endowed with a creative force that affected the viewer's imagination. But what this artist failed to recognize about the multivalent technology of photography is how it can also function as a powerful instrument in shaping imperial agendas.

NOTES

1   Adolphe Otth, *Esquisses africaines, dessinées pendant un voyage à Alger et lith-ographiées par Adolphe Otth* (Berne: J. F. Wagner, *1839*), pl. *30*. I thank Ken Jacobson and Gérard Lévy for their insightful comments on this paper. Special thanks also go to Ken Jacobson for reviewing and augmenting my list of photo studios in Algiers.

2   See the terms of the capitulation rendered to the inhabitants of Algiers when the French occupied it on 5 July 1830, published in Pierre Christian, *L'Afrique française, l'empire de Maroc, et les déserts du Sahara* (Paris: A. Barbier, 1846), 40.

3   Isabelle Bruller, *Algérie romantique des officiers de l'armée française, 1830-37* (Paris: Service Historique de l'Armée de Terre, 1994).

4   R. Jungmann, *Costumes, moeurs et usages des Algériens* (Strasbourg: J. Bernard, 1837), 83.

5   See, e.g., Honoré-Jean-Pierre Fisquet, *Histoire de l'Algérie dépuis des temps anciens jusqu'à nos jours* (Paris: A la Direction, 1842), 11.

6   Rachid Tlemçani, "Islam in France: The French Have Themselves to Blame," *Middle East Quarterly* 4 (1997): 31–38.

7   Daniel Panzac, *Les Corsaires barbaresques: La fin d'une épopée, 1800-1820* (Paris: Centre National de la Recherche Scientifique, 1999).

8   Gabriel Esquer, *Iconographie historique de l'Algérie depuis le XVIe siècle jusqu'à 1871* (Paris: Plon, 1929), passim.

9   Among the early accounts, the best description is presented by Thomas Shaw, who resided in Algiers for twelve years; see his *Travels or Observations Relating to Several Parts of Barbary and the Levant* (Oxford, 1788; reprint, Farnborough, England: Gregg, 1972), 215–318.

10 Printed on the cover of the handbook *British Valour Displayed in the Cause of Humanity: Being a Description of Messrs. Marshall's Grand Marine Peristrepic Panorama of the Bombardment of Algiers* (Manchester: M. Wilson, 1822). Cf. the critical viewpoint on Lord Exmouth's victory presented by Chabaud-Arnault, "Attaque des batteries algériennes par Lord Exmouth en 1816," *Revue africaine* 19 (1875): 194–202.

11 Barbara Maria Stafford and Frances Terpak, *Devices of Wonder: From the World in a Box to Images on a Screen* (Los Angeles: Getty Research Institute, 2001), 315–24.

12 James Jennings, *Description of Lord Exmouth's Attack upon Algiers Painted by Henry Aston Barker: Now Exhibiting in His Panorama* (London: Jas. Adlard and Sons, 1818), 9–11.

13 Ibid., 4.

14 The information on panoramas outside London was generously furnished by Ralph Hyde, who, with Stephan Oettermann, is preparing to publish a dictionary of panoramists.

15 Given the venue, it seems likely that this was a small-scale attraction conceived by

a British artist who was capitalizing on the name of Louis Daguerre and his famous protean diorama staged at this time in both Paris and London, not to mention the recent French invasion of Algiers, which had been currently in the news.

16   Esquer, *Iconographie*, vol. 1, fig. 131.

17   Anon., "Peinture: Alger," *Journal des artistes* 2 (11 July 1830): 25–28. See Marie-Paule Petit, *L'oeuvre algérois de Jean-Charles Langlois*, 3 vols., Thèse de troisième cycle en esthéthique (Université de Paris I, n.d. [c. 1983]), 1:178–79.

18   Anon., "Peinture: Alger," *Journal des artistes* 2 (11 July 1830): 28.

19   Victor Hugo, *Les Orientales* (Paris, 1857), XI–XII. Petit, *L'oeuvre algérois de Jean-Charles Langlois*, 1:301–4, argues that Algiers was not part of the French concept of the "Orient" until after Delacroix exhibited his *Femmes d'Alger dans leur appartement* in the Salon of 1834. John Zarobell shows that the shift had occurred at least by 1833; see his "Framing French Algeria: Colonialism, Travel, and the Representation of Landscape, 1830–1870" (PhD diss., University of California at Berkeley, 2000), 33.

20   F. P., "Peinture: Panorama d'Alger, par M. Ch. Langlois," *Moniteur universel*, no. 59 (28 February 1833), 3d supplement, 557.

21   Germaine Bapst, *Essai sur l'histoire des panoramas et des dioramas* (Paris: G. Masson, 1891), 22–24.

22   Petit, *L'oeuvre algérois de Jean-Charles Langlois*. See also John Zarobell, "Jean-Charles Langlois's Panorama of Algiers (1833) and the Prospective Colonial Landscape," *Art History* 26, no. 5 (2003): 638–68.

23   Eusèbe de Salle, "Le panorama d'Alger," *Revue de Paris* 49 (1833): 179.

24   Augustin Jal, *Panorama d'Alger, peint par M. Charles Langlois, Chef de Bataillon au corps royal d'état major, officier de la Légion-d'Honneur auteur du panorama de Navarin* (Paris: [no publisher], 1833). See also E.-Ch. Bourseul, *Biographie du colonel Langlois* (Paris: P. Dupont, 1874), 19–21.

25   Anon., "Panorama d'Alger, par M. Langlois," *L'artiste* 5, 1st series (1833): 45.

26   Salle, "Le panorama d'Alger," 173.

27   Petit, *L'oeuvre algérois de Jean-Charles Langlois*, 1:145.

28   Ibid., 26–27.

29   The review in *L'artiste* 7, 1st series (1834): 150, notes that, even in the winter when the light was less favorable for viewing the panorama, it attracted visitors to the city who did not want to miss the spectacle.

30   F. P., "Peinture: Panorama d'Alger, par M. Ch. Langlois"; anon., "Beaux Arts: Panorama d'Alger par Ch. Langlois," *La France nouvelle*, no. 2038 (20 March 1833); anon., "Panorama d'Alger," *L'artiste* 7, 1st series (1834): 150.

31   Petit, *L'oeuvre algérois de Jean-Charles Langlois*, 1:256–57.

32   See the study by David Hockney, *Secret Knowledge: Rediscovering the Lost Techniques of the Old Masters* (New York: Viking, 2001), who believes that, although it is not documented in contemporary literature, Ingres, for example, used a camera lucida to sketch many of his portraits.

33 The Navarin panorama drew 42,487 visitors, while that of Algiers had only 27,375. Since the critical reviews of the Algiers panorama were generally favorable, Petit, *L'oeuvre algérois de Jean-Charles Langlois,* can offer no concrete reason for the difference.

34 Although the debates began in late April, the colonization of Algiers, as pointed out by one deputy, was well under way by this time because of private initiatives and in spite of the government's hesitation. See Ministère de l'Instruction Publique, "Extrait du registre des delibérations du conseil royal de l'instruction publique," *Moniteur universel,* no. 120 (30 April 1834): 1075; and Chambre des Députés, "Séance du Mardi 29 avril," *Moniteur universel,* no. 120, supplement (5 April 1834): 1074.

35 "L'importante discussion de la Chambre des Députés sur la question de savoir si la France conservera ou abandonnera cette colonie, ajoute un haut intérêt à ce tableau où M. Langlois a su rendre si habilement et la ville d'Alger et la riche campagne qui l'environne. Aussi l'on s'empresse d'aller les contempler, du moins en peinture, et souvent le plateau destiné à porter les spectateurs est trop petit." Advertisement in *Journal des artistes,* 5 May 1834 (Petit, *L'oeuvre algérois de Jean-Charles Langlois,* 1:184). See also Petit, *L'oeuvre algérois de Jean-Charles Langlois,* 1:170.

36 *Moniteur universel,* no. 121 (1 May 1834): 1696.

37 In defining photography, the *Grand dictionnaire universel du XIXe siècle,* published between 1866 and 1879, described its extended meaning as "Par ext. Reproduction, description d'une exactitude scrupuleuse: Les drames romantiques nous semblent préférables à ces grises photographies de la réalité que le théâtre actuel encadre dans son passe-partout. (Théophile Gautier)" ([reprint, Geneva: Slatkine, 1982], 887). See also the review by Théophile Gautier of Gustave Flaubert's *Salammbô,* in *Moniteur universel,* no. 352 (22 December 1862): 1750, in which he states: "Les types qu'il a créés ont leur état civil sur les registres de l'art, comme des personnes ayant existé véritablement; et rien ne lui était plus facile que d'ajouter à cette collection quelques photographies d'une exactitude non moins impitoyable."

38 Ernest Lacan, the leading photography critic in the Second Empire, described a photograph as "ce tableau si vrai" in *Esquisses photographiques* (Paris, 1856; reprint, New York: Arno Press, 1979), 27; see also 18–23.

39 No complete set of Moulin's work survives intact. The Archives d'Outre-Mer (AOM) in Aix-en-Provence hold the greatest number of his photographs, although these images, which originate from the duc d'Aumale's collection, have handwritten captions, not the captions with short texts produced sometimes for the published series. The AOM (8Fi427) has seventy-eight photographs of the province of Algiers.

40 G. Julien, "L'Algérie photographiée," *L'illustration* 31 (1858): 200.

41 In her study of Moulin's Algerian work, Estelle Fredet could find no recorded reason why Moulin undertook the photographic campaign, although his selection of images supported a colonial outlook. See Estelle Fredet, "L'Algérie photographiée (1856–

1857) de Félix-Jacques-Antoine Moulin, et la politique algérienne de l'Empire," in *Mémoire de maitrise* (n.p.: Université de Provence, 1993–94), not paginated.

42 Julien, "L'Algérie photographiée."

43 As early as 1844, Algeria is described as "la nouvelle France" by F. Gomot, *Guide du voyageur en Algérie* (Paris: J. DuMaine, 1844), 67.

44 The camera obscura in Algiers entertained spectators for the entire second half of the nineteenth century since it was still in place in a late stereo view held by the Getty Research Institute (ZS box 1).

45 Young conscripts serving in the Algiers intervention would have generated a long-term consumer group. Édme-Patrice de Mac-Mahon (1808–93) represents the premier example. After fighting with the expeditionary force in 1830, he commanded the subdivision of Tlemcen from 1848 to 1852 and the division of Constantine from 1852 to 1855, and he was the governor-general of Algeria from 1864 to 1870, before being elected president of the French Republic, a post that he held from 1873 to 1879.

46 This photograph with accompanying caption ("où débarquerent les Français en 1830") is mounted in an album entitled *Tunis-Algerien 1861*, which was assembled by two German-speaking travelers to North Africa and is housed in the Getty Research Institute, 95.R.106. Another print of the same negative exists at Vincennes, Service Historique de l'Armée de Terre, series D 128 (AFN) 53. The oral history on the debarkation was sustained by veterans of the event, who for some ten years after landing at Sidi Ferruch would assemble annually on 14 June at the site to commemorate the landing. See Gomot, *Guide du voyageur en Algérie,* 77. On Moulin's extended visit to Algiers, see Jacobson, *Odalisques,* 254–55.

47 Moulin, "Algérie photographiée," volume for Algiers, photograph no. 27, held by the Service Historique de la Marine, Château de Vincennes. The photograph by Alary is held by the Getty Research Institute (95.R.100, fol. 1r) and the Société Française de Photographie. On the history of Alary's studio, see Jacobson, *Odalisques,* 200–201.

48 *Catalogues des expositions organisées par la Société Française de Photographie, 1857–1876* (reprint, Paris: Éditions Jean-Michel Place, 1985).

49 Getty Research Institute, 91.R.6, fol. 6r.

50 Anne de Mondenard, "L'Algérie, terre oubliée des photographes en Orient," in *De Delacroix à Renoir: L'Algérie des peintres,* ed. Institut du Monde Arabe (Paris: Hazan, 2003), 110, proposes that the photographs of Algiers with Marville's blind stamp are actually prints by Alary that Marville sold in Paris. Mondenard comes to this conclusion because there is no evidence that Marville visited Algiers. However, the photographs with Marville's blind stamp held by the Getty Research Institute are markedly different in tone and character from those made by Alary. See also Jacobson, *Odalisques,* 253–54, who posits why Marville "may have functioned more as a publisher than a photographer with respect to Algeria."

51   All three photographs are held by the Getty Research Institute: Alary 92.R.85 and 96.R.146; Marville 95.R.100; and anonymous 93.R.101.

52   Inscribed "Pavillon du coup d'eventail à la Kasbah," Beaucorp's photograph begins an album of his work that is entitled *Algérie 1858* and is owned by the Wilson Centre, London (97.5587). The photograph's placement suggests that Beaucorps knew the significance of the Casbah portico and purposefully placed it first as an introduction to his visual essay that would illustrate his sojourn in the historical context of the French presence in Algiers. Beaucorps was not a member of the Société Française de Photographie, although he exhibited prints there in 1859, 1861, and 1869. See Marianne Thauré, Michel Rérolle, and Yves Lebrun, *Gustave de Beaucorps (1825-1906): Calotypes "L'appel d'Orient"* (Neuilly: Art Conseil Elysées, 1992), 12 and figs. 13-21. See also the auction catalogue *Photographies modernes et contemporaines, photographies anciennes* (Paris: Drouot Richelieu, 5 June 1992), no. 192.

53   A more general view of the Casbah with this portico is reproduced as a wood engraving after a photograph by Moulin in *Histoire populaire contemporaine de la France* (Paris: A. Lahure, 1864), 1:235, to illustrate the text explaining the French intervention in Algiers.

54   See Émile Cardon's book review of F. Ribourt (colonel d'État-Major), *Le gouvernement de l'Algérie de 1852 à 1858,* in *Revue du monde colonial* 1 (1859): 50-55.

55   First published in 1948, Max Weber's "The Nation" is reprinted in *Nationalism*, ed. John Hutchinson and Anthony D. Smith (Oxford: Oxford University Press, 1994), 21-25.

56   Todd B. Porterfield, *The Allure of Empire: Art in the Service of French Imperialism, 1798-1836* (Princeton, NJ: Princeton University Press, 1998), 7.

57   For a translation of Ducos du Hauron's first treatise, see Philip Hypher, "Colours in Photography: The Problem Resolved," *History of Photography* 23, no. 3 (1999): 281-93. On the career of Ducos du Hauron, see Ariane Isler-de Jongh, "The Origins of Colour Photography," *History of Photography* 18, no. 2 (1994): 111-19; William Marder and Estelle Marder, "Louis Ducos du Hauron," *History of Photography* 18, no. 2 (1994): 134-39; and Ariane Isler-de Jongh, "Louis Ducos du Hauron," *History of Photography* 19, no. 3 (1995): 270-71.

58   N.-P. Lerebours, *A Treatise on Photography* (London: Longman, Brown, Green, and Longmans, 1843), 215.

59   Text of Eugène de Lasiauve, published in Noël-Marie-Paymal Lerebours, *Excursions Daguerriennes* (Paris: Rittner et Goupil, 1841), pl. 1.

60   Getty Research Institute, 94.R.3, pls. 3, 18, and 15 respectively.

61   Bibliothèque Nationale, Département des Estampes et de la Photographie, "Topographie de l'Algérie," P175612 and P175613. The versions owned by the Getty Research Institute are hand-colored, possibly by Théodore Müller, the lithographer credited with making the prints.

62   *Indicateur général de l'Algérie* (Algiers, 1848), 556.

63   Cromer Collection at the George Eastman House, Rochester, NY; see Janet E. Buerger, *French Daguerreotypes* (Chicago: University of Chicago Press, 1989), 211–12, nos. 22.1–22.3, for daguerreotypes signed by Delemotte that depict views of Constantine and Medea. A daguerreotype of the port of Algiers is owned by Gérard Lévy, Paris; see Marie-Claire Adès, *Photographes en Algérie au XIXe siècle* (Paris: Musée Galerie de la Seita, 1999), 25; and Malek Alloula, *Alger: Photographiée au XIXe siècle* (Paris: Marval, 2001), 35. A daguerreotype of Algiers depicting a market near the ramparts on the Bab Azoun side of the city is in the collection of Serge Kakou; see Alloula, *Alger*, 63. These two unattributed views of Algiers, along with another daguerreotype depicting the al-Jadid Mosque housed at the George Eastman House (Buerger, *French Daguerreotypes*, 234, no. 70.12), may have been taken, not by resident studios, but by visitors, since Algiers attracted a number of travelers outfitted with daguerreotype cameras.

64   For example, in a report written to the minister of war on 18 April 1840, Bory de St. Vincent states: "The bad weather that we have had for the last month has interrupted our efforts in taking daguerreotypes, which will be taken up again once the mornings are more sunny" (AOM, F80 1591).

65   "Rapport sur les travaux d'architecture faits en Algérie par Monsieur Ravoisié" (AOM, F80 1591).

66   The daguerreotype camera and forty-two plates sent on 4 December 1839 were supplied by Lerebours. Another forty plates and another daguerreotype camera described as the system "Séquier," supplied by Charles Chevalier, were sent on 19 January 1840. However, according to a letter written by Amable Ravoisié on 6 February 1840, twenty-four plates in this shipment were damaged. Hence, another shipment of forty plates arrived on 1 April 1840 for Ravoisié, in addition to a box of fifteen plates sent on 22 January 1841. See the "Inventaire général des instruments de chimie, de physique et armes, livres, cartes et autres objets," along with Ravoisié's letter, in AOM, F80 1594. Another copy of the "Inventaire des instruments" notes in a later hand next to the daguerreotype sent on 4 December 1839: "ayant beaucoup servi." See AOM, F80 1594, no. 50.

67   AOM, F80 1594, no. 3424.

68   *Bulletin de la Société Française de Photographie* 2 (1856): 324.

69   *Bulletin de la Société Française de Photographie* 4 (1858): 287. A six-part panorama of the port of Algiers dating to the late 1850s and measuring just under one meter is in the collection of the Getty Research Institute (98.R.19*).

70   *Bulletin de la Société Francaise de Photographie* 3 (1857): 164–65.

71   Roger Taylor, *Photographs Exhibited in Britain, 1839–1865* (Ottawa: National Gallery of Canada, 2002), 50–51, 68.

72   Introduction to Charles-Robert Ageron, *Modern Algeria: A History from 1830 to the Present*, 9th ed., trans. and ed. Michael Brett (London: Hurst, 1991), vi.

73   C. A., "Photography in Algeria," *Photographic News*, October 1858, 53–54. The au-

thor experienced far more trouble finding willing sitters when he traveled outside Algiers. See *Photographic News*, February 1859, 256.

74 Mondenard, "L'Algérie," 111 and pl. 53.

75 J. Paul Getty Museum, 84.XP.368.23 and 84.XP.368.24. Tenison's visit to Algiers may have been an extension of his trip to Spain, where he traveled extensively with his wife, Lady Louise Tenison, a noted travel writer. For the photographs that he exhibited at the International Exhibition, Dublin, in 1853 and at the London Photographic Society in 1854, see Taylor, *Photographs Exhibited in Britain*, 709. I am grateful to Roger Taylor for alerting me to these photographs.

76 *Bulletin de la Société Francaise de Photographie* 2 (1856): 214; and Michel Natier and Amélie Lavin, *Paul Jeuffrain, 1809-1896* (Louviers: Musée de Louviers, 2001), passim.

77 Jeuffrain's photographs are held by the Société Française de Photographie, dossier 0464.

78 Eleven photographs of Algeria by Silvy are recorded among a list of photographs that he donated to the Société Française de Photographie in May 1858. See Mondenard, "L'Algérie," 110-11. I am most grateful to Mark Haworth-Booth for not only providing a copy of this unpublished list but also generously sharing his meticulous research on Silvy's trip and known Algerian photographs that will appear in a forthcoming catalogue provisionally titled *A Photographer of Modern Life: Camille Silvy (1834-1910)* to accompany an exhibition organized by Jeu de Paume and to be shown at the Hotel de Sully, Paris, and the National Portrait Gallery, London, in 2010.

79 Natier and Lavin, *Paul Jeuffrain*, 112.

80 I am grateful to Ken Jacobson for pointing out that many of the illustrations in the catalogue by Thauré, Rérolle, and Lebrun, *Gustave de Beaucorps*, are by other contemporary photographers collected by Beaucorps. Without examining these prints in person, I hesitate to attribute them, although the panorama of Algiers may indeed be by Alary.

81 Jakob August Lorent, *Egypten, Alhambra, Tlemsen, Algier: Reisebilder aus den Anfängen der Photographie*, compiled by Wulf Schirmer, Werner Schnuchel, and Franz Waller (Mainz: P. von Zabern, c. 1985), figs. 105-12. His photographs are held by the Société Française de Photographie, dossier 0255. Lorent was a member of the Société Française de Photographie from 1858 to 1884, and he exhibited his work there in 1859; see *Catalogues des expositions organisées par la Société Française de Photographie, 1857-76* (reprint, Paris, 1985), 29.

82 Mondenard, "L'Algérie," 113 and pls. 128-30. I am grateful to Serge Kakou for allowing me to consult the three views by Marès and his extensive early photographic holdings on Algeria.

83 It should not go unmentioned that perhaps this Monsieur Durrieu was related to Eugène Durieu, a founding member of the Société Française de Photographie who from 1855 to 1858 was not only active on their Comité d'Administration but also

functioned as president (*Bulletin de la Société Française de Photographie* 1 [1855]: 277). Durieu is best known for his photographic studies of nudes, including ones he probably supplied to Delacroix. See Sylvie Aubenas, "Les photographies d'Eugène Delacroix," *Revue de l'art,* no. 127 (2000): 62–69.

84   Jules Barbier, *Itinéraire historique et descriptif de l'Algérie* (Paris: Librarie Hachette, 1855), xviii; see also "Home Life in Algiers," *St. James Magazine* 7 (1863): 306.

85   Serge Dubuisson and Jean-Charles Humbert, "Jean Geiser, photographe-éditeur: Alger, 1848–1923, chronique d'une famille," in *L'image dans le monde Arabe* (Paris: Éditions du Centre National de la Recherche Scientifique, 1995), 275–84.

86   Ibid. Continuing to the end of the century, the Geiser Studio was the longest lived in Algiers. An advertisement on 8 January 1867 in *L'akhbar* records that "Geiser frères" are the successors to "Alary et Geiser" and, besides the establishment on the rue Neuve Mahon, an "Exposition nouvelle, rue Bab-Azoun, angle du Lycée," has opened.

87   The location of Klary's studio in 1868 is recorded on a *carte-de-visite* contained in an album representing Zouaves held by the Château de Vincennes, Service Historique de l'Armée de Terre, Fi 178.

88   *Courrier de l'Algérie,* no. 601 (20 January 1863).

89   *Courrier de l'Algérie,* no. 352 (1 November 1863). Trésorier is located at 7, rue Bab Azoun, where Jean Geiser was also located sometime after 1867, suggesting that Geiser took over his quarters.

90   Besides advertising in the *Courrier de l'Algérie* in 1863 and 1868, Portier placed ads weekly from the end of 1863 through the end of 1869 in the *L'akhbar,* while, for example, Clavier advertised only once, on 24 December 1869. Curiously, Portier's ads, starting in May 1868, list that his photographs are also for sale at the Librairie-Éditeur Chalamette, 14, rue Bellechasse, Paris. Perhaps he hoped to capture a market for Parisian travelers who, for whatever reason, were not able to purchase photographs in Algiers. On Portier's photographic career, see Jacobson, *Odalisques,* 261.

91   From the one sweeping photograph of Algiers harbor by Jules Buisson in 1867, it cannot be ascertained whether he established a studio there before he opened one in Cannes or whether it simply records a trip to North Africa. See the photograph by Buisson inscribed in the negative held by the Bibliothèque Nationale, Département des Estampes et de la Photographie, G61755.

92   According to *cartes-de-visite* (Getty Research Institute, ZCDV2, box 1), Mouttet was also located at 22, rue Bab Azoun.

93   In 1866, Leroux was located at 12, rue de Grignan but by the early 1870s had moved to 9, rue de la Lyre. See Jacobson, *Odalisques,* 251–52.

94   From 26 February to 12 March 1865, this same studio advertised in *L'akhbar:* "Charles Leinack et Cie, Villa-Roux à Mustapha, Photographie hippique et portraits." It is unclear whether these two establishments were concurrent or one followed the other.

95   The notice for Moulin's prints ran from October to December 1863 and in March 1864 in *L'akhbar*. The latter advertisement appeared in Sébastien Bottin, *Annuaire-almanach du commerce, de l'industrie, de la magistrature et de l'adminstration* (Paris: Firmin Didot Frères, 1866–), from 1866 to 1870 and also in *L'akhbar* for a few months in 1865 and for most of 1869.

96   Getty Research Institute, 2001.R.20.

97   Charles Desprez, *Alger naguère et maintenant* (Algiers: F. Maréchal, 1868), 47–48.

98   See, for example, the political gathering in the prefecture of Algiers photographed by Guyot and distributed in *carte-de-visite* format by the Disderi Studio in Paris, as illustrated in Elizabeth Anne McCauley, *A. A. E. Disderi and the Carte de Visite Portrait Photograph* (New Haven, CT: Yale University Press, 1985), 128 and fig. 131.

99   *L'illustration* 26 (1855): 56. For the Musée Algérien, which was opened on 20 October 1853, see Jules Duval, *L'Algérie* (Paris: Librairie Hachette, 1859), 455.

100   Émile Cardon and A. Noirot, "Visite à l'Exposition Permanente de l'Algérie et des Colonies," *Revue du monde coloniale* 3 (1860): 60–67.

101   Ibid., 60.

102   On the career of this artist, see Laure de Margerie et al., *Charles Cordier, 1827–1905: L'autre et l'ailleurs* (Paris: La Martinière, 2004).

103   Émile Cardon and A. Noirot, "Visite à L'Exposition Permanente de l'Algérie et des colonies," *Revue du monde coloniale* 4 (1861): 217.

104   Photographs of the Algerian display at the 1867 Universal Exposition taken by an anonymous photographer are housed at the Getty Research Institute, 2003.R.12. The economic importance of Algeria to France is stated in the exposition's official publication: *Exposition universelle de 1867 à Paris: Rapports du jury international publiés sous la direction de Michel Chevalier* (Paris: P. Dupont, 1868), 9, which states: "One cannot deny the importance of Algeria as a commercial enterprise. . . . in 1867 it furnished goods to France having a value of only 71,598,000 francs while those that it imported had a value of 135,562,000 francs, resulting in an exchange between the metropole and the colony of 207,161,000 francs."

105   Grant McCracken, *Culture and Consumption* (Bloomington: Indiana University Press, 1990), 130; see also xiv and xv for an explanation of the relation between culture and consumption.

106   Charles Desprez, "La photographie à Alger," in *Miscellanées algériens* (Algiers: Jules Breucq, 1864/65), 1 (originally published in *L'akhbar*, 7 May 1865). The perception of photography as a marvel is so pervasive at this time that even a Christian interpretation of its wondrous nature is noted by John Reynell Morell: "The regeneration of man is daguerreotyped in characters of light, but we are blind to God's photographic art, the age of reason and the reign of love is rapped out by unearthly hands on our parlour tables, but we are deaf to the summons of the seventh heaven" (*Algeria: The Topography and History, Political, Social, and Natural of French Africa* [London, 1854; new ed., London: Darf, 1984], vi).

4

A LINGERING OBSESSION

THE HOUSES OF ALGIERS IN FRENCH
COLONIAL DISCOURSE

Zeynep Çelik

The French occupation of Algeria in 1830 found an enduring metaphor in Eugène Delacroix's *Les femmes d'Alger dans leur appartement* (1834). As a member of a French diplomatic mission to North Africa and pursuing the tradition of the French artists who had accompanied Napoleon to Egypt, Delacroix was entangled with colonial politics. His entry into the Algerian house through *Les femmes d'Alger* opened a long tradition in French visual culture that complemented other genres of political narratives that equated the domination of Algeria with that of the Algerian family. During the subsequent thirteen decades, the discourse on the houses of Algiers expanded with an intensity that paralleled the importance attached to them. The official argument that the conquest of Algeria could be achieved only if its nucleus (the family unit) could be broken survived throughout the French rule and was reiterated in multiple aspects of visual culture, turning the Algerian house into a persistent focus of attention. Running parallel to the generic harem of Orientalist constructions and in dialogue with them, the preoccupation with the Algerian house was blatantly politicized. Algeria's captive status, it would seem, would have facilitated access to the private life of the colonized society—in contrast to the barriers Europeans had to face in Istanbul and Cairo, for example. Indeed, the appropriation of mansions that once belonged to the Ottoman elite by the French army enabled detailed documentation of the "Islamic house" in an unprecedented manner. Nevertheless, access to residential architecture did not translate into access to life at home, which had to be imagined in the Orientalist tradition, and the colonial condition reinforced the impenetrability of Algeria's domestic realm.[1]

Algerian nationalist, scholarly, and literary writing after independence emphasized the political significance of the house and the crisp division between the public and private realms during the colonial period. According to sociologist Djamila Amrane, in the everyday struggle against colonialism, the house served as the unique place where Algerians recovered their identity away from the gaze of the colonizers ever present in the public spaces of the city. The house became and remained "the inviolable site, the place of refuge where the Algerian, perpetually exposed to colonialism, [found] his identity."[2] As argued by Joëlle Bahloul, it also served as a space of knowledge that defined the forms of social exchange and that was transmitted over generations through memory.[3]

The architecture of the house and the massing of the housing fabric facilitated this phenomenon because the introverted spaces organized around the courtyard turned away from the political realities and social promiscuity of the street. Where the house opened up to the outside world by means of its roof terraces, it deleted the foreign presence in the city visually. The complicated built topography on the roof level, formed by adjacent terraces that descended gradually toward the lower town, framed restricted views that concealed the presence of the colonizer in the lower town and in the neighboring extensions. Lucienne Favre, a populist writer whose illustrated books on Algiers enjoyed wide reception during the interwar period, observed that views from the terraces toward the harbor eliminated the marks of "vandalism and militarism that had accompanied the conquest." She added that the houses, holding each other tightly, seemed as if they were one body, united in solidarity.[4] In his 1985 study of the Casbah, Djaffar Lesbet revisited this notion by interpreting the totality of the housing fabric as a collective voice. Echoing Amrane's concept of "inviolable site," he qualified the Casbah as a "counter-space" (*espace contre*) that represented the Algerian opposition to the colonial power.[5]

The architecture of the Casbah enabled an alternative circulation. As the rooftops were accessible from neighboring structures, passage from house to house was easy and constituted a common fact of daily life, especially among the women of Algiers, who were the main users of the terraces. Challenging the primacy of the street for communication, this network accommodated patterns of movement, exchanges, and displacements hidden from the colonizer, which only served to heighten European apprehensions regarding the Casbah, its architecture, and its denizens. The architecture of their houses enabled Algerians to exert their own subtle control over the urban domain, against the background of radical French interventions that carved straight arteries and squares into the precolonial fabric and devised sophisticated administrative and legal mechanisms to subjugate the city.

From the earliest French accounts to the end of the occupation, the Algerian house emerges as a main theme in colonial discourse, not only because of its social and political significance and alleged impenetrability, but also because of its formal and aesthetic otherness. An enduring textual genre from generation to generation reiterated the image of the Algerian house and etched the same pictures in the metropolitan consciousness from the same frames with the same cultural references. The first accounts set the tone. For example, an army officer summarized the image of Algiers in 1830 as fixed by the housing mass of a "dazzling whiteness" slashed by "narrow and tortuous streets where two mules could not pass side by side" (see fig. 3.5). The exteriors of the houses consisted only of "high walls," with a few small rectangular windows on the upper levels, while the interiors displayed "all the elegance of Moorish architecture, with its luxurious marble columns." A line from Montesquieu explained the Algerian house: "In despotic states, each house is a separate empire."[6] Another description from 1830 attributed the relation of the house to the outside world to "jealousy," arguing that this "bizarre [configuration] was universally common to regions dominated by the Quran,"[7] in an early manifestation of a common leitmotif in colonial writing on "native" Algerian (and Arab or Muslim) culture that found it flawed, perverse, and incapable of civilization because Arab or Muslim men suffered from an exaggerated sense of jealousy toward their women.

Again in the 1830s, French army engineers started documenting the houses of Algiers in architectural drawings—in response to practical needs. The army, consisting of well over 30,000 men in 1830, needed buildings. The easiest and fastest solution was to use the existing stock, making the necessary transformations for new uses. A detailed plan of the city that showed the newly opened place d'Armes recorded at the same time all the buildings that had belonged to Ottomans and that had been taken over by the military, namely military structures, palaces, and mansions of the ruling elite, who had fled the country in the aftermath of the occupation. The majority of the mansions were situated in the lower town, close to the newly opened place d'Armes and the harbor (fig. 4.1); others were in the higher parts of the old city, in the vicinity of the dey's palace (the Casbah proper). The mansions in the lower part of the city were adapted mostly for official functions. For example, Dar Mustapha Pasha (the house of Mustapha Pasha) was converted into the "Museum-Library" in 1839 (see fig. 4.13). The ground floor accommodated the museum, and the four rooms on the second level that opened to the gallery were linked to each other and turned into reading rooms.[8] High-ranking officers claimed the villas on the hills as their private residences.[9]

4.1 Plan of Algiers, 1832; buildings appropriated from the Ottomans are shown in blue (Service Historique de la Défense, Château de Vincennes, Paris)

The French occupation hence enabled a systematic and precise documentation of houses that belonged to Muslims, arguably for the first time. The carefully rendered architectural drawings dating from the 1830s and the 1840s in French military archives depict the buildings in their entirety, parts, and contexts; they consist of floor plans, sections, façades, and details. The transformation of residential buildings involved moving walls to enlarge interior spaces, but the more dramatic interventions concerned the regularization of the exterior façades. With the straight line as the guiding principle, the buildings were adjusted to widen streets and, whenever possible, appended with an arcade on the lower level and an entirely new façade with large and regularly distributed windows.[10] Therefore, although the buildings maintained their introverted organization around courtyards, their façades were pierced by rows of fenestration, and their regimented exterior appearances now addressed the public realm. These rehabilitation designs present double identities as witnesses of the early years of the occupation when abrupt acts of modification aimed to define a new urban image by throwing a French mantle over the "Islamic" city.

Targeting a new market in the metropole, thirsty for information on the newly conquered territory, a surge of illustrated literature on Algeria began in the first decade of the occupation. Such books focused on the city of Algiers and brought together the residential architecture and the people in narrative and visual formats, setting the precedent for "*scènes et types*" (and "*métiers*") that would become a familiar category in the visual representation of all French colonies, especially in postcards. One of the earliest books of this genre, *Costumes, moeurs et usage des Algériens* (Strasbourg, 1837) by R. Jungmann, considered "un des plus beaux albums sur l'Algérie" ("one of the most beautiful albums on Algeria"), helped establish a presentation format and provided a page of simple architectural drawings, perhaps the first in a publication on Algeria addressed to popular audiences (fig. 4.2). Emphasizing the key elements of the house, the drawings present an interior perspective, a plan, and a cross section. The courtyard was rendered in detailed perspective, down to the serpentine columns and the decorative tiles. The schematic plan focused on it as well, together with the surrounding rectangular rooms, while ignoring the irregularities of the spaces that would normally define the outer layers of the building. The section, again in a simplified fashion, showed the arcade around the courtyard on both levels and the roof terraces. However, the largest, most memorable, and most appealing was the drawing of the courtyard, which would ultimately dominate the image of Algerian houses in French discourse.

Despite his participation in the French invasion of 1830 as noted in the introduction to his book, Jungmann's Algerian house was not based on his own observations and documentation; it recycled an already-generic image, published a century ago in Thomas Shaw's travelogue, *Travels, or Geographical, Physical and Miscellaneous Observations &c. or Travels, or Observations relating to Several Parts of Barbary and the Levant* (Oxford, 1738; rev. ed., 1757).[11] Jungmann reprinted the plan and the section of Shaw's "one of the houses of Barbary" but gave a new frame to the courtyard, now focusing on the corner in contrast to Shaw's drawing, which represented one frontal side in a symmetrical manner and included equal parts of the adjacent sides. The "intertextuality" between Jungmann and Shaw, a common practice in the tradition of travel literature of the eighteenth and nineteenth centuries, situates Jungmann's book as an intriguing bridge. Building upon the contribution of early travel literature, *Costumes, moeurs et usage des Algériens* takes a step further toward the development of the Orientalist discourse and colonial representations.

A much more elaborate and scholarly documentation of an Algerian house appeared in Pierre Trémaux's *Parallèles des édifices anciens et moderns du continent africain* (Paris, 1861). Described as the "Ancient Residence of the Secretary

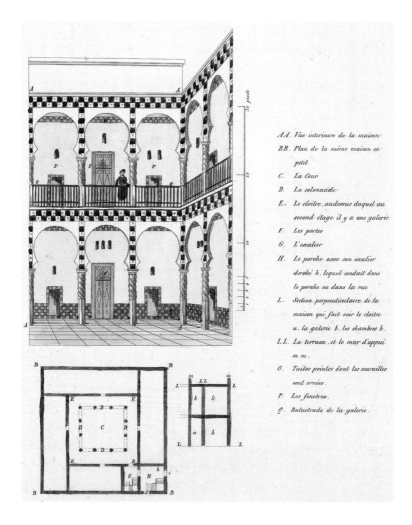

AA. Vue intérieure de la maison

BB. Plan de la même maison en petit

C. La Cour

D. La colonnade

E. Le cloître, au-dessus duquel au second étage il y a une galerie

F. Les portes

G. L'escalier

H. Le porche avec son escalier derobé h. lequel conduit dans le porche ou dans la rue

I. Section perpendiculaire de la maison qui fait voir le cloître a. la galerie b. les chambres k.

LL. La terrasse, et le mur d'appui m m.

O. Tuiles peintes dont les murailles sont ornées.

P. Les fenêtres.

Q. Balustrade de la galerie.

4.2 A typical house of Algiers, courtyard perspective, plan, and section, Robert Jungmann, colored lithograph (Jungmann, *Costumes, moeurs et usages des Algériens* [Strasbourg: J. Bernard, 1837], pl. 24)

of the Bey of Algeria," hence clearly belonging to an Ottoman notable, the mansion occupied a site on the waterfront. Trémaux's plans situated it in its immediate context and showed all the rooms, giving a complete picture of the main and ancillary spaces that allowed for an understanding of the relationship between them (fig. 4.3). A section that cut through the courtyard cast further light on the complexity of the spatial organization but also underlined the significance of the courtyard (fig. 4.4). It was enlivened by formulaic "scenes" from domestic life, including the patriarch of the house being fanned by a woman and an intimate vignette that featured the inevitable reclining odalisque in the section. A detailed interior perspective from the second story conveyed the beauty of the architecture, enriched by another gendered Orientalist touch that showed a woman leaning over the balustrade of the second-story arcade, with a male servant leaning against the wall, attending and supervising her (fig. 4.5).

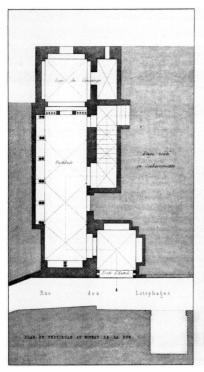
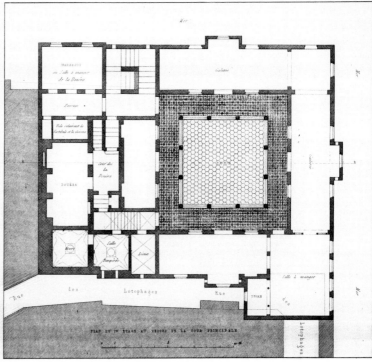

4.3 "Ancient Residence of the Secretary of the Bey of Algeria," plans of the ground and first floors, Pierre Trémaux, lithograph (Trémaux, *Parallèles des édifices anciens et modernes du continent africain* [Paris: L. Hachette, 1861], pl. 13)

Trémaux's architectural training, as a student at the École des Beaux Arts, is obvious from the meticulous attention he pays to describing and illustrating the Algerian house. As though to make an argument for a typological approach, he included a set of plans that showed four other houses in Algiers, drawn on the same scale to provide a comparative framework (fig. 4.6). They share the same design principles: access from the street to the interior is indirect and layered, a central courtyard acts as the organizational space, and the main rooms open onto it. Yet, depending upon the scale of house, each house differs in the distribution of the spaces and the relationships between them. One, on a small and crowded street, is explored in more detail. To explain the complicated configuration of this house, Trémaux drew plans for all five levels, from the basement to the roof terraces, as well as a section through the courtyard.[12]

Trémaux complemented his visual documentation of the Algerian house with a commentary that emphasized its difference from the European house and associated this difference with social customs and climate. The residential streets "in the Orient," he stated, were antipodes of "our streets, modern and straight." They did not meet well their primary goal of moving traffic along, yet they had a highly picturesque quality derived from the irregularity of the façades that lined

4.4 "Ancient Residence of the Secretary of the Bey of Algeria," section through the courtyard, Trémaux, lithograph (Trémaux, *Parallèles des édifices*, pl. 14)

them. Unlike a French street, which bore passersby along, the "Oriental street" offered an array of surprises with its "thousand detours and movements." The houses barely opened to the street, and their randomly placed small and grilled windows gave them the look of prisons. Trémaux pointed out that the grills on the windows seemed to have been placed there, not for the security of the household, but to prevent the women and the slaves from escaping their hopeless conditions. Inside, if the tightness of residential spaces, the careful filtering of light, and the provision for shade were in part responses to climate, they were also shaped by social norms. The latter were allegedly dictated by the Moor, "defiant [and] egoist," who desired to "hide his luxury and his pleasures from the jealousy of his neighbors by the appearance of his house, as simple on the exterior as it was rich in the interior."[13]

With the invention of photography in 1839, the history of photography becomes intertwined with the history of colonialism. Algiers was represented with a validity that brought further "reality" to the depiction of the houses of Algiers. To cite Roland Barthes, "photography (that is its *noeme*) *authenticates* the existence of a certain being."[14] In the case of the French Empire, the "certain being" was Algeria. Judging from the scale and nature of its photographic documen-

4.5 "Ancient Residence of the Secretary of the Bey of Algeria," courtyard perspective, Trémaux, chromolithograph (Trémaux, *Parallèles des édifices*, pl. 16)

tation, Algeria was one of photography's privileged subjects, and the conquest was repeated by capturing Algeria with the new technology, a manifestation of France's superiority over its colonies.[15]

The colonial photographer coded the photographs so that they were associated with certain meanings, often determined by an imperial agenda that was instilled—consciously or unconsciously—in the photographer. Surveying a series of themes and ordering them into simple categories, photographers developed a "stock of signs" and "cognitive connotations" that enabled a shorthand identification of France's most significant possession *outre-mer*.[16] As argued by Frances Terpak in this volume, the immediacy of photography—which differed from other illustrative techniques—furthered the colonial endeavor by helping the French public assimilate Algiers into its consciousness.

The photographic documentation of Algiers conveys a collective image of the houses; the compressed nature of the residential fabric made it an irrelevant exercise (and more or less an impossibility) to try to frame a single building. Using the topographic complexity of the city, photographers captured the exteriors of houses from several perspectives: looking down from the heights toward the sea to depict the entire urban fabric (as in Charles Langlois's 1833 panorama) and looking at the city from the sea. A photograph by the studio of Alary and Geiser, taken from the north, showed the white, cubical masses that make up the residential fabric, densely packed within the fortifications that surrounded the city and that soon would be demolished by the army engineers; the religious complex of Sidi 'Abd al-Rahman stood outside the walls (fig. 4.7). This view of old Algiers also revealed the French presence in two interventions: a European-style building in front of the complex of Sidi 'Abd al-Rahman and, more significantly, a new type of public space, a park. Jardin Marengo, built in 1833 on several terraces on the waterfront, testified to the urban transformations that accommodated a European way of life suitable for the settlers; its location outside the fortifications made a statement about the forthcoming expansion of the city. The French occupation was also made clearly visible in this photograph by a group of European men and women sitting along the water's edge.

Street views showed groups of houses for which it was difficult to figure out where one house ended and another began. The picturesque possibilities of the residential streets of Algiers made them favorite topics for photographers, despite the technical difficulty caused by the lack of sunlight. According to Félix-

4.6 Four houses in Algiers, plans, Trémaux, lithograph (Trémaux, *Parallèles des édifices*, pl. 21)

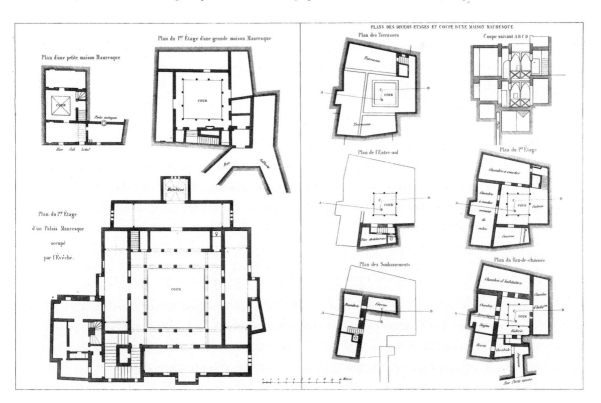

4.7 View of Algiers, showing the old city within the Ottoman fortifications and, outside, the complex of Sidi ʿAbd al-Rahman and the Jardin Marengo on the waterfront, Jean-Baptiste Alary and Geiser, albumen print (photograph album: *Algérie*, 1850s; Getty Research Institute, 96.R.146)

Jacques-Antoine Moulin, the narrowness of the "hideously curious" streets and the projecting eaves on two sides complicated his work. He complained, "no sun, no photographs," but added, "I managed to take a few."[17] It is hence not surprising that the majority of the early photographs of the streets of Algiers are devoid of people. They gradually became staged with local "types" to accentuate the feeling of authenticity. To pose children was common (and, presumably, the easiest) (fig. 4.8), but women were essential for the photographers to convey the most convincing message about the "reality" of the colony (fig. 4.9). Covered from head to toe in their white veils, they complemented visually and metaphorically the concealing character of the houses. A page from an 1881 album, discussed earlier in another context by Terpak, framed Algerian women "types" with street views and brought a gendered reading to residential neighborhoods (fig. 4.10).

4.8 A street view, albumen print (photograph album: *D'Alger à Tunis*, c. 1880–1900; Getty Research Institute, 94.R.51)

Photographs that depicted the housing fabric in a collective manner make implicit references to the concept of *hawma*, or neighborhood, explored by Isabelle Grangaud in this volume. On the one hand, the views from a distance, taken from the sea or from the heights, underline the amorphous quality of the boundaries between the neighborhoods because the unity and the continuity of the built forms give no indication of physical separations. They seem to express the concept of *hawma* defined from the center and not the boundaries—as understood by the residents of the old city and as argued by Grangaud. On the other hand, and again following Grangaud's interpretation, street views supported the definitions of neighborhood imposed by the colonial order by sug-

4.9 A street view, albumen print (photograph album: *D'Alger à Tunis*, c. 1880–1900)

gesting that they served as boundaries and broke up the residential fabric into identifiable units. Unintentionally, colonial photography represented both notions.

Photographing the interiors was a problem, as the photographers could work only in houses occupied by the French, resident Europeans, or in some cases Jewish families and in those that had been transformed for other uses. Views of interiors remained reductive and ultimately dominated by a standard representation: a corner of the courtyard. Only vaguely connected to its function and meaning in the Algerian context, the courtyard became a "representational space" for the French, explained by Henri Lefebvre as "directly lived through its associated images and symbols. . . . This is the dominated space which the imagination seeks to change or appropriate. It overlays physical space, making symbolic use of its objects."[18]

Being open to the sky, the courtyard was relatively easy to photograph. Yet, its scale made it difficult to be seized in its entirety by the camera. Faced with one of the main problems of depicting architecture without losing its spatial character, photographers concentrated on the corner. They were thus able to convey a feeling of depth and perspective while building on an image already common in drawings. Through the act of framing the camera, the Algerian domestic realm became fixed on a single dominating image, whose visual power,

4.10   Houses and women of Algiers, albumen prints (photograph album: *Algeria/Tunisia*, 1881; Getty Research Institute, 2001.R.20)

4.11 *Rich Lady and Her Servant*, attributed to Claude-Joseph Portier, albumen print (photograph album: *Views and Peoples of Algeria*, 1868, pl. 21)

simplicity, and connotations would extend its symbolism to encompass eventually all dimensions of Algerian culture and society.

Many versions of this view simply show the architecture. However, inserting figures in the foreground complicated the message. Frequently, *mauresque* women in "authentic" costumes filled the center of the composition and repeated the metaphorical entry into the Algerian house.[19] The corner became a stage for women in various poses and engaged in all kinds of activities. Playing music, smoking, and drinking coffee, all associated with the imagined generic harem life and disseminated widely by postcards, featured most prominently (fig. 4.11).[20] Scenes of production, such as carpet weaving, also entered the repertory. Significantly, the "serious" production activities were associated with the French presence. Several photographs of Luce Ben Aben's artisanal school, which was founded to teach Algerian girls "indigenous" crafts in a systematic and "scientific" way, showcase the symbolic transformation of the courtyard from a place of "hanging out" to one with a useful mission. In one, children focus on their embroidery; in another, young women prepare couscous (fig. 4.12).[21]

The French presence filled the corner in other ways as well. In photographs of

4.12   Luce Ben Aben's École des Broderies Arabes, hand-painted photograph, c. 1900 (Prints and Photographs Division, Library of Congress)

the Musée d'Alger (which also sheltered a library), the spacious courtyard was lined with Roman statues (fig. 4.13). A residential structure was hence assigned a foreign and public function, as well as being linked to Algeria's Greco-Roman patrimony, a major colonial enterprise that sought to legitimize French North Africa by casting France as the successor to Rome.[22] Politically charged photographs of French men continued to convey the message regarding the power structure. Examples include several photographs taken during Napoleon III's visit to Algeria in 1865 that feature key French officers, as well as the emperor himself (fig. 4.14). A photograph from 1867 showed the bishop of Algiers consulting with three Frenchmen on an official mission; the figures sit around a table in a courtyard, the typical corner columns defining the background.[23] The building, Dar ʿAziza, was a sixteenth-century Ottoman palace that was turned into the seat of the archdiocese in 1838; it was situated in the lower part of the city close to the Ketchaoua Mosque, which had been converted into a cathedral. The two structures operated as the religious anchors of the colonizer, linked to

4.13   Interior of the Library, albumen print (Joseph Armstrong Baird Collection of Architectural Photographs, c. 1870 and 1890; Getty Research Institute, 88.R.8)

4.14   Napoléon III and his entourage, albumen print (photograph album: *Napoléon III in Algeria*, 1856–1865; Getty Research Institute, 96.R.117)

4.15 The courtyard of the Algerian pavilion, Universal Exposition, Paris, 1900 (*L'Exposition de Paris* [Paris, 1900], vol. 3)

the administrative apparatus (even though the majority of the European settlers, colonial officialdom, and sections of the military were anticlerical). Another photograph depicts the courtyard of the Algerian pavilion erected in Paris for the 1900 Universal Exposition (fig. 4.15). In front of the familiar corner, recycled here to represent Algeria at large, a group of men sat around a table, tasting Algerian wines. This act stood for another level of French conquest, as it promoted the new product designated for the consumption of the colonizers while referring to the transformation of the Algerian agricultural pattern from cereals to grapes.

Colonial photography contributed to the development of stereotypes and flattened the diverse human, cultural, and visual landscapes of Algeria into simplified and comparable categories,[24] but not everything fitted into its frame neatly. A photograph (c. 1884) with the generic title *Cour mauresque* (Moorish courtyard) by an unidentified photographer tells an alternative story about the Algerian house and family life (fig. 4.16). It shows a modest but architecturally refined courtyard. The "family members" crowd the small space in a seemingly informal manner, creating an intimate scene. The man of the house sits on the

899 COUR MAURESQUE. ALGER

4.16 *Moorish Courtyard*
(photograph print: *Algé-
rie 1884;* Getty Research
Institute, 95.R.95)

steps behind a low table with coffee cups on it, and three women and a girl
surround him in relaxed poses. He comes across, not as the essential omnipo-
tent and jealous Muslim patriarch, but as an ordinary husband and father. The
presence of four coffee cups suggests a recreational break shared by the family
and challenges the rigid gender hierarchy, a favorite topic in Orientalist art.
An ambiguity about the family structure dominates the scene. As there are no
clues given, no references made to the expected scenes in the courtyard, one
can only speculate about the relationships between the people in the frame.
Are the women all wives, for example, or one wife and three daughters? Is the
black woman a servant? While the Orientalist harem and its hierarchies are
evoked, the pervasive everyday quality muddles the phantasmagoric and sexu-

alized cliché. The practical summer dresses of the women, their composure, and the ordinary objects strewn around the courtyard turn this photograph into a contradiction of the generic harem, the locus of ultimate laziness, but also distance it from its opposite, the choreographed workshops of Ben Aben's school. The cat sitting on the steps completes the picture of domestic coziness and normalcy. While the social setup in this photograph is as artificial as all the others and reveals little about the Algerian home and family, the image slips out of the codes established by visual culture and provokes other interpretations. At the same time, it continues to perpetuate and strengthen the common agenda by supplying it with a new vitality, supposedly providing a unique, "true" entry into an ordinary house and the lives of ordinary people.

The "types" of representation established in the nineteenth century remained remarkably stable until the end of French rule, with rare approaches that offered complicated arguments. Among the latter is the Grille de CIAM-Alger, an architectural and urbanistic study of the *bidonville* (squatter settlement) Mahieddine in Algiers. Dating from the last decade of the French occupation, the settlement brought an alternative vision to the Algerian house.[25] Presented to the 1953 congress of CIAM (Congrès Internationaux d'Architecture Moderne) in Aix-en-Provence, Grille de CIAM-Alger was an interdisciplinary study that deduced lessons for modern architecture from the *bidonville*. It proposed new readings of the Algerian house, now in the form of a squatter house. Deleting all associations to the Orientalist harem, the squatter house was understood as a building that successfully responded to social, cultural, topographic, climatic, and environmental issues. For example, the exteriors, still turning blank faces to the street, nevertheless displayed "in-between" elements, such as a built-in bench on the façade—in a generous gesture to the street that linked the public and the private realms (fig. 4.17). While the architects who conducted the research pointed to the miserable conditions, they also saw great merit in many aspects of the squatter houses. They admired their simplicity, lightness, geometric abstraction, clean lines, and whitewashed façades. They appreciated the built-in furniture for its functionalism, lightness, flexibility, and spatial efficiency, as well as the standardization of construction materials.

The courtyard continued to be a key space in the squatter house, but it was now examined in its multiple functions. Aesthetically and climatically, it epitomized the relationship between nature and built forms. A tree was the "indispensable complement of the courtyard, the element of life and poetry in the heart of the *bidonville*." One panel at the exhibition showed a rooftop with a tree bursting through the patio and a cat sleeping in the sun; others explained the climatic advantages of planting a tree in a courtyard and adding a "summer

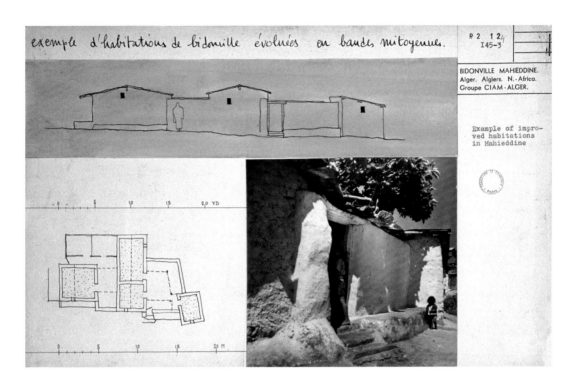

4.17 *Bidonville* Mahieddine, street façade, unit plans, and street view, multimedia exhibition plate (Grille de CIAM-Alger, 1953, Fondation Le Corbusier)

room" overlooking it (figs. 4.18 and 4.19). Often shared by more than one unit, the courtyard was the realm of the women, where their household chores were performed. Inspired by anthropological methodologies, the CIAM team studied the food preparation and cooking patterns, including the ingredients and the utensils, and filled the courtyards with scenes that differed from the staged ones in ben Aben's school. In an unusual episode in the history of French colonialism in Algeria, European men were invited into Algerian homes. Architect Roland Simounet (who worked on the study), reported that women talked to them, offered them coffee, and even allowed themselves to be photographed.

The houses of Algiers became highlighted with yet another twist during the Algerian War. When the Battle of Algiers began on 7 January 1957, the city turned into a war zone. During the months that followed, the duality that had characterized the public spaces of Algiers became more acute than ever. According to a letter to the editor in *France outre-mer* at the time, the city was completely split into two: "the cafés, cinemas, restaurants, where the Muslims do not go," and "the neighborhoods of the Casbah practically barred from the French [civilians]." The military operations, considered "inevitable," accen-

4.18 *Bidonville* Mahieddine, a rooftop (Grille de CIAM-Alger, 1953, Fondation Le Corbusier)

tuated the already-existing scission. The letter writer's justification for these operations blatantly summarized the official stand: "the patrols, raids, searches that continue day and night, have nothing else as goal but to watch, to control the Muslims. They all are figures of suspicion and the almost daily attacks do not allow for other courses of action."[26]

The Algerian house played a major role during the war, serving as a cell of resistance, as an "impregnable barrier," in Pierre Bourdieu's words.[27] Domestic rituals became politicized in unusual ways. For example, musical receptions at home changed character. Performed by ensembles commonly composed of several musicians who played the *raïta* (a kind of clarinet), the *tambour,* and the *darbuka* (a smaller tambour) and accompanied by a singer, the songs traditionally concerned the "torments of love."[28] Yet, during the war, certain orchestras began to include *nashîd* (nationalist songs) in their repertoires, imbuing celebrations such as marriages and circumcisions with political overtones. As they circulated from house to house, these musicians formed a connective thread between various groups.[29]

The architectural and urban forms of the Casbah made it an unusual battle-

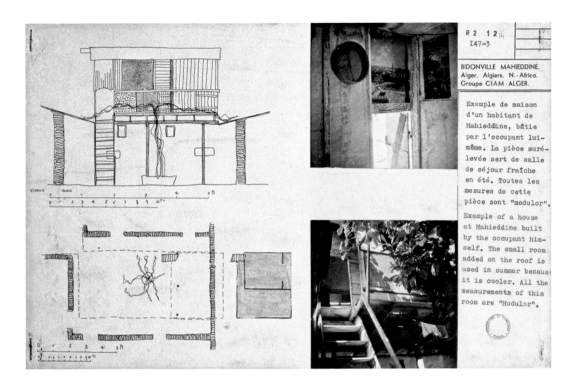

Inside the image, the following text is visible:

R 2 12₁₄
I47-3

BIDONVILLE MAHIEDDINE.
Alger. Algiers. N.-Africa.
Groupe CIAM-ALGER.

Exemple de maison
d'un habitant de
Mahieddine, bâtie
par l'occupant lui-
même. La pièce suré-
levée sert de salle
de séjour fraîche
en été. Toutes les
mesures de cette
pièce sont "modulor".

Example of a house
at Mahieddine built
by the occupant him-
self. The small room
added on the roof is
used in summer because
it is cooler. All the
measurements of this
room are "Modulor".

4.19 *Bidonville* Mahieddine, courtyard (Grille de CIAM-Alger, 1953, Fondation Le Corbusier)

ground and favored the resistance fighters. They could take refuge in houses and devise circulation patterns inaccessible and incomprehensible to the French army officers as they found their way from one house to the other, using the adjacent roof terraces. As described by journalist Henri Marchand at the end of French rule, the "terrorists, . . . familiar with routes that the French troops would have great difficulty detecting, could go freely from one end of the Casbah to the other." There were instances, he continued, when an "assassin," seen entering a house in the lower town, reappeared in the upper town several hours later, "sometimes even dressed as a woman."[30] The entire built fabric seemed to participate in the war—a phenomenon that film director Gillo Pontecorvo captured so effectively in his memorable epic *The Battle of Algiers*.

It was during the war that the French finally entered the Algerian houses, in search of the fighters of the National Liberation Front. In the process, the army photographers recorded the capture of the Casbah. In these photographs, smiling soldiers waved at their companions from the rooftops, and the famil-iar image of the courtyard reappeared, now occupied by the troops, their war gear strewn everywhere (fig. 4.20). The frames of reference were unmistakable:

4.20 French soldiers in a courtyard, 1960 (Établissement Cinématographique et Photographique des Armées, Paris)

the French had broken into the core of Algerian life, transforming Delacroix's metaphorical entry into a harsh military reality. Across the Mediterranean, as they gazed at photographs on printed pages as war news, or more intimately as memorabilia sent home by soldiers on duty, French citizens could easily comprehend the message. Thirteen decades of visual breaking and entering had prepared them historically.

NOTES

1 Algerian domestic life is difficult to construct, and historic studies on residential architecture have remained restricted to formal and spatial analyses. For the Ottoman period, the archives have scattered data only on upper classes—a situation recently confronted by scholars. For example, in her extensive analysis, Sakina Missoum opted for a typological classification of houses and did not deal with family structure and activities. See Sakina Missoum, *Alger à l'époque ottomane: La médina et la maison traditionnelle* (Aix-en-Provence: Édisud, 2003), especially 191ff. Tal Shuval, who looked at Ottoman families in Algiers, stated that "we find no description of the Ottoman household [in Algiers]." Shuval nevertheless managed to piece together enough data to trace some developments over a period of three hundred years to maintain that "the households were indeed a key feature of the Algerian Ottoman elite." He concluded: "many questions remain open." See Tal Shuval, "Households in Ottoman Algeria," *Turkish Studies Association Bulletin* 24, no. 1 (Spring 2000): 41–64 (quotations from 64). The scarcity of data on the Ottoman elite is also indicative of the difficulty of research on the private lives of other communities in this multiethnic city in the precolonial era. Accounts of the Algerian War and oral history have shed some light on household activities during the last years of French rule. Novels also cast retrospective looks onto this period. Joëlle Bahloul's ethnological study *The Architecture of Memory* (Cambridge: Cambridge University Press, 1996) does that for the years 1937–62, but the house she studies is in Sétif, in eastern Algeria, a place very different from Algiers.

2 Djamila Amrane, *Les femmes algériennes dans la guerre* (Paris: Plon, 1991), 45. The fears that the Arab home and house provoked on the part of colonial officials and male gaze theory as it applied to Algerians are discussed in Julia Clancy-Smith, "Islam, Gender, and Identities in the Making of French Algeria, 1830–1962," in *Domesticating the Empire: Languages of Gender, Race, and Family Life in French and Dutch Colonialism, 1830–1962*, ed. Julia Clancy-Smith and Frances Gouda (Charlottesville: University Press of Virginia, 1998), 154–74.

3 Bahloul, *Architecture of Memory*, passim.

4 Lucienne Favre, *Tout l'inconnu de la Casbah d'Alger* (Algiers: Baconnier Frères, 1933), 252.

5 Djaffar Lesbet, *La Casbah d'Alger: Gestion urbain et vide sociale* (Algiers: Publications Universitaires, 1985), 39–48.

6 Quoted in Edouard Dalles, *Alger, Bou-Farik, Blidah et leurs environs* (Algiers: Librairie Adolphe Jourdan, 1888), 25–26.

7 A. M. Perrot, *Alger: Esquisse topographique et historique du royaume et de la ville* (Paris: Librairie Ladvocat, 1830), 33–34. To refer to one other example among many, a similar description that shares many phrases with Perrot's account appears in *Alger: To-*

pographie, population, forces militaires de terre et de mer, acclimatement, et ressources que le pays peut offrir à l'armée d'expédition, par un français qui a résidé à Alger (Marseille: Typographie de Feissat aîné et Demonchy, 1830), 54–55.

8   Dalles, *Alger, Bou-Farik, Blidah*, 87. Golvin mistakenly gives the date of the conversion of Dar Mustapha Pasha as 1863, not 1839. See Lucien Golvin, *Palais et demeures d'Alger à la période ottomane* (Aix-en-Provence: Édisud, 1988), 47.

9   Louis-André Pichon, *Alger sour la domination française; son état présent et son avenir* (Paris: Théophile Barrois et Benjamin Duprat, 1833), 252–55.

10 For urban design concerns in these interventions, see Luc Vilan, "Les arcades de la Casbah: Alignements dans Alger," in *Paris s'exporte: Modèle d'architecture ou architectures modèles*, ed. André Lortie (Paris: Picard, 1995), 116–17.

11 I am thankful to Nebahat Avcıoğlu for bringing Thomas Shaw's book to my attention. Avcıoğlu discusses Shaw's drawings in her PhD dissertation, "Peripatetics of Style: Travel Literature and the Political Appropriation of Turkish Architecture in Britain, 1737–1862" (PhD diss., Cambridge University, 1997).

12 As an example of a relatively inaccessible house type, the house on rue Rabah Raiah has a unique place in the documentation of the residential architecture of Algiers. Trémaux's drawings have been reproduced in Golvin's *Palais et demeures d'Alger*. This is the only house from the upper Casbah that Golvin includes in the chapter entitled "Une maison commune en médina," and he argues that the other houses in the Casbah were similar (75–78).

13 Pierre Trémaux, *Parallèles des édifices anciens et modernes du continent africain* (Paris: L. Hachette, 1861), n.p.

14 Roland Barthes, *Camera Lucida: Reflections on Photography*, trans. Richard Howard (New York: Farrar, Straus, and Giroux, 1981), 107.

15 For a version of the discussion on photographs of houses in Algiers, see Zeynep Çelik, "Framing the Colony: Houses of Algeria Photographed," *Art History* 27, no. 4 (September 2004): 616–26.

16 The concepts are borrowed from Barthes. See Susan Sontag, ed., *A Barthes Reader* (New York: Farrar, Straus, and Giroux, 1982), 207, 208.

17 Moulin, "La photographie en Algérie," *Lumière* 6, no. 12 (22 March 1856): 46.

18 Henri Lefebvre, *The Production of Space*, trans. Donald Nicholson-Smith (Oxford, UK, and Cambridge, MA: Blackwell Publishers, 1991), 39.

19 It was common practice for photographers to hire prostitutes to pose for them.

20 Depicting women as smoking carried an additional transgressive message since respectable women in Europe did not smoke at the time.

21 On artisanal education in North Africa, including Luce ben Aben's school, see Julia Clancy-Smith, "A Woman without Her Distaff: Gender, Work, and Handicraft Production in Colonial North Africa," in *A Social History of Women and the Family in the Middle East*, ed. Margaret Meriwether and Judith Tucker (Boulder, CO: Westview Press, 1999), 25–62.

22 See Nabila Oulebsir, "La découverte des monuments de l'Algérie," in "Figures de l'orientalisme en architecture," special issue, *Revue du monde musulman et de la Méditerranée* 73/74 (1994): 57–76, especially 57–65; and Nabila Oulebsir, *Les usages du patrimoine: Monuments, musées et politique coloniale en Algérie, 1830–1930* (Paris: Éditions de la Maison des Sciences de l'Homme, 2004), 233–60.

23 *Histoire de l'Algérie et voyage du Napoléon III, 1867*, Bibliothèque de la France, Paris, Vh509 (G61771).

24 Paul S. Landau underlines this point in reference to photography in "Africa" in general. See Paul S. Landau, "Empires of the Visual: Photography and Colonial Administration in Africa," in *Images and Empires: Visuality in Colonial and Post-colonial Africa*, ed. Paul S. Landau and Deborah Kaspin (Berkeley and Los Angeles: University of California Press, 2002), 161.

25 For detailed studies of the CIAM-Alger project, see Zeynep Çelik, "Learning from the Bidonville: CIAM Looks at Algiers," *Harvard Design Magazine*, Spring 2003, 69–74; and Zeynep Çelik, "Bidonvilles, CIAM et grands ensembles," in *Alger: Paysage urbain et architectures, 1800–2000*, ed. Jean-Louis Cohen, Nabila Oulebsir, and Youcef Kanoun (Paris: Éditions de l'Imprimeur, 2003), 186–227. The discussion in this essay is derived from those publications.

26 Letter to the editor, *France outre-mer* 43, no. 326 (1957).

27 Pierre Bourdieu, *The Algerians*, trans. Alan C. M. Ross (Boston: Beacon Press, 1962), 156–57.

28 Ironically, this description is given in the midst of the Algerian War. See Henri Marchand, *La Musulmane algérienne* (Algiers: Éditions Subervie, 1960), 76–78.

29 Amrane, *Femmes algériennes*, 54–57.

30 Marchand, *Musulmane algérienne*, 52.

5

THE INVISIBLE PRISON

REPRESENTING ALGIERS ON FILM

Eric Breitbart

Our cafés and the streets of our big cities,
our offices and furnished rooms, railway
stations and factories—all seem to
imprison us without hope of liberation.
Then, along comes the cinema . . . and
explodes this closed universe so that now,
lost among the far-flung debris, we can
undertake new journeys, new adventures.

—Walter Benjamin, *Essays II, 1935–40*

Motion pictures offer us more than passive entertainment and escape; they provide a two-sided language of cultural communication, functioning both as a mirror for anyone living within a particular society and as a window for outside observers. Movies do more than reflect or project images; they also influence the way we behave, how we judge each other, and how we see the world around us. Appearing on film also confirms one's existence—whether "one" is a person or a place. Movies possess magical power because they appear to be *real*, occupying both physical space and depth on the screen and psychological space in our minds. As spectators in a movie theater we do not just watch what takes place on the screen but rather fabricate reality from what we know are nothing more than two-dimensional images on a piece of celluloid.

This complex interaction between spectators and spectacle has not gone unnoticed. In his early study of motion pictures, psychologist Hugo Münsterberg observed that "we see actual depth in the picture and yet we are at every instant aware that it is not real depth and the persons are not real. . . . we perceive movement too, but it is only a suggestion. Depth and movement alike come to us in the moving picture world, not as hard facts but as a mixture of fact and symbol. They are present and yet they are not in the things. We invest the impressions with them."[1]

Like architecture, movies have a visual grammar that creates complex, three-dimensional structures and a sense of place. A film's story line provides the framework, while lighting, lenses, camera angles, sets or locations, music, and editing all contribute to the way a film is perceived by an audience. These various elements may come together seamlessly, or they may be revealed intentionally, just as the structural elements of a building may be. Filmmaking is selective, choosing certain elements over others, then rearranging them into an artistic vision. "To direct a film is to redirect the viewer's attention, to give objects new meaning. . . . The power of cinema can make us believe in a whole while showing us only a part."[2] This is particularly true of cities. Once filmed, a city is no longer the "real" city it was before; it has become a subjective place of the imagination, whether it is an actual location or a set built in the studio. Through lighting and camera angles, a city can also evoke the psychology of a character, what sociologist Edgar Morin called "anthrocosmomorphisme."[3]

An intimate relationship between movies and urban life has existed since the invention of cinema. From the beginning, motion pictures found their subjects and their audiences in large cities like Paris, New York, and London. Over time, the cinema created artificial worlds, part dream, part reality, that offered both a reflection of the city and an escape from it. This interaction was explored in Cités-Cinés, an exhibit originating in the Centre de la Villette in Paris in 1987 that combined clips from feature films with re-created movie sets.[4] In his introduction to the exhibition catalogue, François Barré wrote that "there are cities that are 'real' because they have made the fictional world of film concrete, attempting to solidify the halo, the breath of fresh air, that floats over the movie cities in which we have all lived."[5] Can we think of New York City without the images created by Woody Allen and Martin Scorsese? Is it possible to imagine Paris divorced from the films of Marcel Carné, René Clair, or Jean-Luc Godard? Does Rome exist without Fellini, Tokyo without Ozu and Kurasawa? Certain cities used as locations are so identified with their film images—Shanghai and Casablanca, for example—that the name alone is enough to evoke mystery and adventure. Algiers, on the other hand, was relatively sheltered from media attention until 1967, when *The Battle of Algiers* was released. Since then, the city's image has been fixed as the site of urban guerrilla warfare.

The Lumière Brothers sent newsreel cameramen to Algiers as early as 1896. The short films they brought back to Paris—ships in the harbor, market scenes, the narrow streets of the Casbah—were little more than animated versions of photographs found in travel journals or on turn-of-the-century postcards. This image of Algiers as a backdrop, a mysterious location in which the Algerian people were blended in with the scenery, continued when the first Algerian fiction films were produced during the 1920s and 1930s; there was no incentive for the French to portray the city in any other way. These films, the more than fifty features shot in Algeria between 1918 and 1954, were intended primarily for export to France, which meant that certain things, like Algeria's colonial status, were taken for granted. "In the cinema," one critic wrote, "the French are present in Africa as if they had always been there, and it would never occur to a filmmaker to think otherwise."[6]

In colonial Algeria, motion pictures played a small yet essential role in supporting the empire by exporting a particular image of the country as an exotic haven whose benign, colorful subjects could prosper only under French control. The local population was treated as raw material that could be molded to fit the needs of the motherland. In his book *Les Algériens au miroir du cinéma colonial,* Abdelghani Megherbi points out how "everything that was undertaken in the country [during the colonial period], infrastructure or superstructure, was done because of the direct needs and interests of the Europeans who lived there—including the cinema."[7] France had little interest in developing an indigenous film industry since by the 1930s Algeria was considered not so much a colony as an integral part of France. In spite of this, both the FLN (Front de la Libération Nationale, National Liberation Front) and the GPRA (Gouvernement Provisoire de la République Algérienne) considered it important enough to set up a production unit in 1957 that was able to release a few films dealing with the struggle for independence, mostly in rural areas. In France, strict government censorship ensured that few motion pictures about the war reached the French public during the 1950s and 1960s; those dealing with it directly were usually shot in Morocco or Tunisia because of security concerns. Films about Algeria, both before independence and during the war, do exist of course, and war photographs were regularly published in magazines like *Historia*, but the war was not a popular subject with the French film industry. The Établissement Cinématographique et Photographique des Armées, at Bois d'Arcy, outside Paris, for example, contains over 300,000 photos and thousands of documentary films produced during the 1940s, 1950s, and 1960s, mostly by the French army, but these films are not easily accessible, even to historians.

The difficulties in establishing an Algerian cinema independent from French control are discussed in detail by Roy Armes in his recent book *Postcolonial Images: Studies in North African Film*. Suffice it to say that a lack of financing or a production infrastructure, along with strict government control, severely restricted the number of films released after 1962. Though a few foreign co-productions, like Gillo Pontecorvo's *The Battle of Algiers* (1965) and Luchino Visconti's *The Stranger* (1968), were filmed in Algiers, Algerian cinema itself was primarily a cinema of exile, even before the bloody civil war of the 1990s. Historian Benjamin Stora takes a more extreme view of the situation. For him, by the end of the twentieth century, Algeria was a country deprived of its own film history. In an interview with *Cahiers du cinema*, Stora remarked that the relative absence of images has served to create an unreal Algeria, a fantasy country that never existed. "We live in a world of images, we are bombarded by images," Stora wrote, "and should remember that the contrast between this flood of images and absence of images on Algeria produces a kind of vertigo—and an enormous amount of anxiety. Even before the tragic events of the 1990s, Algeria was already an abstraction, a black mark that had disappeared from the collective consciousness of France."[8]

Whether or not one agrees with Stora's negative assessment, the cinematic image of Algeria (and of Algiers in particular) is worth considering, since the rerelease of *The Battle of Algiers* in the United States and France has brought the city back into public consciousness. For the purposes of this essay, I will focus on the portrayal of Algiers in five films: *Pépé le Moko* (1937), *Algiers* (1938), *The Battle of Algiers* (1965), *Omar Gatlato* (1976), and *Bab El Oued City* (1994). Of course, such a small number does not provide a comprehensive survey. Still, since these are all films that have had successful commercial distribution in France and the United States (as well as Algeria in the case of *Omar Gatlato*) either in their original release (or, in the case of *The Battle of Algiers*, rerelease) or on VHS or DVD, one could argue that they are the primary source of the image of Algiers in the popular consciousness. Despite having been made by directors from four different countries over a period of sixty years, the films are consistent in depicting the crushing psychological burden French colonialism has imposed on the Algerian people. Algiers is identified with the Casbah, the old city, and depicted as a closed space, a virtual prison from which there is little or no chance of escape—and which offers nothing more than despair or death.[9] Only *The Battle of Algiers* offers the possibility of liberation. At the end of the film, eight years after the FLN leadership has been killed or imprisoned, the Algerian people rise up in mass demonstrations, demanding independence.

In his preface to *Le cinéma colonial*, Guy Hennebelle describes North Africans in motion pictures as strangers in their own land, appearing in European films either as background scenery, like palm trees, camels, and mosques, or as villains whose base nature fights needlessly against the civilizing mission of France. Europeans, on the other hand, are usually "déclassé elements—legionnaires, bartenders, or petty criminals—who have come to the colony looking for the magic ladder that will permit them to find a place in society denied them in the mother country."[10] It would be hard to find a better description of Julien Duvivier's now-classic film *Pépé le Moko* (1937) and its lesser-known Hollywood remake *Algiers* (1944), directed by John Cromwell. Like Fanon's portrait of the colonial city in *The Wretched of the Earth*, this cinematic Algiers is divided between the European quarter, a "well-fed town, an easy-going town; its belly always full of good things," and the native town, "a crouching village, a town on its knees, a town wallowing in the mire." In this divided city, "it is the policeman and the soldier who are the official, instituted go-betweens, the spokesmen of the settler and his rule of oppression."[11]

Pépé le Moko opens on a close-up of a wall map of the Casbah, then moves back to reveal the office of the chief of the Algiers police. A Parisian colleague has come to chastise the French police officers for not capturing the infamous criminal Pépé le Moko, played by Jean Gabin. When the Parisian asks why they just do not go in and arrest Pépé, one of the detectives provides a short illustrated lecture on the Casbah, as if we were watching an educational documentary (almost the same footage is used for a similar scene in *Algiers*). The narrator describes it as both a labyrinth and a teeming, putrid, lice-infected anthill, linked by inner courtyards and terraces, populated by a heterogeneous mix of races and nationalities. Algerians are conspicuously absent from the list. The Casbah we see is a self-contained world, closed to outsiders, including the authorities. While the French may control Algeria, the Casbah is a separate territory, a law unto itself. Policemen enter at their own risk, with a good chance of not coming out alive. Unconvinced, the Parisian detective organizes a raid that very evening based on information supplied by Régis, an Algerian informer.

Even though the raid catches Pépé and his men by surprise, the police are clearly out of their element. After an exchange of gunfire, Pépé and his men escape through a hidden doorway, then flee over the rooftops—in much the same way FLN guerrillas will move around the city twenty years later. One of the striking elements in this scene is how much the architecture of the Casbah has insulated the local population from the French police, who may represent the power of the state but are confined to street-level patrols. This, of course, is Pépé's dilemma: he is a free man as long as he remains imprisoned under the Casbah's protective umbrella. As Denise Brahmi notes in her article "Le cinéma colonial revisité," the colony plays the role of ultimate refuge for those who have no place else to go—a refuge that is both an impasse and a trap.[12] Inez, Pépé's Algerian girlfriend, underlines the point when she tells him that he is already under arrest because he cannot leave the Casbah.

A possible way out appears when he meets Gaby, a beautiful Parisian whose companion, a rich older man, has brought her on a cruise with a few of his friends for a taste of the danger that the Casbah can provide. Even though criminals and fugitives populate the Casbah, the old city is not threatening. French tourists do not seem to be afraid to walk the streets, even when gunfire breaks out. Pépé and Gaby meet when Pépé is wounded during the police raid, and it is his attraction to her and all that she represents—the Paris that he cannot go back to—that leads to his downfall. Once he ignores her jewels, rejecting his identity as a thief, we sense that he is doomed. At one point he tries to leave the Casbah to meet Gaby but is unable to go down the final steps that lead to the French quarter; it is as if he is paralyzed. At the end of the film, when he tries to board the ship that is taking Gaby back to France, Pépé is seized by the police and taken away in handcuffs. He watches the ship sail off, framed by the bars of the port's giant gates that close around him. Faced with this symbolic prison, he commits suicide. Death is his only chance of escape.

In her book on Algiers, Zeynep Çelik argues that the myth of the Casbah developed around the concepts of gender, mystery, and difference—Algiers was seen as a "wise and dangerous mistress."[13] In *Pépé le Moko*, Inez and Gaby represent the poles of Pépé's life, Algiers and Paris; it is Gaby, however, the Parisian temptress, who incarnates danger and death. In Pépé's mind, Inez is a beneficent jailer whose only threat to him is boredom. Film historian Georges Sadoul has noted both the similarities and differences between *Pépé le Moko* and Howard Hawks's *Scarface*, the American film that defined the 1930s gangster genre.[14] But where Hawks's crime boss, played by Paul Muni, was an uncontrolled, overwhelming force, Pépé le Moko has been defeated from the outset—not by the police but by his nostalgia for Paris, by his exquisite boredom, and by fate. At the end, unable to embrace Inez and his life of exile, Pépé dies in front of the gates separating him from the symbolic ship that was supposed to take him away from Algiers.

The denizens we meet in *Pépé le Moko*—Slimane, the Algerian policeman, Pépé's girlfriend Inez, and Régis, the informer—symbolize the subservient relationship between France's colonial power and its subjects. Aside from the occasional stray child and street merchant, we never see families or anything re-sembling normal daily life. Although one aim of colonial cinema was to make European audiences feel protective toward the indigenous population, *Pépé le Moko* gives us the image of the Casbah as a tourist attraction where the local population is invisible. Gaby and her tourist friends are in Algiers for a taste of danger; their cloistered view of the Casbah has as much to do with the real Algiers as did "La rue d'Alger" in the World Exposition of 1900. While *Pépé le Moko*'s last sequence on the docks was shot on location, set designer Jacques Kraus re-created the Casbah in Pathé's studios. As photographed by Jules Krüger, the Casbah's narrow stairways and passages have a warm, luminous quality that seems to contradict the film's earlier description of it as a gritty, lice-infested labyrinth. One can imagine what the film would have been like if it had been lit and photographed like a "film noir," but this would have made the city less inviting to tourists.

In *Les Algériens au miroir du cinéma colonial*, Abdelghani Megherbi situated *Pépé le Moko* in both the 1930s "realist" film tradition of Jean Renoir and Marcel Carné and the literary realism of Balzac and Zola. Of course, realism had its limits in this instance, since it could not denounce French colonialism or show it explicitly. Megherbi questions the image of the Casbah as a refuge for petty criminals, arguing that the Casbah had no larger share of the world's crimi-nal element than any other city in Algeria—but reality was beside the point. "Duvivier contributed enormously to maintaining the image of the Casbah as a fearful place in the minds of Europeans—a reputation that did this beautiful and tranquil city no good at all."[15] Megherbi also characterizes Pépé's rapport with the local population as benevolent, yet anchored in the principles of colo-nial power. He strolls through the streets of the Casbah as a lord inspecting his fiefdom. He sleeps with Inez but shows her little affection; other Algerians are there essentially to follow his orders. Pépé never makes the least gesture of gratitude toward those who serve him, as when he takes a drink from a water carrier in the street. Slimane, the Algerian detective, plays a more complex and ambivalent role. Even though he serves the French, he is not really trusted by them, and in the end, it is unclear what Slimane achieves by bringing Pépé to justice—except the personal satisfaction of having outwitted both Pépé and his French colleagues by using what we might call his "native intelligence."

It is hard to imagine anyone other than Jean Gabin playing Pépé le Moko, and Charles Boyer, star of *Algiers*, is a pale copy of the original.[16] Heddy Lamar, on the other hand, gives us a stunning Gaby, particularly in the close-up shots of her face and hands provided by legendary Hollywood cinematographer James Wong Howe. Even Jean Gabin would have been tempted. *Algiers* is worth seeing for these scenes alone, as well as for the overhead tracking shot as Pépé runs through the Casbah and for the dream/fantasy sequence when he walks toward the dock, and his doom, at the end. *Algiers* is also noteworthy for its script credits. Though totally derivative of *Pépé le Moko*, *Algiers* was written by John Howard Lawson, later to become famous as the most uncooperative member of the Hollywood Ten, while mystery writer James Cain contributed additional dialogue. One major difference between the two films, possibly in deference to the tastes of American audiences, is that Pépé does not kill himself at the end of *Algiers*. Instead, he is shot by one of the detectives as he runs toward the departing ship. "I thought he was trying to escape" is the policeman's all-too-familiar rationale.

Both movies rely heavily on studio re-creations of the Casbah to achieve the desired mood. Rather than portray the dark rabbit warren described in the police headquarters, this Casbah is clean, quiet, and softly lit, permitting the main characters to float along on its surface rather than be integrated fully into the life of the city. Even though we know on some level that what we are seeing is not "real," both films create a world—Münsterberg's mixture of fact and symbol—that is nonetheless absolutely convincing.

Turning to *The Battle of Algiers* (1965), we find ourselves immersed in a different kind of realism—that of Algiers itself, since the film was shot entirely on location. In fact, the film seemed so "real" that its American distributors, with director Pontecorvo's permission, inserted a title card at the head declaring that not one foot of newsreel footage was used in making the film. After its initial release *The Battle of Algiers* was screened at festivals in Venice (where it won the Golden Lion Award, over the objections and walkouts of French critics), London, Acapulco, Moscow, Edinburgh, and New York. In 1967, the film was nominated for Academy Awards for Best Foreign Language Picture, Best Director, and Best Original Story and Screenplay. Though banned in France for five years, it enjoyed fairly wide distribution in the late 1960s and 1970s in the rest of the world as one of the best examples of left-wing political filmmaking. By the 1980s and 1990s, however, *The Battle of Algiers* was old news and the film had almost disappeared from distribution. The film was rereleased in January 2004, with a new 35 mm print and new subtitles, and played in New York and several other cities to large crowds. Some of the publicity around the film, however, came from another, less public screening. In the summer of 2003, the Pentagon's Office of Special Operations and Low Intensity Conflict had shown *The Battle of Algiers* as a staff training film, advertising it as a textbook case in "how to win a battle against terrorism and lose the war of ideas."[17] One might also imagine a Pentagon audience taking notes during the realistic torture scenes.

When *The Battle of Algiers* was released, it received many accolades characterizing it as a stirring epic film. As a sign of how times have changed over the past forty years, Stuart Klawans, writing in the *New York Times* in 2004, described it as "the legendary epic about terrorism and counter-terrorism."[18] Words like "revolution," "liberation struggle," and "colonialism" have been eliminated from the twenty-first-century critic's vocabulary. Klawans also remarked on the importance of the physical setting, suggesting that "architects could spend a happy two hours concentrating on *The Battle of Algiers* just for the winding staircases, inner courtyards and rooftop lookouts of the Casbah."[19] To focus on the architecture as architecture, however, would be to miss the point. One reason the film succeeds on a dramatic level is that the architecture is integrated into the narrative and treated as a living presence affecting how people interact. The insular, closed quality of the Casbah is captured by camera angles that emphasize the narrow streets with their unexpected twists and turns that catch people unawares. An outsider will not know what awaits him around the corner—a single person, armed or unarmed, or an angry mob.

Nevertheless, the "realistic" depiction of the Casbah in *The Battle of Algiers* is, in fact, far removed from the realism of a documentary. Everything we see in the film was staged for the camera. Pontecorvo and his director of photography, Marcello Gatti, constructed the "look" of the Casbah in *The Battle of Algiers* as carefully as Julien Duvivier and his set designer and cameraman did for *Pépé le Moko* thirty years earlier. In the interview that accompanies the published screenplay, Pontecorvo outlined the elements he used to achieve this impression of realism, what he called "the dictatorship of truth." First, he chose black-and-white film instead of color because most people experienced world events in the early 1960s through newsreel footage. Paradoxically, black and white was more "real" than color. Second, he discarded the normal lenses of 32 or 50 mm focal lengths, which approximate the field of vision of the human eye, in favor of telephoto lenses of 200, 300, and 600 mm, because most newsworthy events were filmed from a distance with telephoto lenses that flattened out the perspective. Light was the third element. Visitors to Algiers always seem to talk about the blue sky and bright sun reflecting off white buildings, yet *The Battle of Algiers* appears to have been shot entirely on overcast days. "It seemed to me," Pontecorvo told his interviewer, "that shade, diffused light, was much more dramatic. So all the exteriors were shot without sun."[20] Marcello Gatti covered the areas to be filmed with yards of gauze sheeting to diffuse the light, allowing occasional slivers of sun to provide depth and contrast. Pontecorvo often waited to shoot until late afternoon when the sun disappeared behind buildings. Finally, he and Gatti asked the film laboratory to lower contrast and increase grain when the film was developed, giving the film a gray, gritty, almost dirty texture. Of course, as Pontecorvo points out, there was no need to convince the French army that the film was fiction since they easily recognized the rifles and tanks used in the film as those supplied to the Algerians after independence by the Czech government.

The Battle of Algiers depicts the liberation struggle of the FLN in Algiers in the mid-1950s essentially as a flashback, opening with the occupation of the Casbah by French paratroopers in the fall of 1957. Most of the FLN leadership has been killed or captured, or is in exile abroad, except for Ali la Pointe, who is trapped, along with three comrades, in a hiding place behind the wall of an apartment. An older Algerian has revealed their hiding place after being tortured. The soldiers give Ali and his comrades an ultimatum: surrender or be blown up. After this prologue, the film moves back three years to the beginning of the urban guerrilla war. Unlike the impotent police in *Pépé le Moko*, the French army under General Massu isolated the Casbah with barbed wire and conducted house-by-house searches; they broke down the FLN cells by sheer numbers and brute force. The genial collaborators and informers from twenty years earlier, men like Slimane and Régis, were long gone, intimidated, tortured, or killed by the French or by the FLN.

Although the Casbah became, to use Djaffar Lesbet's term, "a 'counterspace' that represented the opposition to the colonial power,"[21] it could not offer a permanent haven from overwhelming military force. Nonetheless, this separation of the European city from the Casbah and the isolation of the Algerian population were captured by Pontecorvo in several scenes. When we first see Ali la Pointe, he is a card dealer on the street in the French quarter. A woman points him out to a policeman. Ali folds his cards and begins to run. As he passes a group of young Frenchmen, one of them sticks out his foot and Ali sprawls on the ground. Instead of getting up and escaping, he punches the French youth in the face. He is then pummeled by an angry crowd and has to be rescued by the police. Brahim Haggiag, the nonprofessional who played Ali la Pointe, perfectly captures the rage of the oppressed as the camera holds on his face as he is marched off to jail.

Later in the film, after two policemen are shot in an ambush, Pontecorvo cuts to an old man on the street with a cart, obviously out of place in the European quarter. He emphasizes this by shooting the scene from the other side of the street so the man is dwarfed by the buildings behind him; the wide street and open space contrast with the close quarters of the Casbah. People start calling out from the windows that he is the perpetrator; fearful and disoriented, the man begins to run. Unlike Ali la Pointe, he does not fight back and is quickly surrounded and taken away by the police. These scenes illustrate the colonial city as described by Fanon: "The zone where the natives live is not complementary to the zone inhabited by the settlers. The two zones are opposed, but not in the service of a higher unity. Obedient to the rules of pure Aristotelian logic, they both follow the principle of reciprocal exclusivity. No conciliation is possible."[22] The two sides ultimately communicate only through violent confrontation.

The realism of *The Battle of Algiers* is not merely a product of the technical aspects of the film but results from its adaptation of the personal experiences of FLN leader Yacef Saadi, who plays himself in the film. Saadi wrote the first draft of the story while he was in prison, worked closely with Pontecorvo on the script, and helped secure permission to shoot in the actual locations. While Pontecorvo was careful not to demonize the French (though this did not stop the film from being censored) and shows violent acts perpetrated by both sides, his sympathies are clearly with the FLN. Saadi wrote a book about his real-life role in *The Battle of Algiers* that was published in 1962.[23] At the time of the film's rerelease in 2004 he seemed to be more concerned with correcting the historical record for what he feels is his lack of credit in creating the film.[24] As for what constitutes the "real" story of the "battle of Algiers," this is open to question. Accounts by French officers involved in the action of 7–8 October 1957 on the rue Abdérames paint a much less heroic picture of Saadi's actions.[25]

In one sense, *The Battle of Algiers* is the story of a defeat, since the soldiers dynamite the building where Ali la Pointe and his comrades are hiding. The Casbah that had provided a haven for the FLN for so long has become a tomb. In a way, this echoes Eugene Fromentin's nineteenth-century travel journal, in which he described Algiers residents as "more or less like the national burnoose [cloak] that they wear, in a uniform and crude envelope . . . a single mass of masonry, compact and confused, built like a sepulcher. . . . I spoke the truth when I mentioned a sepulcher. The Arab believes he lives in the white town; he is in fact buried there, hidden in a lethargic state that drains him . . . shrouded in doubt and dying of inaction."[26]

While the FLN may have lost the battle for the city in 1957, they won the war. Five years later, at the end of the film, the people rise up in the mass demonstrations that ultimately drove the French out of the country. Here too, Pontecorvo masterfully uses the city's architecture to make his point. The people of Algiers appear almost spontaneously, coming out of the mist into the large open space in front of one of the government buildings. Thus, the film's final confrontations with the French army do not take place in the narrow dark streets of the Casbah but in one of the large public squares, as if Pontecorvo is saying that only by coming out of the closed city can liberation take place.

Twenty years after the events depicted in *The Battle of Algiers,* and fifteen years after independence, the world depicted in Merzak Allouache's two films *Omar Gatlato* (1976) and *Bab El Oued City* (1994) is as circumscribed and limited as Pépé le Moko's was in the Casbah of the 1930s. Allouache's films concern the postindependence struggles of daily life as seen through the eyes of two young men, who are, in a real sense, the children of the revolution. For them, the psychological legacy of colonialism, and the failures of the postrevolutionary government, are a heavy burden. *Omar Gatlato* is fiction, yet the film has the feel of a documentary. Omar, who is both the narrator and the main character, begins the film by directly looking at the camera. When we first meet him, he is living in a small apartment in a housing project, sharing a room with his sister and her children. He has no privacy. Although he physically resembles Ali la Pointe in certain ways, whatever anger Omar may have once had has been drained away by a relatively well paying, though boring, desk job and replaced by empty machismo. Omar's one escape is a bulky recorder that he carries around everywhere to capture the sounds of concerts and movie soundtracks on tape. At one point, however, he receives a tape with a mysterious woman's voice on it. Enamored with her, he eventually finds out who she is and calls to set up an outdoor rendezvous. When she appears, his lack of self-esteem prevents him from even crossing the street to talk with her. In both *Omar Gatlato* and *Bab El Oued City,* Algiers is no longer divided horizontally into the European quarter and the Casbah but is divided vertically: the rooftops belong to the women, the streets to the men, and communication between them seems to be impossible. No neutral, intermediate space exists.

The lack of privacy that we see in both films helps determine the characters' lives and behavior and depicts the housing crisis in Algiers that resulted from a tripling of the population between 1962 and 1992. A written version of this appears in *Algérie, 30 ans: Les enfants de l'indépendance.*[27] Based on a series of interviews with young Algerians done in 1991, Tewfik Hakem wrote about the problems of housing and privacy.[28] Réda, a twenty-year-old, explains that his thirty-five-year-old brother is still living at home, and when he gets married next year, his wife will come to live with them. Like Omar, Réda shares a room with his two sisters and younger brother. He has no place to go with his girlfriend. Every month there are fewer movie theaters; those that remain are so filthy that no women will go there. Many cafés have also closed, and since they are not welcoming to women, this is not a great loss. Tea salons are too expensive. The only time Réda can spend with his girlfriend is when he meets her after school and they walk together, exchanging CDs. When he hangs out with his friends, they play dominoes, which are more acceptable to the fundamentalists than card games. For Omar Gatlato, the only escape from sadness and despair is Indian movies and the occasional folkloric concert.

Bab El Oued City takes its name from the working-class quarter that one sees on the map in the beginning of *Pépé le Moko*. Like *Omar Gatlato*, the film focuses on a disaffected youth, Boualem, who works in a bakery and lives, like Omar, in a cramped apartment. When we first see him, he is on the roof of his building, tearing a loudspeaker broadcasting religious programs or sermons from its anchor outside his window. The constant intervention of the religious leaders provides an interesting parallel with the bullhorns used by the French army in *The Battle of Algiers;* the voice of authority comes only as an amplified, disembodied voice. Like Omar Gatlato, Boualem has no privacy in his apartment or outside in the street. Neither does anyone else. Coming off work at ten in the morning, Boualem and his coworker wake a friend who is sleeping in his car outside the bakery. Boualem tells him how lucky he is to have a car; his friend says that he lives in a two-room apartment with sixteen people; the car serves as an extra bedroom. The housing crisis in Algiers is deftly referred to again when Boualem returns home and his mother has to get his younger brother out of bed early to go to school so Boualem can go to sleep. When he wants to speak to his girlfriend in private, they go to the European cemetery—"the only secure place in Algiers" is how she describes it. But even here they are followed by one of the members of Bab el-Oued's fundamentalist cadre, whose leader happens to be his girlfriend's brother. When Said, the brother, hears of this, his suspicions of Boualem as being the one who stole the speaker are confirmed and he forces the baker to fire him. In a society on the verge of disintegration, there is no place for Boualem to go after he loses his job. Ripping the speaker from its mounting post and throwing it into the ocean was an act of rebellion by an isolated individual, not the beginning of a revolutionary movement. Even the local imam, who appears as a voice of reason, decides to leave Algiers for a less violent place. At the end of the film, Boualem leaves Algiers as well and boards a ship for an unknown future in France. Ultimately, *Bab El Oued City* is a depressing portrait of life in the postcolonial society. The closed world of the Casbah has come full circle to a dead end. Life in such a society is impossible; the only outlets are escape or death.

Of course, things have changed in the ten years since *Bab El Oued City* was released; a generation of younger filmmakers have begun to extricate themselves from the cloud of despair that afflicted their elders. In Nadir Moknèche's *Viva*

Ladjérie (2003), the main characters are a young single woman, her mother, who is a former well-known cabaret dancer, and a ten-year-old girl in the upstairs apartment. Still, the more things change, the more they stay the same. The older woman relives her past glory and dreams of reopening the nightclub that made her famous, while the daughter vents her frustrations in casual sex and an affair with a married doctor. What future awaits the young neighbor is unknown, but the film ends on a hopeful note as the daughter seems to begin a tentative new relationship with a young man who has been following her throughout the film.

Algeria's painful history has not disappeared, but it is no longer an unbearable burden leading inexorably to exile or death. We all carry the past within us. We can read about the past; we can visualize it in our minds and see it reflected in the streets of the cities in which we live. But the past does not have to determine how we live. Pépé le Moko lived in an Algiers that was a prison—a product of French colonialism and one that was self-imposed by his own inability to establish human relationships. This new cinematic vision of Algiers is telling us that the city may yet provide the seeds for a new life.

NOTES

1   Hugo Münsterberg, *The Film, a Psychological Study: The Silent Photoplay in 1916* (New York: Dover Publications, 1970), 30.

2   Thierry Flamand, "Adapter la ville à l'écran," in *Visions urbaines: Villes d'Europe à l'écran* (Paris: Centre Georges Pompidou, 1994), 9. The same could be said of world's fair attractions like "La rue du Caire" and "La rue d'Alger." For further discussion of this point, see Sylviane Leprun, *Le théâtre des colonies* (Paris: L'Harmattan, 1986); and Zeynep Çelik, *Displaying the Orient: Architecture of Islam at Nineteenth-Century World's Fairs* (Berkeley and Los Angeles: University of California Press, 1992).

3   Edgar Morin, *Le cinéma ou l'homme imaginaire* (Paris: Seuil, 1962), 82.

4   Cités-Cinés was a popular exhibit on film and the city, first seen in Paris in 1987. Architectural design and motion picture clips re-created a triple illusion of the real, the reel, and the imaginary. However, except for Tokyo, the Cités-Cinés urban vision was Eurocentric and American.

5   François Barré, "Le vrai-faux passeport," in *Cités-Cinés* (Paris: La Villette/La Grande Halle, 1987), 9.

6   Marcel Oms, "L'imaginaire coloniale au cinéma," in *Images et colonies: Regards sur l'Afrique; Actes du colloque 22 janvier 1993 à la Bibliothèque Nationale à Paris* (Paris: Syros/ACHAC, 1993), 103. See also Roy Armes, *Postcolonial Images: Studies in North African Film* (Bloomington: Indiana University Press, 2005), 15–17.

7   Abdelghani Megherbi, *Les Algériens au miroir du cinéma colonial* (Paris: Société Nationale d'Édition et de Diffusion, 1982), 249.

8   Interview with Benjamin Stora, "Où va le cinéma algérien?" *Cahiers du cinema*, hors série, February–March 2003, 8.

9   This image of Algiers can also be found in William Klein's 1970s documentary *Eldridge Cleaver in Algiers*, as well as recent films like *Viva l'Aldjérie*.

10   Guy Hennebelle, *Le cinéma colonial de "L'Atlantide" à "Lawrence d'Arabie"* (Paris: Seghers, 1975), 9–10.

11   Franz Fanon, *The Wretched of the Earth*, trans. Constance Farrington (New York: Grove Press, 1968), 39, 38.

12   Denise Brahmi, "Le cinéma colonial revisité," *Cinémas du Mahgreb, CinémAction* 111 (2004): 36–48.

13   Zeynep Çelik, *Urban Forms and Colonial Confrontations: Algiers under French Rule* (Berkeley and Los Angeles: University of California Press, 1997), 21.

14   Sadoul quoted in Hennebelle, *Cinéma colonial,* 130.

15   Megherbi, *Algériens au miroir du cinéma colonial,* 250.

16   Algerian critic Abdou B. describes the remake *Algiers* as "un film américain sans importance." See Abdou B., "Alger au cinéma, de *Pépé le Moko* à *Bab-el-Oued City,*" *La pensée de Midi,* no. 4 (Spring 2001): 93.

17 Stuart Klawans, "Lessons of the Pentagon's Favorite Training Film," *New York Times*, 4 January 2004.

18 Ibid.

19 Ibid.

20 Gillo Pontecorvo, *The Battle of Algiers* (New York: Scribners, 1973), 171.

21 Çelik, *Urban Forms and Colonial Confrontations*, 38; Djaffar Lesbet, *La Casbah d'Alger: Gestion urbain et vide sociale* (Algiers: Publications Universitaires, 1985). See also Çelik's "The Houses of Algiers in French Colonial Discourse," chapter 4 in this volume.

22 Fanon, *Wretched of the Earth*, 38.

23 Yacef Saadi, *Souvenirs de la bataille d'Alger* (Paris: Julliard, 1962).

24 Gary Crowdus, "Terrorism and Torture in *The Battle of Algiers:* An Interview with Yacef Saadi," *Cineaste* 29, no. 3 (Summer 2004): 30–37.

25 See, e.g., Capitaine Blonnel, "Comment finit Ali La Pointe," *Historia* 233 (January 1958): 1201–7.

26 Eugène Fromentin, *Une année dans le Sahel* (Paris: E. Plon-Nourrit, 1888), 31–32.

27 Merzak Allouache and Vincent Colonna, eds., *Algérie, 30 ans: Les enfants de l'indépendance*, Éditions Autrement, hors série, no. 60 (Paris: Autrement, 1992).

28 Ibid., 26–29.

PLACES

6

MASKING AND UNMASKING THE HISTORIC QUARTERS OF ALGIERS

THE REASSESSMENT OF AN ARCHIVE

Isabelle Grangaud

Ottoman Algiers appears to belong to the distant past. This is especially so when weighed against the backdrop of contemporary history, namely the French conquest, which shook precolonial society to its roots and continues, even today, to efface most traces or representations of that earlier period. The distance not only is the work of time but can be measured in turns and twists that have left their mark on a tormented past. Therefore, contemporary Ottoman historians can never be neutral but rather are obliged to recognize the intervening colonial practices. Due to the reordering of archival data following the French occupation, historians cannot move along a simple chronological path. Rather, they must find the means to resurrect hidden historical processes, seek that which has been forgotten, reveal that which no longer makes sense. In bringing to light how former institutions in Ottoman Algiers functioned and assumed meaning, historians may benefit to some degree from contemporary configurations. In turn, present-day systems may be better understood when compared with their historic counterparts.

This study investigates the modalities by which a largely centralized urban institution under the Ottomans, the *hawma* (Arabic for "quarter" or "neighborhood"), present in Algiers from the early sixteenth century until 1830, was transformed under colonial rule. My goal is to comprehend the semiconcealed sociopolitical practices and idioms of spaces that shaped relations between the inhabitants of a particular neighborhood and the wider city. I begin with an overview of the ways in which neighbors and neighborhoods function in today's Algiers, paying attention to the critical question of how the members of a certain city quarter recognize as well as express their belonging to a delimited space and community of people. Both the space and the sense of identity with it and its inhabitants are signified by the notion of *hawma* (in the plural, *hawmât*).

Earlier studies of Ottoman urban organization in Algiers tended to analyze the *hawma* solely as a spatial entity, neglecting its internal—and external—social dynamics. This approach reduces the question to administrative guidelines passed down over the ages and based upon colonial models of Islamic and/or Maghrebi cities that were imposed on urban society. Another, related perspective, inspired by anthropology, has sought and found popular social practices frequently interpreted as folklore and often regarded as "coming from elsewhere." I will argue that the dynamics of social practice, even the most fluid, have to be carefully situated within their particular historical context and also in relationship to the institutions of their time. Indeed, the official medieval texts organizing urban life in North Africa provide details on the various social and political consequences of one's place of residence and on the physical limits of the city.

Next, I explain why previous generations of historians had such difficulty in grasping the meaning of the *hawma* as enunciated in the Ottoman texts. By consulting the principal source of documentation from that era, the Fonds Ottomans (Ottoman Archives) at the Centre des Archives Nationals (Center of National Archives) in Algiers, established at the very beginning of the French conquest, I was able to reconstitute the organizational history of the documents. It became obvious that the category *hawma* employed in the French public domains administration after 1830 did not coincide exactly with that of the Ottoman documents. The creation of this category makes no sense unless it is interpreted as the consequence of the conquerors' imposition of new urban spatial relationships, which was an especially urgent task given the massive French presence in the city from 1830 on, mainly the army and military personnel. The effect of these modifications in legal and social meanings was to negate the *hawma* as an urban institution by making it invisible.

Finally, I discuss the spatial transformations introduced by the colonial regime during the nineteenth century, transformations that have generally been perceived as the result of profound urban reform. In contrast, I argue that the changes in the center of Algiers undertaken in the months immediately following the conquest were not the consequence of attempts at city reorganization as much as they were the product of ignorance and chaos combined with the physical necessity of occupying the capital city and its suburbs. Ignoring pre-1830 urban institutions and relationships undermined the preexisting social space and, further, provoked a collective loss of memory regarding the *hawma*.

The significance of any reference to a *hawma* by residents of Algiers—or to a *hawma* of any other Algerian or North African city—for the purpose of characterizing certain neighborhood relationships has generally gone unnoticed by contemporary social historians,[1] probably for two reasons: first, the *hawma*, both in oral tradition and practice, seems relevant only incidentally, in reference to precise and very personal experiences of city life, and second, other forms of expression of urban identity, more in tune with the colonial administrative framework of the urban landscape, have overshadowed it. This probably explains why sociological studies regard the neighborhood as irrelevant for any formal definition of identity (family or professional). Where space is concerned, other categories and dual oppositions hold sway, among them administrative spaces versus informal spaces, rich versus poor neighborhoods, old versus recent housing. The *hawma* does not appear in the language of mainstream sociological or urban discourse, the latter influenced more by state planning and generally by the social dynamics in place since the nineteenth century.

The fact that the *hawma* predates the modern era leads historians to classify its manifestations as archaic or, at best, as traditional and atavistic urban social forms, hence detrimental to the vitality of the contemporary city.[2] However, by investigating the present reality of the *hawma*—fluid as that may be—it becomes possible to grasp the nature of the old quarters, to understand their roots, and, thereby, to attempt to reconstitute the evolution of this urban phenomenon.[3]

The root *ha-wa-ma* suggests the notion of environment, a circular perimeter within the eye's purview; it also connotes dense mass or density of place. In declining the root, several directions are possible; however, it is only in the Maghreb that the term *hawma* is the equivalent of the word "quarter," the usual translation. Dictionaries of classical Arabic, such as Ibn Manzur's *Lisan al-ʿArab* (The Arab Language), Kazimirski's *Dictionnaire arabe-français* (1860), and Reig's *Dictionnaire arabe-français, français-arabe* (1983), either ignore or do not retain this definition of the term, at least not for the Mashriq (the eastern Arab world), thus relegating it to spoken or dialectical Arabic. In point of fact, in Algiers, the literal translation of *"Wash hiyya hawmtak?"*—"Where do you live?"—is "Which is your *hawma?*" In this sense, the term refers to the fact of living together in the city rather than to specific spatial units, as the notion of quarter or neighborhood suggests, anchoring people to physical spaces.[4] This definition of *hawma* pertains to the residential area, be it the old urban center (Casbah), the residential quarters of the colonial era, or the housing projects that now occupy the outskirts of the city. The members of the *hawma* hence are not fixed in place; one can take one's quarter with him/her by retaining those intricate social ties with other citizens of the *hawma*.

When people say they no longer have a *hawma*, it does not mean that they are homeless or that they have lost track of a former place of residence, but rather that they have lost sight of those who had been part of their daily lives.[5] The *hawma* is often the memory of experiences shared with other children or young people within a common place of residence and play.[6] *Hawmti* (my quarter) refers to one's childhood residence, one's playmates and classmates. In this context, the term implies tiny neighborhood units—a block, an alley, a building—unrelated in any way to the much larger districts designated by administrative terminology. The *hawma* is the place one goes back to every day to chat or to play. The *hawma*'s children identify with the common practices of their place of residence. As adults, they recognize each other at gatherings or receptions, such as marriage ceremonies. For the individual, the *hawma* is as much a social reality as it is a geographic one; in social circumstances, it must always be considered or, at least, recognized.

The *hawma* is one of the social languages shared by the people of a city. It forms a space with a center rather than a border; its formal existence is not actually geographic but rather defined by those who are part of it. Active proximity constructs the space of a *hawma*. The sense of belonging to the city emanates from the *hawma*: it defines one's group recognition, founded not on family ties but neighborhood relationships, and makes a distinction between itself and "strangers," the *barrânî*, or those from "outside." Relationships within the *hawma*, while not strictly based upon kinship or family, should not be confused with friendship or professional ties. Other subtle practices refine the *hawma*: it is not a place for flirtation; and relations between young people are limited to the community they form among themselves. Young women and girls—*banât al-hawma* (girls of the quarter)—are treated with deference and respect. The same codes of honor apply to the quarter's inhabitants as to the family: with respect to both, reputations are defended against attack by outsiders.

Certain rights are associated with one's membership in the *hawma*: the right to defend it and circulate within it, and the right to certain forms of appropriation of the space—at least symbolically. Anecdotal evidence supporting this definition comes from a televised message concerning road safety in residential neighborhoods. A man driving the wrong way on a one-way street is stopped by the police. The driver explains that he is in his own neighborhood: *rânî fî hawmtî* (I am in my quarter), thereby signifying that he should not be penalized. Certain rights, as well as duties or responsibilities, are accepted as inherent in neighborhood relations. Thus, belonging to a *hawma* is a local experience of life in the city, a way of representing urban space through social practices, with obligations of shared language and rights. While it receives no official recognition—and it may even find itself in opposition to the nation's laws—the *hawma* nevertheless weighs heavily upon social relations and urban organization and may even make claims to a form of legitimacy.[7]

The language and customs of the *hawma* are seen by those who practice them as popular expressions of the local dialect and folklore, as tools of one's private world.[8] Its definition as an urban space is one of informality; its boundaries fluctuate with the intensity of social interactions, rendering "scientific" mapmaking practically impossible. This is all the more true in Algiers, in contrast to Moroccan cities, in that the word is absent from any municipal terminology, which relies on other terms to define the urban landscape, in particular, the modern term *hayy* (residential sector) to designate different areas of a neighborhood.

The description of the *hawma* in Algiers today closely resembles that given by the French scholar Roger Letourneau in his study of the neighborhoods of Fez prior to the establishment of the French protectorate in Morocco in 1912. He observed two types of quarters. He called the first the "official" and produced a map of the city based on "official" quarters. The second, the "social quarter," was "a small cell that owes its life to the personal ties the neighborhood establishes among its inhabitants and that, in the case of significant events, can play a certain political role."[9] The administrative and political outlines of Letourneau's "real quarters," the second type, as opposed to the more abstract administrative and fiscal entities, are remarkably similar to those of the Algiers *hawmât*, in particular the significance of the social bonds created in one's place of residence. Letourneau underscored the difference between this type of social entity and the neighborhoods of French cities: the boundaries of the "real quarters" were defined not by the streets in front of the blocks of houses but by the rears of buildings, the street constituting not a frontier but the very heart of the quarter.

Letourneau's description is useful, but it is limited to the organization of space, borrowed from familiar European hierarchies; he neglected to delve further into the historic foundations. New light has been shed on this question in a recent study of the organization of urban space in North African cities undertaken by Jean-Pierre Van Staëvel, historian of medieval law.[10] Basing his research on a tenth-century document, he has analyzed the rulings of Maliki jurists concerning the claims of property owners on thoroughfares, as well as relationships between the owners and the authorities; these rulings remained the basic guidelines for town and city planning in the Maghreb until the nineteenth century.[11]

Van Staëvel stresses the importance of rights associated with the use of urban spaces and the underlying notions of physical organization and hierarchy. He outlines the process by which the public thoroughfare intervenes and leads to a proliferation of dead-end streets, generally considered characteristic of the anarchic development of the Islamic city.[12] The misreading, he insists, is based on ignorance of the juridical underpinnings of spatial transformation, which stems from attributing an inalienable quality to the public realm and linking any interference of unwarranted privatization to judicial laxness.[13] This interpretation of the urban environment is based on Roman law, according to which the public domain is inalienable and imprescriptible, principles that do not apply under Maliki law. The essential criteria depended on how thoroughfares were frequented. The road networks were not, at the outset, part of the public domain but spaces of common good and as such "not subject to individual appropriation." A distinction was made, however, between thoroughfares used by everyone and others, such as alleys and dead-end streets, that were frequented solely by their residents, which meant that building owners might install a doorway at the entrance to their alley. Moreover, the inhabitants living on a thoroughfare could petition for the right to dispose of their space as a group. Van Staëvel remarks that the use of public byways "is more a question of the logic and strategies for circulation, logic and strategies shared by all the inhabitants," jurists included.[14] Therefore, the city is composed of areas of proximity with recognized rights of usage that in the long term contribute to spatial transformations.

Seen from this angle, practices represented as folklore assume significant dimensions. The *hawma*, far from being a simple, archaic community practice, with its back turned to the city, becomes a means of appropriation of urban space based on local residency and neighborhood networks, the epitome of urbanity. At the time of Ottoman rule the term was also employed in *'udûl* (notarial) texts and other legal documents as a reference for the location of buildings.[15]

This notion of the neighborhood as an institution founded and empowered by social relationships and joint rights to a common living area (and not as a territorial unit or a unit associated with a particular ethnic group) has been investigated by contemporary historians, and not only in the Maghreb. Recent studies have revealed its existence in Ottoman cities, in particular in Anatolia, where quarters called *mahalle* presented an alternative to classifications according to the confessional and ethnic *millet* (forms of community that for a long time were privileged in urban studies); the term *mahalle* belonged to an urban language and was often used in the courts, traces of which can be seen in popular urban culture today. The institutional dimensions of social practices, largely invisible in historical records or contemporary sources, oblige the modern scholar to probe deeper into seemingly discontinued social manifestations that actually reoccur over time and entail shared languages and legally recognized moral behaviors.[16] They provoke the historian to question, in particular for the Algiers *hawma*, the historic processes that brought about the loss or proscription of the institution.

"SPACE INVERTED"

Studies of North African cities under the Ottomans present a very different image of the *hawma* from the one derived from the observation of present-day manifestations of urban identity.[17] Presented either as an extended family or ethnic space of a proto-urban type (along the lines of the "segmented city") or as an apparatus of the central authorities forced upon the city, the *hawma* has most often been seen as a fixed structure broken down into systematic and regular divisions (possible to map) without consideration of the practices and social dynamics that shaped it.[18] On the one hand, such a biased interpretation of the *hawma* of a city like Ottoman Algiers is connected to the endurance of the "Islamic city" model, which presents an overly stable, mechanical view of urban institutions in the Muslim world. According to this perception, there can be no link between the quarters of the precolonial era and those of today. On the other hand, the relative invisibility of today's *hawma* in analyses of urban space is the result of research blinded by the effects of colonial modernity on present-day realities of the city—physical as well as social.[19]

This truncated vision of urban space under the Ottomans is based, more than is realized, on archives born of the French conquest. The tendency has been to accept the early administrative texts of the conquerors as emanating from the Ottoman era. After all, the French denied that they intended to reform the city and also claimed to maintain the documents as organized by the Ottomans, which was all the more believable since the texts were in Arabic. Not only relating to questions of urban space and the *hawma*, a variety of information gathered at the beginning of the French conquest has been considered to represent the precolonial situation, especially because the records were the product of an administrative organization that quickly disappeared. The paper files classified as pertaining to the *hawma*, including files on corporative bodies, trade organizations, and property ownership, exert a lasting legacy, masking much that occurred prior to 1830.[20] Although this documentation is accepted by historians as reliable, the people of that era lived another story, which must be told.

Algeria's state and religious archives contain vast quantities of land titles (pri-

vate and *habûs,* or Muslim pious endowments) covering various types of trans-
actions—inheritance, sales, legacies, gifts, rights of succession, and rentals of all
sorts.[21] A large majority concern Algiers and its hinterland. The information is
recorded in sizable registers that separate *habûs* and private assets according to a
geographic classification by *hawma,* both within the city's walls and without.

Historians have generally considered these documents as strictly Ottoman,
since the classifications in Arabic refer to an Ottoman nomenclature and go
back as far as the sixteenth century, when Algeria was incorporated into the
Ottoman Empire; some, however, date from the first years of the French conquest. After the independence of Algeria, this collection of documents has been
called the "Fonds Ottomans" and has been interpreted by nationalist historians
as providing continuity to Algeria's national history.[22] Because of the concern
to locate the roots of the "nation" in the Ottoman past, the manner in which the
collection was constituted and archived and how its contents relate to Ottoman
history have not been questioned. Moreover, the tendency has been to clean up
the collection for the purpose of eliminating disorder and to contribute to its
"Ottomanization." In so doing, it has been presumed, somewhat naively, that
the French colonial authorities were determined to preserve the historic documentation of the country *in extenso.*

Of prime importance for the French conquest, the collection was actually
created sometime after the summer of 1830. Building the archive was the work
of the public domains administration set up in October of that year, whose task
was to evaluate public properties and to control the conditions of appropriation
of private property, with the caveat that, in case of default, private property
would be given over to the public domain. The operation was limited to Algiers,
since it was the first city seized from the Ottoman state and represented, in those
early years, the only real area from which the policies of colonization could be
developed. In addition, the agents of the public domains administration considered Algiers the model for the creation of an administration covering the entire
country.

Obviously, the elements required to establish an inventory of properties were
not available. The very notion of public domain contradicted existing legal concepts of property and ownership, which were not as immediately adaptable as
had been supposed. The documentation at our disposal is, therefore, the result
of the systematic effort to establish an inventory of properties and to lay the
groundwork for the creation of a category of public domains—previously nonexistent.

Since no property roll or its equivalent existed, the authorities undertook to
contact owners demanding that they show their property titles or be dispos-

sessed. The superintendent of the War Ministry declared in January 1831: "To establish the Domains definitively and to amass more exact data on the city's structures, it will be necessary to demand that all titles of property be produced, a careful inventory made, that they be rented out, leased, and the revenues collected on the Treasury's behalf."[23] Such were the concerns and activities that led to the geographic classification of the documentation. The exact measurements of a property were not recorded, but its (often approximate) location was. As a result, classification was by neighborhood.

The fact of borrowing terms from the former vocabulary and nomenclature (*hawma* for "quarter") has led to their acceptance as Ottoman spatial categories. Quarters with toponyms received numbers: for example, certain properties would be classified as *hawma* number 9 rather than by their local toponyms, which might have referred to a lineage or to an economic activity or to some event from the distant past. There was the astonishing *hawma madkûra*, meaning "the above-mentioned *hawma*," a designation in the absence of a name. Property titles that were incomplete or in fragments and that bore no identifying location (it was sometimes noted that the property title had been burnt or torn) were subsumed under this heading. In other words, grouped under the category "*hawma madkûra*" were properties whose titles contained no address. It is clear from the analysis of these registers of property titles that they were created by French colonial officials for the purpose of regrouping neighboring properties. Furthermore, the *hawmât* did not necessarily coincide with the localizations referred to in the titles collected, and localization was far from systematic. On the one hand, in the records created during the Ottoman era, the localization of a property did not require a reference to a *hawma*. The address on many titles was one of proximity, such as above, below, next to, across from a mosque, a market, a public bath, a fountain, etc. Such spatial references could also be replaced by association within a *hawma*: for example, "next to" could replace "in the *hawma* of" and vice versa. On the other hand, the *hawma* under which a property was classified might not be the one on the title if the one on the title had been incorporated into another *hawma*. In other words, a *hawma* might have encompassed several quarters. The issue is that, while the *hawma* as used in Ottoman era property titles was not a precisely mapped spatial reference, the French, upon their arrival in Algiers, strove to systematize a classification by *hawma*, which resulted in adding a different dimension to each *hawma*, more administrative and less social than what it had theretofore encompassed. This would end up causing confusion within spatial nomenclatures that had been used prior to that time.

Lastly, the organization of the documentation does not coincide with local spatial concepts. It is clear from certain documents in the collection that a distinction was made between the *hawmât* identified by the public domains administration and those explicitly designated under the heading "Arab quarters" (that included both references of proximity and *hawmât*). In addition, the term *hawma* itself was applied not only to areas in the city but also to its outskirts, urban and rural.

These manipulations prove that orderly documentation was the intention. For the agents of the French administration, who were completely unfamiliar with local spatial and legal language, the idea was to create larger and more stable units of spatial classification, as attested to by the registers. Furthermore, nothing testifies to the correspondence of the units to a new administrative structure, especially because the rapid and large-scale transformations undertaken in the city have left no trace of such a reorganization. Nor is there any evidence that the geographic boundaries of urban quarters were strictly defined. It would seem, therefore, that legal viability was the goal sought by the classification of the property titles in order to expropriate property from the inhabitants of Algiers and transmit that property to Europeans, who, however, required proper legal titles.

This endeavor ignored the physical dimensions closely associated with the social space of the Algiers *hawmât,* and it delegitimized a basic urban institution, whose existence from then on would be an informal one. The "spatial inversion" was made possible by a seemingly insignificant event with enormous consequences: the naming and numbering of the city's streets.

The taxonomic battle was not between two conceptions of the *hawma,* one that was Ottoman in origins and founded on common local residency and the rights associated with the community thus formed, and the other imposed after 1830 for the purpose of reorganizing and rationalizing the urban administration. But, another organization of urban space, founded on the primacy of the road network—not on the neighborhood—had been mandated. The street became the vector for the spatial organization of the city.

THE POWER OF IGNORANCE

The street is very present in the archives of the public domains administration. It constitutes the backbone of a classification of properties also listed by *hawma.* Since the classification is in French, Ottomanists have paid little attention to the significance of how the precolonial archive was continued after 1830.[24] One might rightly ask whether the classification of properties by street was not the goal of the whole operation. The creation of the registers by *hawma*, referenced at times with street names, was obviously the point of departure for the classi-fication. However, the classification of properties by street could not have been done before 1835, the year when an intensive street-naming operation, using the store of national and military names, mostly drawn from the Algerian campaign, was launched.[25] This operation was not the first of its kind.[26] It followed a more precipitous one begun in a climate of violence and widespread chaos barely a few days after the French troops entered the city on 5 July 1830. A report ad-dressed to the minister of war by his superintendent, Baron Volland, dated 12 January 1831, presented an optimistic view "of the method of government estab-lished provisionally in the Kingdom of Algiers," limited at the time to the city and its outlying districts. It emphasized the progress of the occupation and took part in the acrimonious debate on the future of the conquest then provoking an uproar in the French Parliament. Volland wrote concerning the administration inside the city: "A large number of projects of public utility have been conceived [but] few have been implemented because time has not permitted. However, we have managed to provide street designations and to undertake an inventory and the numbering of houses."[27]

Naming streets and numbering houses were, therefore, among the first ini-tiatives of the conquerors. Although these operations were presented as suc-cessful initiatives of the new municipal authorities to promote the public good, the urgency with which they were actually accomplished is not obvious. Yet, five months and one week to the day after entering Algiers, Volland's predeces-sor, Baron Denniée, had addressed a report to the commanding general of the French army that laid out the questions dealt with by the government commis-sion over which he had presided in its daily meetings since 7 July. Judging from a series of events cited on 12 July 1830, the French administration was far from securely established. The commission "had heard several senior civil servants of the former government" and expressed "the need to have immediate and deeper knowledge of the details of the former administration." It had also decided "to designate agents to proceed without delay to the examination of [the Ottoman] registers." The same day, the same commission proposed nominating a domains committee for the overall management of property.[28] One of the first objec-tives of the commission since 7 July had been to find housing in the city for the troops, who numbered in the tens of thousands, which explains the measures taken to establish an inventory of the public domain. However, the occupation of the city was far from stabilized. The commission report also dealt with the question of streets and referred to a decision taken still earlier regarding their sweeping and the removal of garbage.[29] Furthermore, the committee proceeded with the numbering of houses and the posting of names at both ends of streets.

The next step would be lighting. On 11 July, a military order was promulgated requiring that "each inhabitant light, at his expense, the front of his house," while the administration's "responsibility was only the maintenance of twenty lanterns along the main streets."[30] Thus, the initial principle of naming streets was ordered early on, although under conditions that left considerable leeway to the indigenous inhabitants since the expeditionary forces in 1830 lacked the means to implement urban decrees.

The first street names were inspired directly by local toponyms and were traced on the fragile walls of the buildings; they were so faint that by 1835 they had practically disappeared, thereby erasing the impact of the intervention.[31] The initiative to name the city streets, the "spatial inversion," went largely unnoticed, in contrast to the highly visible military urban operations taking place during the same period and associated, quite naturally, with the need to control the native population. Far from being a conscious or planned military initiative, these early interventions into the social and physical spaces of Algiers were the product of a profound ignorance of realities on the ground.

Given the brutal nature of the invasion and the lack of familiarity with the workings of the society, control over the city's street network was both crucial and pragmatic: finding one's way through totally unfamiliar terrain was critical, yet the invaders knew virtually nothing about the city's topography, organization, and languages. In this strange maze or labyrinth that was Algiers in 1830 street names and numbers were to serve as stepping stones.[32] It should be noted that the French military had understood only recently the importance of street names as the most rapid, the most efficient, and the most natural means of penetrating a city. At the time of the Egyptian expedition, thirty years earlier, Cairo's quarters, not its streets, had been delineated.[33] Even in Paris, street nomenclature was not well established, and numbering had not been imposed. It was only in 1805, a few years after Napoleon's troops left Egypt, that the change occurred in Paris.[34]

Within a few decades, Algiers too was subjected to a series of measures aimed at its appropriation.[35] Immense arteries were cut through the city. The lower quarters were gutted, and a large square, place d'Armes, was fitted out. In October 1830, plans for a theater were drawn up and the program of its repertoire announced: ballet and Italian opera.[36] The remarkable pace of urban interventions in 1830, even before the first survey had been executed by the army engineers, testifies to the importance of conquering the city spatially.[37] In other words, the army had transformed something incomprehensible into something seemingly manageable. One of the spokesmen of Algiers, Hamdan Khûdja, in a report addressed to the War Ministry in 1833, denounced the destruction of buildings in Algiers and concluded: "this city has no need of squares."[38]

It might be useful here to compare the military officers' relationship to urban space with the systematic deportation of former Ottoman authorities out of the country. Once again, space had to be made for the new conquerors. In the same way that this measure was later regretted, the large-scale transformations to which Algiers was subjected were subsequently denounced.[39] They were the consequence of a blindness not typical of the French, Ernest Feydeau said in 1860.[40] The precolonial city was not adaptable to such intervention. Historian René Lespès attributed this rigidity to the character of the urban fabric: "the Barbary Coast city was made for an absolutely different civilization than ours. Huddled and wary behind its walls, it was the midwife of its space. The street—neither a promenade for passersby nor a showplace of houses for their residents—was limited to the absolute minimum width."[41] While he criticized the early French operations for not understanding the city, Lespès did not question colonization but simply pointed to the differences in aesthetic and cultural values and argued for alternative approaches to French urbanism in Algeria. For European travelers the brutal transformations divested Algiers of its picturesque charm.

The appropriation of the city took place without the support of scholarly experts such as Napoleon's *armée des savants* that had followed him to Cairo some thirty years earlier. Genty de Bussy, in 1839, insisted on the importance of the alliance between conquest and science: "While he [Napoleon] was capturing the pyramids and Cairo, other members of the expedition were studying the climate and the soil, and still others inventoried monuments and different time periods; each one filled his bag." He then asked: "Why, immediately following the occupation [of Algeria], did we not follow this example?" Genty de Bussy then proposed the creation of a scientific commission that "could render immense service to real science as well as to colonization."[42] It took ten years for this colonial wisdom to take hold and for scientific curiosity about Algeria to develop.[43] This delay explains in part the relative scarcity of documents on the major spatial transformations undertaken. It also sheds light on the tremendous brutality of the conquest. The priority of the conquerors was to carve out space for themselves. The naming of streets played a crucial role in this violent process: it disavowed other ways of practicing space—physically, socially, and politically—and it obliterated the very significance of the inversion, rendering it natural.

Following the independence of Algeria in 1962, the streets of Algiers were renamed to celebrate the nation and its recovered or reimagined past. But this act was merely symbolic. The colonial nomenclature, which signified domination par excellence, remains etched in the Algerian landscape and in the archive. The name changes lost sight of the deeper stakes at play: in eroding the *hawma*, the colonial order had dismantled the very logic of the city.

Translated from the French by Elaine Mokhtefi.

NOTES

1   It is striking how rarely the *hawma* is mentioned in studies of the city. Special issues of *Insaniyat: Revue algérienne d'anthropologie et de sciences sociales* devoted to the study of urban phenomena are representative. See "Villes algériennes" (May–August 1998) and "Oran, une ville d'Algérie" (January–June 2004). By comparison, Moroccan studies give more prominence to this urban phenomenon. See, e.g., Mohammed Naciri, *La medina de Fès: Trame urbaine en impasses et impasse de la planification urbaine, Présent et avenir des médinas (de Marrakech à Alep)* (Tours: Urbama—Université de Tours, 1982), 237–54; M'hammed Idrissi Janati, "Les images identitaires à Fès: Divisions de la société, divisions de la ville," in *Les divisions de la ville,* ed. C. Topalov (Paris: UNESCO and Maison des Sciences de l'Homme, 2002), 347–72. It should be noted that the *hawmât* of Moroccan cities have been institutionalized. A *shaykh al-hawma* is responsible for issuing residence documents and certificates of good conduct to inhabitants of the *hawma.*

2   Larbi Icheboudene, "De la Houma à la cité: Une évolution historique de l'espace social algérois," *Revue algérienne des sciences juridiques, économiques et politiques* 40 (2002): 59–74. The model of the tribal *soff,* or clan, has also been applied to the city to describe the origins of opposition between neighborhoods during the colonial era.

3   See my entry, under the heading *hawma,* in the encyclopedia *Trésor des mots de la ville,* to be published by UNESCO. It is based on a brief survey carried out in Algiers and Constantine.

4   This detail is all the more remarkable in that, outside Algeria, the *hawma* characterizes the neighborhoods of old cities and medinas.

5   Alfred-Louis de Prémare, *Dictionnaire arabe-français—langue et culture marocaines* (Paris: L'Harmattan, 1994–98), points out that the expression "he has no *hawma*" can even be used to designate a "stateless person."

6   On the question of social activities of young people in the neighborhoods and their role in the formation of political and militant identities during the colonial era, see Omar Carlier, "Espace politique et sociabilité juvénile: La parole étoiliste en ses quartiers, contribution à une étude du 'nous,'" in *Lettrés intellectuels et militants en Algérie, 1880–1950,* ed. Omar Carlier and Fanny Colonna (Paris: Office des Publications Universitaires, 1988).

7   The example cited is an illustration of the outlawing of shared customs as well as the contrary: the situation that was televised places emphasis on the neighborhood rights of the individual that may authorize driving the wrong way down a one-way street.

8   A type of popular protest music called "*rap houma*" has been in existence for several years. The term *hawma* is often adopted by city associations: for example, by the well-known Ouled Houma, a sports and cultural association of Algiers.

9   Roger Letourneau, *Fès avant le protectorat* (Casablanca: Société Marocaine de Librairie et d'Édition; Paris: Firmin Didot, 1949), 213. In addition, the same author has written a synthesis of the characteristics of Maghrebi cities, starting from his extensive knowledge of that old city: *Les villes musulmanes de l'Afrique du Nord* (Algiers: La Maison des Livres, 1957).

10   Jean-Pierre Van Staëvel, "Les usages de la ville dans l'occident musulman médiéval (9ème–14ème siècles)" (PhD diss., Université de Lyon II, 2001). See also by the same author "Le Qâdî au bout du labyrinthe: L'impasse dans la littérature jurisprudentielle mâlikite (al-Andalus et Maghreb, 3/IX–9/XV siècles)," in *L'urbanisme dans l'Occident musulman,* ed. P. Cressier, M. Fierro, and J.-P. Van Staëvel (Madrid: Casa de Velâzquez–CSIC, 2000), 39–63.

11   Isâ ibn Musa ibn al-Imâm al-Tûtilî (323/934–35 to 380/990), *Kitâb ʿalâ l-qadâ wa nafy al-darâr ʿan al-afniya wa l-turfîq wa l-mabânî wa l-sâhât wa l-shajâr wa l-jâmʿî.* One of the manuscripts of this text can be found at the National Library in Algiers under the title *Solutions de Malik relatifs aux propriétés urbaines et rurales et aux rapports des propriétaires entre eux et à la voirie, 1252 (1837).* It was first translated into French by Jules Barbier, "Des droits et obligations entre propriétaires d'héritages voisins," *Revue algérienne, tunisienne et marocaine de législation et jurisprudence* 16 (1900): 9–15, 17–23, 42–56, 93–104, 113–44; 17 (1901): 65–84, 89–108. In his thesis, Van Staëvel proposes a revision of the translation of much of the text. The text covers all forms of legally admissible urban spatial transformation. It should be noted that it was after the French occupation of Algiers and the considerable transformation of the urban landscape that the last copy of this medieval text was uncovered.

12   Van Staëvel, "Le Qâdî au bout du labyrinthe," 39–40. An abundant bibliography exists on the question of urban anarchy, a basic element of the Orientalist analysis of Muslim cities. See E. Wirth, "Villes islamiques, villes arabes, villes orientales," in *La ville arabe en Islam,* ed. A. Bouhdiba and D. Chevallier (Tunis: Cérès, 1982), 193–225; André Raymond, *Grandes villes arabes à l'époque ottomane* (Paris: Sindbad, 1985); R. Ilbert, "La ville islamique: Réalité et abstraction," *Les cahiers de la recherche architecturale* 10–11 (1982): 6–14. They all insist on the Islamic city's inability to take historic contingencies into account.

13   For a discussion that opposes Van Staëvel's ("Le Qâdî au bout du labyrinthe," 39–40) and R. Brunschvig's ("Urbanisme médiéval et droit musulman," *Revue des études islamiques,* 1947, 127–55) argument, see H. Nejmeddine, "La rue dans la ville de l'occident musulman médiéval d'après les sources juridiques malikites," *Arabica* 50, no. 3 (2003): 273–305.

14   Van Staëvel, "Le Qâdî au bout du labyrinthe," 41.

15   The term *hawma* could be used to designate vast areas but most often it referred to narrow units with changing boundaries in the immediate vicinity of a mosque or houses in a single small street. For a definition of the *hawma* in Constantine during the Ottoman era, see Isabelle Grangaud, *La ville imprenable: Une histoire sociale de Constantine*

au 18e siècle (Paris: Éditions de l'École des Hautes Études en Sciences Sociales, 2002), 90; on Algiers, see Isabelle Grangaud, "Alger au miroir de ses sources: Ce que le fonds d'archives de la Régence est à son histoire ottomane," in *Actes du colloque international du 4 au 6 mai 2002 à l'École Polytechnique d'Architecture et d'Urbanisme* (Algiers: Éditions Dalimen, 2004), 35–42.

16 This approach has been illustrated authoritatively by Claude Cahen using an urban social grouping, the *ahdât*, founded on local residency in Baghdad in the ninth to twelfth centuries; its political role was evident in periods of crisis. See C. Cahen, "Mouvements populaires et autonomisme urbain dans l'Asie musulmane du Moyen-Age," *Arabica* 5 (1958): 225–50; 6 (1959): 25–56, 233–65.

17 The title of this section alludes to the work of geographer Marc Côte, *L'Algérie, ou l'espace retourné* (Paris: Éditions Flammarion, 1992), which emphasizes the double inversion of massive proportions that took place in Algeria with colonization and then independence.

18 Recent work, though interesting, seems caught up in that mechanical reading of the city; see, e.g., Sakina Missoum, *Alger à l'époque ottomane: La médina et la maison traditionnelle* (Aix-en-Provence: Édisud, 2003); and Tal Shuval, *La ville d'Alger vers la fin du XVIIIème siècle: Population et cadre urbain* (Paris: Éditions du Centre National de Recherche Scientifique, 1998).

19 See Côte, *L'Algérie*, as well as S. Benkada, "Savoirs militaires et modernité urbaine coloniale: Le rôle des ingénieurs du génie dans les transformations des villes algériennes, le cas d'Oran (1831–1870)," *Insaniyat, Oran, une ville d'Algérie*, nos. 23–24 (January–June 2004): 135–50.

20 A. Henia, *Propriété et stratégies sociales à Tunis (XVI–XIX siècles)* (Tunis: Publication de la Faculté des Sciences Humaines et Sociales de Tunis, 1999). This study of Ottoman Tunisia, equally relevant for Ottoman Algeria, attests to the fact that Ottomanist historians have erroneously considered the categories established at the time of the conquest as Ottoman categories.

21 *Habûs* and *waqf* (the latter term used more frequently in the Arab East) are endowments of property or of any income-producing entities in perpetuity and, unlike private property (*malk*), are inalienable. They may, however, be rented, even in perpetuity (*'anâ'*). Before such endowments arrive at their final destination (generally an institution whose functioning is underwritten in this way), the donor names beneficiaries—usually direct descendants—who exercise their right of usufruct until extinction of the line of heirs, which may take several generations.

22 For a discussion of the naming of this collection of Ottoman archival material, see Fouad Soufi, "Les archives, une problématique de patrimonialisation," in "Le patrimoine," *Insaniyat: Revue algérienne d'anthropologie et de sciences sociales*, no. 12 (September–December 2000): 129–50, especially 142.

23 Baron Volland, "Notice sur le mode d'administration établi à Alger, 12 janvier 1831," Centre des Archives d'Outre-Mer, Aix-en-Provence. Part of this collection was not

the result of notarial activity under the Ottomans but of the requirement that property owners provide proof of their holdings to French authorities. On this question, see Pierre Genty de Bussy, *De l'établissement des Français dans la Régence d'Alger* (Paris: Firmin Didot, 1835); Hamdan Khûdja, *Le miroir, aperçu historique et statistique sur la Régence d'Alger*, ed. S. Djeghloul (Paris: Sindbad, 1985); as well as the bilingual report of Hamdan Khûdja to the War Ministry in Paris ("Mémoire de Hamdan Khûdja à l'adresse du Ministre de la Guerre," 3 June 1833 [19 pages], followed by "Analyse et commentaires sommaires" [23 pages], Fonds du Ministère de la Guerre, Division du Fonds et de la Cté gale, Politique et administration générale, Demandes et réclamations des indigènes, Centre des Archives de Vincennes 1H20).

24 The data are presented in the form of tables. See, in particular, *Fonds des archives de la Régence d'Alger*, microfilm 1M1 70, Centre des Archives d'Outre-Mer.

25 For these names, see the list and the conditions for its creation in Comité du Vieil Alger, *Feuillets d'El-Djezaïr* (1910 edition by Henri Klein; reprint, Blida: Éditions du Tel, 2003), 53.

26 It is considered so officially, for at that date the principle of the conquest had been approved, and the administrative measures applied to the entire country. See M. P. de Ménerville, *Dictionnaire de la législation algérienne: Code annoté et manuel raisonné des lois, ordonnances, décrets, décisions et arrêtés publiés au bulletin officiel des actes du gouvernement suivi d'une table alphabétique des matières et d'une table chronologique des lois, décrets, etc. . . . 1. 1830–1860* (Paris: Durand; Algiers: A. Jourdan, 1866), 671.

27 Baron Volland, "Notice sur le mode d'administration établi à Alger, 12 janvier 1831." For the events of this period, see Charles-André Julien, *Histoire de l'Algérie contemporaine*, vol. 1, *La conquête et les débuts de la colonisation (1827–1871)*, 2d ed. (Paris: Presses Universitaires de France, 1979).

28 The report also mentioned the lack of water in the city due to damage to the drainage system by soldiers stationed at the gates, who were probably dying of thirst under the July sun.

29 The Central Committee of City Property Managers (*syndics*) was composed of seven Algiers notables named by the Government Commission on 8 July for the purpose of garnering information on the requirements of an urban administration: "They will, first of all, be able to provide all the information required by an administrative system, territorial and local. In addition, they will be held to satisfy, by every means at their disposal, the most urgent needs of the army and to indicate any special resources of the Regencies and the City of Algiers" ("Procès verbaux de la Commission du Gouvernement," 7 July 1830, Centre des Archives d'Outre-Mer).

30 Comité du Vieil Alger, *Feuillets d'El-Djezaïr*, 53.

31 At that date, the more formal city authority then in place required that the inhabitants replace the fading names, most of which were of *hawmât*.

32 Use was also made of stripes of paint, each color representing a particular destination (Comité du Vieil Alger, *Feuillets d'El-Djezaïr*, 55).

33   A. Raymond, "La géographie des hâra du Caire au XVIIIème siècle," *Livre du cente-naire de l'Institut Français d'Archéologie Orientale,* 1980, 417–31.

34   In Paris at the end of the eighteenth century, a first attempt at numbering was under-taken privately, financed by a German diplomat. Numbers were inscribed on horse-shoes hung on the houses, beginning on one side of the street and returning in the other direction, so that the first and last numbers faced each other. The present system dates from 1805.

35   The minutes of the meeting of the Government Commission on 23 July state: "the Su-perintendent of Algiers reported to the commission on the difficulties of communica-tion between the different parts of the city, making hospital and subsistence services almost impossible. He demanded, therefore, that the main arteries, which he named, be broadened by destroying the shacks that encumber them."

36   12 November 1830: "Ministerial order establishing that the direction of the theater of Algiers will be under private concession and that performances will be of ballet and Italian opera."

37   André Raymond, "Le centre d'Alger en 1830," *Revue de l'Occident musulman et de la Méditerranée* 31, no. 1 (1981): 73–84. This article underscores the impossibility of reconstituting a precise map of the city center in the absence of a topographic render-ing.

38   Centre des Archives de Vincennes, 11120.

39   Genty de Bussy, *De l'établissement des Français dans la Régence d'Alger,* 57.

40   Ernest Feydeau, *Alger, étude,* ed. F. Pouillon (Paris: Bouchène, 2003).

41   René Lespès, *Alger: Esquisse de géographie urbaine* (Algiers: Félix Alcan, 1925), 116. See also Comité du Vieil Alger, *Feuillets d'el Djazaïr;* and Feydeau, *Alger, étude.*

42   Genty de Bussy, *De l'établissement des Français dans la Régence d'Alger,* 213–15.

43   M.-N. Bourguet, B. Lepetit, D. Nordman, and M. Sinarellis, *L'invention de la Méditer-ranée: Egypte, Morée, Algérie* (Paris: Éditions de l'École des Hautes Études en Sciences Sociales, 1998).

7

HISTORIC INTERSECTIONS

THE CENTER OF ALGIERS

Zeynep Çelik

The image of Algiers is famously remembered for the clashing divisions introduced under French rule. First marked by the cutting and slicing of the lower
town in Haussmannian operations before Haussmann, then by the construction
of the "European" quarters adjacent to the old town, the urban forms stand as
an embodiment and a metaphor of colonial policies (fig. 7.1). However, a closer
reading reveals that power relations were already engraved into the spaces of
the city, albeit under the auspices of the Ottoman Empire, whose decentralized
structure allowed its provinces to have a considerable degree of autonomy. Incorporated into the empire in 1529, Algiers served as an important port for the
Ottoman navy. The Ottoman principles of domination in Algeria may have been
very different from the French ones, but the reliance on urban forms and architecture to express the imperial presence was common long before 1830.

A historical examination of one urban fragment over two centuries, covering the Ottoman, French, and the postcolonial periods, unveils certain threads
that ran through the seemingly oppositional regimes. Studying the "tangible
substance, the stuff of the city," that is its "physical mass,"[1] with the understanding that urban spaces and buildings are social-political documents, reveals the agency of built forms in shaping history. In this essay I will survey the
actual transformations along with a series of unrealized projects for the center
of Algiers that housed the precolonial souks, the colonial place d'Armes (later,
place du Gouvernement), and the postcolonial place des Martyrs, exploring the
patterns, forces, and processes at work. The microhistory of the urban fragment

7.1   Algiers, aerial photograph (*Chantiers*, March 1935)

opens up questions on the sometimes blatant, sometimes ambiguous ideological role played by architecture and urban design, the overlapping expressions for differing programs, and the intersections of visual, spatial, and social-political practices through time.

The Ottoman city, developed on the foundation of an Arab-Berber settlement that went back to the Zirid dynasty in the tenth century, was surrounded by sixteenth-century fortifications, crowned by a citadel (the Casbah) at its highest point.[2] Nestled on a hill facing the Mediterranean, the site conditions had produced a straightforward zoning: the flat part on the waterfront (the lower town, or *al-wati'*, "the plains") and the slopes descending toward it (the upper town, or *al-jabal*, "the mountain"). Two main streets, Bab Azoun leading to the city gate in the south and Bab el-Oued to the gate on the north, divided the upper and lower parts. A third artery (later called rue de la Marine) led to the port. Public life, a concept well acknowledged by Muslim jurisprudence and spatially associated with the presence of through streets, markets, and religious monuments, concentrated in the lower city; residential neighborhoods occupied the heights.[3]

The markets, organized according to different productive activities, centered at the juncture of the Bab Azoun and Bab el-Oued axis and stretched to the north and the east.[4] The main mosques of Algiers, which also served as educational centers and courts (*mahkama*s), were located nearby: Ketchaoua (1612), al-Sayyida (reconstructed in 1794), al-Jadid (1660), and al-Kebir (eleventh century). The Ottoman buildings commonly conformed to longstanding traditions and blended into the architecture of the city. Among them, al-Jadid Mosque stood out in its references to classical imperial monuments; while it had certain features typical to the region (such as the square minaret, the whitewashed exterior, and the decorative elements), its cross-plan with a centralized dome and adjacent vaults, prominently expressed on the exterior, gave it a touch of Istanbul (see figs. 3.1 and 3.9). The radical changes to Ketchaoua Mosque during its conversion into a cathedral in the 1830s make it difficult to speculate on its original character, but its large dome suggests again another nod toward the Ottoman capital. Although the Ottoman presence was only rarely expressed in the city's architecture, its use in centrally located monuments worked well as a constant reminder of the power structure at the empire's edge in the western Mediterranean.

The key buildings of the Ottoman administration were placed to the east of the souks, continuing a pattern that dated from the "Berber" period.[5] Most notable was the Janina Palace, the headquarters of the Ottoman dey until 1817, the date when the administrative functions were consolidated in the Casbah. Noted as "very remarkable" if not "as rich and sumptuous as the palaces of some Christian kings and princes" by Diego de Haëdo, who had lived in Algiers between 1578 and 1581, it was organized around two interior courtyards and had a small garden (see fig. 1.1).[6] The palace faced a square plaza covered by a trellis on the city's main artery; the square had a fountain in the middle and was surrounded by structures that harbored the government functions, including the offices of the *bölükbaşı* (the officer in charge of the janissaries) and the *shaykh al-balad* (the officer in charge of urban affairs).[7] Mansions of Ottoman dignitaries, organized around courtyards as the Janina Palace was, were gathered in the area, further enforcing the image of the dominating power in the city.[8] While these residential structures did not depart from local architectural norms and did not share any similarities with the upper-class houses in the Ottoman capital, they still stood out as "Ottoman" due to their size and the names of their owners—high officials representing the sultanate. Seven military barracks that sheltered around

3,500–4,000 janissaries at the end of the sixteenth century were situated at the periphery of the "administrative" zone, reiterating the imperial character of the area.[9] They concentrated around the Azoun Gate in the south and the Jazira Gate near the harbor.[10]

The urban fabric of the lower town displayed a different pattern from the residential neighborhoods. The many residential neighborhoods of the upper town, crowded by different ethnic and religious communities, offered a remarkably unified image. The white cubical masses of the houses that abutted each other coalesced into a picturesque ensemble, frequently referred to in the nineteenth- and twentieth-century literature as an amphitheater that opened up to the Mediterranean. The streets were narrow, irregular, and often dead-ended (see figs. 4.8 and 4.9). Religious buildings and commercial establishments (bakeries, grocery stores) were small in scale and scattered amid the residential tissue. The scale and architectural grandeur of the monuments and mansions in the lower town, as well as the relative spaciousness of the circulation network, culminated in a visual entity that distinguished itself from the "private" city above the Bab Azoun–Bab el-Oued axis. Nevertheless, the division did not translate to a sharp contrast, due to the use of similar building principles (such as continuous fabrics, as observed in the markets), similar architectural elements, and similar construction materials.

Colonial interventions to Algiers took place in the lower town and capitalized upon the already-existing division, articulated during the three centuries of Ottoman rule but most likely begun earlier. As the French administrative structure replaced the Ottoman one, the duality between the public and private cities grew into a visual and spatial confrontation, producing "Arab" and "European" settlements. Starting immediately after the occupation, French army engineers widened the main arteries, pierced new streets through the old fabric, and, most prominently, carved a place d'Armes in order to accommodate the assembling of the troops, to enable the movement of carriages, and to provide an open marketplace (fig. 7.2; see also figs. 3.13 and 3.19). This operation, carried out during the early 1830s, razed part of the souks, as well as the minaret of al-Sayyida Mosque, considered the most beautiful in the city.[11] A report at the time summarized: "We demolish many ugly shops, several houses, and promptly obtain a very useful space for the troops, the carriages, [and] the markets."[12]

Lacking any formal order in its original configuration, the plaza provoked successive designs that attempted to endow it with an image befitting the French Empire. The myriad projects revolved around the idea of a geometrically coherent open space surrounded and regularized by arcades. An early project from 1830 defined the plaza uniformly by colonnaded structures that would block the

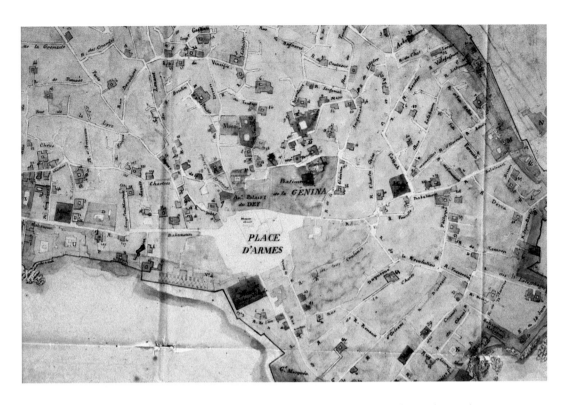

7.2 Plan of Algiers (detail), mixed media, 1832 (Service Historique de la Défense, Château de Vincennes, Paris)

messy architecture of the existing monuments—al-Jadid Mosque and the Janina Palace. A rectangular proposal by government architect Luvini called for the demolition of al-Sayyida and al-Jadid Mosques in 1831 (fig. 7.3). Luvini defined the south and north sides respectively of the place d'Armes by a government palace and a theater; three-story-high buildings with arcades on the ground level recast the eastern and western sides with a new façade. Rows of trees lined the plaza all around. Aiming to start construction at the northeastern part of Luvini's plan, Général Berthézène, the commander in chief of the Armée d'Afrique, authorized the demolition of 806 square meters here, leading to the demolition of al-Sayyida Mosque.[13] In a curious appropriation, an interior arcade from al-Sayyida was integrated into the façade of al-Kebir Mosque on rue de la Marine, creating a rue de Rivoli effect, albeit an "Islamic" one that adapted to the city's architectural heritage. This façade, unusual in the history of the building type, visually complemented the arcades of the nearby place d'Armes (fig. 7.4).[14]

The extent of demolitions reached a critical point when al-Sayyida Mosque was torn down, creating great resentment and sorrow among Algerians, already engaged in a fierce resistance to the occupation. Beginning to grasp the need to

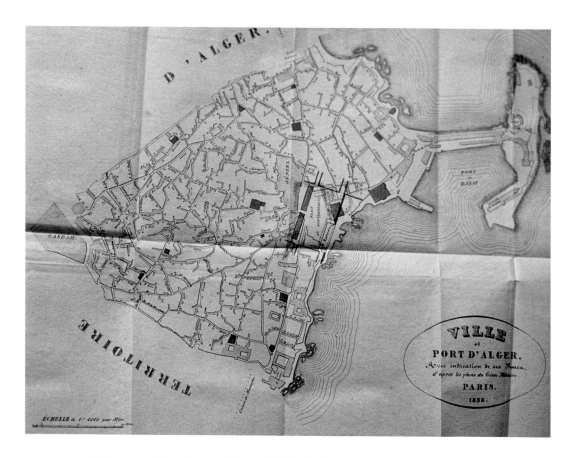

7.3   Project to regularize the place d'Armes (detail), mixed media, 1831 (Louis-André Pichon, *Alger sous la domination française; son état present et son avenir* [Paris: Théophile Barrois et Benjamin Duprat, 1833])

acknowledge and respect the values of the colonized society with some sensitivity and foresight, Lieutenant Colonel Lemercier was the first to criticize the demolitions. He argued in 1831 that tearing down religious buildings was politically problematic; to gain the sympathy of the local population it was key "not to hurt the religious sentiments of the Moors."[15] Lieutenant Colonel Lemercier, as the representative of the corps of engineers, exerted his power to stop Luvini's project from further implementation. Thanks to Lemercier's intervention and because of its relatively tangential location, al-Jadid Mosque survived the demolitions and ultimately served as an anchor for all projects. After the rejection of Luvini's 1831 proposal, the subsequent designs struggled to bring a monumental (and European) character to the place d'Armes while preserving this "unfitting" building. Nevertheless, Luvini's project established the guidelines: symmetry and regularity (to be enhanced by landscaping), continuous façades with ar-

7.4 Al-Kebir Mosque, view from rue de la Marine, Charles Marville, salted-paper print,
1850s (photograph album: *Belgique, Angleterre, Suisse et Algérie*, Getty Research Institute,
95.R.100)

cades on the ground level, and buildings whose functions were intertwined with
the French presence, such as a government palace and a theater—both unrealized.

An 1832 scheme proposed a symmetrical pentagon, rearranging the juncture of the regularized Bab Azoun and Bab el-Oued streets with the plaza and
introducing a third main artery that cut the longer façade in the center and
that extended into the upper city, the latter intervention pointing to the drive
to forge physical links to the autochthonous residential neighborhoods and to
pierce them with wide and straight streets, a policy that probably had military
or policing motivations. The project blocked the alien architecture of al-Jadid
Mosque by interposing an unnamed structure between it and the plaza.[16] The
idea of concealing the mosque from the public space endured for another couple

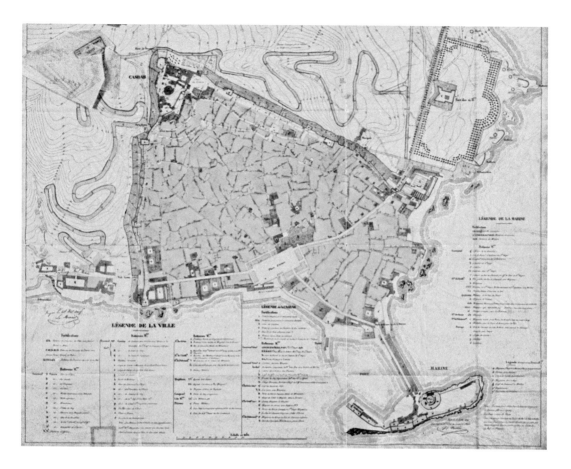

7.5   Project to regularize the place d'Armes, mixed media, 1834 (Service Historique de la Défense, Château de Vincennes, Paris)

of years, taking on different configurations. For example, an 1834 design placed a church right in front of the mosque, aiming to etch the supremacy of the occupier's religion on the cityscape by a neoclassical façade that fronted the plaza (fig. 7.5). Meanwhile, the projects freely sliced up the Janina Palace, used by the army, and concealed it from view.

The proposal to block the mosque with a church (not realized) gave way to another juxtaposition expressing the current power relations. In 1845, an imposing, five-meter-high equestrian statue of the Duke of Orleans, the heir to the throne who had fought and was wounded in Algeria in 1836 and died in a carriage accident in Neuilly in 1842, was erected on the plaza (fig. 7.6). While sculptor Carlo Morochetti's work reflected the nineteenth-century "statumania" in the metropole, it acquired specific layers of political meaning in the colonial setting. Twisting the rules regarding the siting of memorials, it was strategically situated, not in the center of the plaza, but to the side—right in

7.6 *Place du Gouvernement*, Jean-Baptiste-Antoine Alary, albumen photograph (photograph album: Jean-Baptiste-Antoine Alary, *Views of Algeria*, c. 1857; Getty Research Institute, 92.R.85*)

front of al-Jadid Mosque so that a close relationship was established between the two monuments. Elevated on a high base and contrasting in its blackness and dynamic shape with the serene mass of the white mosque, and with its back toward the mosque, it conveyed a straightforward message about who ruled Algeria. The gaze of the duke, turned away from the plaza to face the old city, underlined the statement of French control over Algerians. A public art form that was totally foreign to local norms, the statue dominated the major perspectives toward the plaza, thereby reiterating its message. In 1852, al-Jadid Mosque acquired an unusual feature when French authorities placed a clock on its minaret. The treatment of the minaret as a clock tower was another act of appropriation: although the Muslim monument was left to stand in the main public square of the city, it was transformed, secularized, and forcibly brought into modern time.[17]

Once the relationship between the statue of the Duke of Orleans and al-

Jadid Mosque was established, the following projects had to address it. For example, Pierre-Auguste Guiauchain's (unrealized) 1846 design opted for a pentagonal plan, keeping the idea of symmetry and regularity on three sides by means of continuous arcades.[18] Facing the statue/mosque pair, a theater dominated the longitudinal side; its construction would have meant the demolition of Dar 'Aziza, an Ottoman palace. The Janina Palace, whose northern parts were destroyed in a fire in 1844, had been left to crumble and its demolition did not raise any controversy. The project obeyed the guidelines that had been set the same year by official bodies responsible for the city's administration and the regularization of the street network (namely, the Conseil d'Administration et de la Commission des Alignements) and that had allocated the western part of the plaza to public buildings lacking in Algiers, such as a town hall, library, museum, treasury, post office, and theater.[19]

The passage from the military regime to a civilian one in the 1870s led to the renaming of the square as place du Gouvernement. By then its shape was fixed as a pentagon, with arcaded buildings on three sides and the mosque on the east side. The plaza opened to the Mediterranean on the fifth side (see figs. 3.13 and 3.19). Three sides of the pentagon (i.e., all but the mosque and waterfront sides) were planted with rows of trees. The considerable change in elevation between the public space and the entrance level of the mosque was kept, and a stone balustrade marked the edge on the waterfront. The balustrade proved to be a special place in Algiers, turning the plaza into "a vast balcony over the sea."[20] As noted by Charles Desprez, a passionate observer of the city in the 1860s, its popularity owed a great deal to the design. At any given time, a line of individuals leaned on the balustrade meditating on the view, and groups of workers, women, and children sat beneath the overhang, creating a longitudinal scene of human display.[21] The plaza itself was the inevitable crossroads for the residents of the city, situated as it was at the juncture of the "grand arteries of the new quarter and the thousands of small streets of the old indigenous perch [i.e., the Casbah]"; it also functioned as a promenade and became especially crowded on Sundays and evenings.[22]

During French rule, the place du Gouvernement served as the city's most prominent locale and the view toward the mosque/statue complex became a shorthand representation for the city—as celebrated by the postcard industry and crystallized in a "satirical" image that featured a native shoeshine boy, another symbol of colonial Algiers, against the background of the dual structures (fig. 7.7). In the words of Desprez, the plaza was "the theater of our times of leisure, our ceremonies, [and] our celebrations," in short, "the real forum of the colony" that encapsulated the history of the city of Algiers in its entirety.[23] In

Porquoi ci la fite di jor di l'an. Ji ti souhati oune boune annie vic la boune santi ! Ti gagni bocoup di l'ardjane por ti mangi la couscous vic ton famill. Boune annie pour moi aussi.

7.7 Satirical postcard showing the place du Gouvernement, colored photomechanical print, c. 1900 (Getty Research Institute, 93.R.99)

his comprehensive monograph of Algiers published on the occasion of the centennial of the occupation, historian René Lespès underlined its significance for public ceremonies, which ranged from commemorative gatherings to funerary processions, proclamations of changes in the political regime, and civic and patriotic banquets; he singled out its historic importance as "the theater of the most passionate discussions on colonization and the future of our conquest" and as the site where "all emotions provoked in Algeria by the great events of its history and that of France were transcribed."[24] As we will see later, the role of the plaza as the incubator of history extended into the postcolonial period, when it became the setting of "great national demonstrations, [and] commemorations of the past struggles."[25] Its name changed to place des Martyres after independence, the plaza would at the same time continue to provide informal meeting places in the everyday life of the city.

Even though the square itself did not experience any transformations during the rest of the French period, it was affected by the plans that attempted to modernize the Marine quarter to the north (fig. 7.8). The triangular peninsula, of crucial importance to Algiers because of its proximity to the harbor, had de-

7.8   Aerial photograph of Marine quarter (*Chantiers,* March 1935)

veloped very fast into a crowded settlement where low-income Europeans (from southern Italy, Spain, France, and Malta), Jews, and some "indigenous immigrants" lived side by side. The issues of "hygiene," linked with high densities, troubled the municipality, which sought to cleanse the neighborhood by "razing whatever existed" here as early as the 1880s.[26] A project, developed by Eugène de Redon in 1884, proposed to depopulate the quarter significantly and replace its narrow streets with wide arteries lined by luxurious buildings that would attract a wealthier group of people and a different lifestyle; a casino on the waterfront would enhance the gentrification of the quarter (fig. 7.9). Revived several times, Redon's project was not implemented, but it did establish guidelines for the future.

It was in the aftermath of the centennial of the French occupation and in accordance with the new enthusiasm for "urbanism" among French administrators and technocrats in the 1930s that the replanning of the Marine quarter became a priority, stimulated by the first French law on urbanism, dated 14 March 1919.[27] By that time, the street network of the Marine quarter was inaccessible

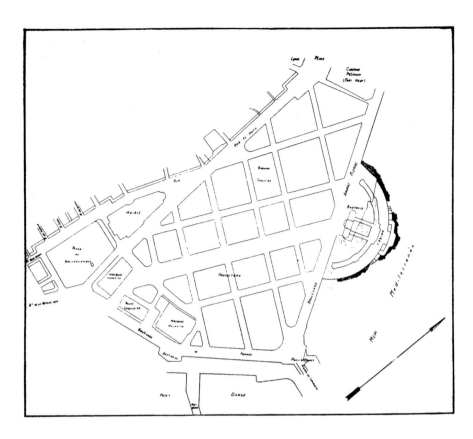

7.9 Project for the Marine quarter by Eugène de Redon, 1925 (*Chantiers*, no. 14 [1954])

to motor vehicles and its neglected buildings were in truly poor condition, as witnessed by a building collapse on rue des Consuls in 1929 that killed over fifty people. Considered "the charter of modern urbanism," the 1919 law called for a master plan for every town having more than ten thousand people in order to regulate growth and enable "beautification" (*embellissement*).[28] The notion of a master plan for Algiers brought back Redon's proposal in full force. For example, Jean Alazard proclaimed in an editorial that "the old Marine quarter must be demolished and reconstructed" to accommodate an uninterrupted circulation pattern for the city, which was "destined to become the grand metropole of North Africa." Alazard argued against a sentimental preservation of old fabrics even though tourism in Algiers was expected to increase because of the upcoming centennial to celebrate the occupation. Predicting the disappointment of visitors, who would find a modern Algiers where they looked for "the Algiers of Fromentin's time," he nevertheless advocated against "shedding tears for the past" but instead supported a forward-looking program that would "intelligently guide the development of a great Mediterranean port."[29]

7.10 Project for the Marine quarter by Le Corbusier, photomontage (Le Corbusier, *La ville radieuse* [Paris: Vincent, Fréal, 1933])

One hundred years after the occupation, with French confidence and security in Algeria well established, the colonial urban and architectural forms no longer needed to convey direct iconographic messages. The debate on urban transformations shifted to modern urbanism versus traditional European urbanism; the latter was characterized by the colonial interventions to the lower part of old Algiers and by the patterns of European settlements that had developed outside the Ottoman fortifications. This was not simply a confrontation between the old and the new: the architects of the 1930s were divided about what it meant to be "modern." In Algiers the battle was between two architects: Henri Prost (working with René Danger and Maurice Rotival) represented the more conventional vision, and Le Corbusier, the avant-garde (fig. 7.10). In the debates about modernizing Algiers, the place du Gouvernement presented a complicated situation. It had an idiosyncratic design integrity that did not easily accommodate new urban design ideas. Furthermore, the presence of al-Jadid and al-Kebir Mosques nearby, two monuments by now universally accepted as part of the historic heritage, perpetuated the duality engraved into the colonial city. The modernity of the proposals dwarfed and dominated the mosques, sharpening the confrontation.

The best-known and the most controversial of the proposals are Le Corbusier's unimplemented designs.[30] In his 1932 project, the architect turned to the Marine quarter, which he wanted to transform into a "Cité d'Affaires"/civic center dominated by skyscrapers that would be connected to the new residential quarters on the hills by a "bridge" over the Arab town. He proposed to demolish the entire built fabric and rebuild it with new structures that left ample space for parks and public gardens, some behind al-Jadid Mosque. Le Corbusier's plans did not touch the place du Gouvernement but overrode its previous prominence by treating it as an enclave that could be viewed from the skyscrapers and the bridge above, thereby turning it into a space subsidiary to the modern structures above. In other schemes, Le Corbusier did away with the bridge and schematically showed the mosque and the statue of the duke as isolated objects among his modern structures. Nevertheless, his project totally overlooked the plaza—which was, for him, an example of outmoded urbanism.

Henri Prost and Tony Socard's project from the same period may have pursued more conservative aesthetics, but it was based on the same idea of an entirely new Marine quarter. They, too, hollowed out the area around al-Jadid Mosque, inserting another landscaped public plaza between al-Jadid and al-Kebir. Ultimately, the resulting space would be an immense, three-partite plaza with al-Jadid Mosque floating in the middle. To the east, they proposed an institutional compound, with the chamber of commerce, stock market, palace of justice, library, and possibly a national school of fine arts. The project's proposed circulation patterns and its distribution of built and open spaces were well received (fig. 7.11).[31]

Maurice Rotival, Prost's partner on the master plan, projected an alternative vision for the Marine quarter that picked up on Le Corbusier's skyscrapers (fig. 7.12) rather than Prost and Socard's conservative building blocks. Toward the end of French rule, Gérald Haning offered a similar image in the context of another master plan, his photomontage showing a double square divided by al-Jadid Mosque (fig. 7.13). Calling the area of the place du Gouvernement and the two mosques a "historic" enclave, Haning argued that completely isolating the monuments from the new modern buildings would put an end to their long "suffering" and give them back their religious and artistic value. The plaza would be enclosed on the north side by horizontal blocks four stories high that would relate to the scale of the mosques and provide a gentle transition to the high-rises.[32]

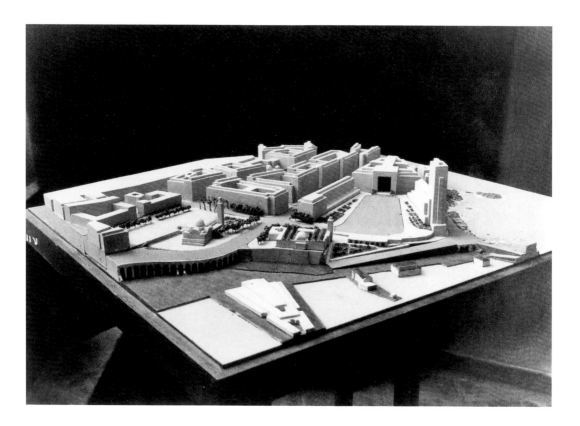

7.11   Project for the Marine quarter by Tony Socard (model), 1951 (photography: Albertis, from Jean-Louis Cohen, Nabila Oulebsir, and Youcef Kanoun, eds., *Alger: Paysage urbain et architectures, 1800-2000* [Paris: Éditions de l'Imprimeur, 2003])

In spite of much heated debate, no project was implemented in its entirety — for several reasons: economic (most important), administrative, and political (linked to the demolition controversy). Nevertheless, Prost's scheme was chosen and the ensuing demolitions were heralded as "the birth of a new Algiers." By 1945, an area of 45,800 square meters had been cleared to enable the construction of a central avenue; this involved the destruction of 340 buildings and the displacement of 11,000 people, including 380 shopkeepers.[33] The operation encountered much criticism from citizens of all ethnicities, who feared the loss of their historic heritage. For example, a French journalist suggested a photographic survey of the quarter as a last resort to conserve its memory: "photographs of all these streets and interesting corners will serve as precious documents for the future."[34] In a public letter, the Algerian theologian and intellectual Omar Racim (artist Mohammed Racim's brother) likened the destruction of Algiers to that of Hiroshima. He wrote that the mosques had been "chipped" away by the opening of the new avenue and they now found themselves as "old people

7.12   Project for the Marine quarter by Maurice Rotival, sketch, 1931 (*Chantiers nord-africains,* January 1931)

deformed by age who in vain tried to hide their shapes caused by their infirmities." Racim wondered sarcastically when the city officials would "bury Algiers alive" by demolishing whatever was left of the old city in order to sell its pieces to tourists as relics.[35]

A second wave of demolitions came in the 1950s, initiated by the city's energetic and controversial mayor Jacques Chevallier, best known for undertaking some of the most remarkable housing projects in Algiers during his three-year tenure between 1953 and 1956.[36] By 1959, an area of about 90,000 square meters had been razed in the Marine quarter, and about 20,000 people had been evacuated from buildings deemed "unsalvageable" (fig. 7.14).[37] At the conclusion of the war for independence in 1962, after eighty years of grand visions for the Marine quarter, the Algerian administration inherited an urban wasteland —

7.13 Project for the
Marine quarter by Gérald
Haning, photomontage,
1959 (*Alger-revue*, Spring
1959)

largely demolished but not coherently reorganized, with only the main avenue
lined by new buildings. The situation seemed to confirm Lespès's observation
of the place du Gouvernement thirty years earlier as a mirror of French policies:
"The history of the place du Gouvernement is one of the most typical [cases]
where perpetual incertitude and reshuffling, marked by an absence of clear
viewpoints and decisions, aggravated by shortage of money, condemned our
work in Algiers."[38]

The built and unbuilt urban design history of the place du Gouvernement
can be summarized as follows. Despite many ambitious plans, the earlier interventions were done incrementally in response to sporadic practical and politi-

7.14   Aerial photograph of Marine quarter, c. 1960 (Établissement Cinématographique et Photographique des Armées, Paris)

cal questions and concentrated on the plaza and its immediate surroundings, whereas the projects from 1930 on were part of "master plans" that aimed to regulate the overall city by zoning and that treated the square as one of its focal points. During the colonial era the place du Gouvernement was regarded as a meeting place of different functions—commercial, administrative, and cultural—but, perhaps more importantly, as the juncture of the colonizer and colonized cultures.

In the aftermath of independence, the most significant urban practice was the occupation of the "colonial city." The physical appropriation of urban space reverberated with a highly symbolic value of "taking possession of the city," which signified "taking possession of power." Otherwise, Algerians continued the urban design practices of the French and kept the same administrative structure.[39] A graduation thesis, which aimed to "revalorize old Algiers" and was submitted to the prestigious Institut d'Urbanisme of Paris University in 1969, serves as an unlikely mirror both to dominant trends in independent Algeria and to continuing French interest in the capital, revealing new shifts in ideological agendas behind urban planning.[40] The study's author, Guy Tombarel, had profound ties to Algeria: his father, Louis Tombarel (1901–71), was an architect in Algeria from the 1930s to the 1960s, in charge of major projects that included sports facilities, parks, and schools. Guy Tombarel had grown up there and begun his architectural studies in Algiers, but he moved to France after independence.[41] Professor Jean Royer, who supervised Tombarel's work, was a prominent name in colonial urbanism and architecture: he was the editor of the two-volume collection *L'urbanisme aux colonies et dans les pays tropicaux* (1932), which brought together the papers presented at an international congress on the occasion of the 1931 Colonial Exposition in Paris. Together with Henri Prost, another key figure in colonial urbanism and architecture, he had also founded the *Revue urbanisme* in 1932 and continued to serve as its editor.

With these links to the colonial period but admittedly enthused by vibrant social and cultural movements taking place in Algeria in the 1960s, Tombarel took on the challenge to address the Algerian mission to re-own the city and make it a reflection of the independent nation. His thesis, entitled "Proposition d'aménagement des abords de la Casbah pour une revalorisation du vieil Alger" (Planning Proposal for the Areas Surrounding the Casbah in order to Revalorize Old Algiers), consisting of a report accompanied by drawings and photographs, aimed to contribute to Algeria's economy by initiating a new type of political tourism, based on the positive response of many foreigners to the Algerian revolution. Tombarel's study quoted an article published in the periodical *El Djezair* in 1964: "It is clear that Algeria benefits from a moral quality due to the revolution—advantageous to attracting large groups of 'social tourists' or tourists who are curious about a country with new socialist structures."

The student-architect relied on urban design as an effective tool to ameliorate the economic difficulties of the postindependence years, stemming from "the massive departure of Europeans," who had left behind "a machine whose many wheels were no longer working," serious unemployment, and a very young population. Algeria's history of tourism, which had attracted the French and the English especially between 1918 and 1930, and its traditional crafts justified the project. The crafts (embroideries and carpets), first destroyed with the souks in the 1830s, then "saved" and promoted by the French especially around the 1930s, were finally reorganized after independence under the auspices of the Office National de l'Artisanat Traditionel Algérien (ONATA). The postindependence boom in hotel buildings in Zeralda, Sidi Ferruch, and Tipasa (most notably by architect Fernand Pouillon, whose commissions spanned the colonial and the postcolonial periods) testified to the government's commitment to tourism.

7.15 Photograph show-
ing the demolished house
where Ali La Pointe and
his compatriots were
killed (*Historia*, no. 232
[1972])

The place des Martyrs was at the center of the tourism zone. It connected to the old town on the adjacent hill and opened to the Mediterranean. The historic and picturesque city on the hill was a natural attraction for foreigners. The legendary role it played during the Algerian War would attract the particular kind of politicized tourist Tombarel referred to (fig. 7.15). Tombarel does not recall being influenced by Gillo Pontecorvo's powerful film *The Battle of Algiers*, released a few years earlier, but its popularity had enhanced the fascination with the Casbah among Europeans, and even North Americans, pointing to the possibility of a specialized tourism along the lines he suggested.[42] Responding to the political climate of the time, Tombarel stated that the old town should

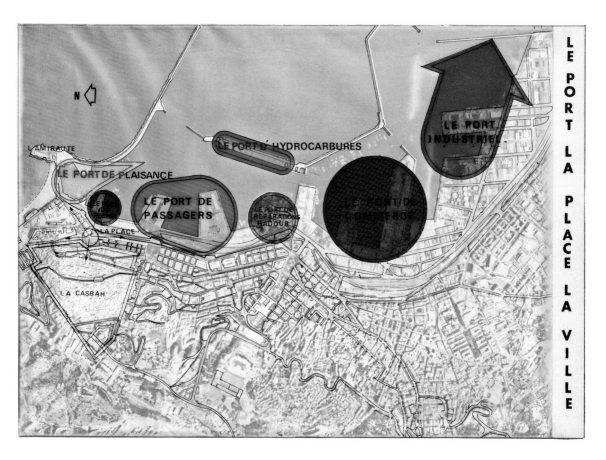

7.16 Proposal for the development of the waterfront, mixed media (Guy Tombarel, "Proposition d'aménagement des abords de la Casbah pour une revalorisation du vieil Alger," 1969; Getty Research Institute, 2003.M.10)

not be frozen into an "objet de musée" (museum piece) but should maintain its life and respond to the "needs of its residents." The right approach was to treat it as a large "operation of restoration," without changing the street pattern to accommodate modern circulation—an error that had destroyed the lower city's fabric.

Tombarel developed the plaza's waterfront connections (fig. 7.16). He preserved the colorful *port de péche* (port of fishing), immediately to the east, reached by steps leading down to the water level, and endowed it with "a dozen small restaurants with picturesque décor." He zoned the harbor level, with the port for passenger boats adjacent to the fishermen's harbor and a *port de plaisance* (port of recreation) to the north in the bay facing the old Admiralty. The *port de plaisance*, complete with a yacht club, nautical club, and rowing club, would form part of a "leisure zone" that extended along the waterfront. An ar-

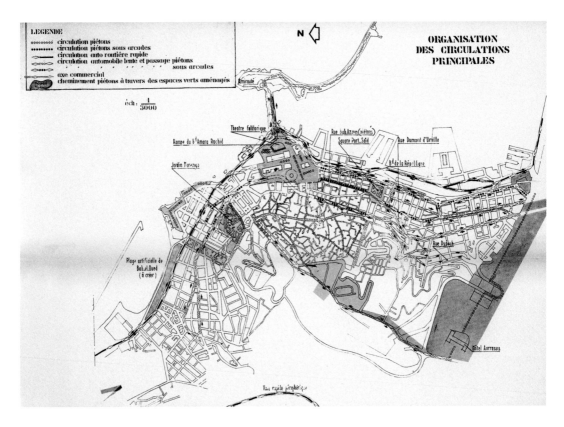

7.17   Proposal for the circulation system, mixed media (Tombarel, "Proposition")

tificial beach would be created in the bay of Bab el-Oued, picking up a concept developed in a project by Raymond Coquerel and Pierre Renaud that went back to 1938.[43] Tombarel pointed out that now the task was doable, as the buildings on the waterfront were mostly vacant and belonged to the state.

A citywide circulation system that separated different kinds of traffic adhered to the conventions of master plans (fig. 7.17). Fast motor traffic was relegated to the coastline, while other roads, with slower motor traffic and sidewalks in arcades, were in the west and the south. The traffic on the place des Martyrs and on all its connections was restricted to pedestrians, encompassing the streets of the old town on the heights in the west and the harbor in the east (rue de la Marine), as well as Bab Azoun and the former avenue de l'Impératrice (then, avenue de la République, now Avenue Che Guevara) in the south. The arcaded streets from the French period, such as rue Bab Azoun and avenue de l'Impératrice, worked particularly well in accommodating pedestrians. Place des Martyrs and its immediate surroundings also formed parts of a citywide system of "green spaces" linked by pedestrian streets (fig. 7.18).

Focusing on the plaza itself, Tombarel noted that during the last years of

7.18 Proposal for a system of green spaces, mixed media (Tombarel, "Proposition")

French rule it had become a parking lot, necessitated by the great need for parking stemming from the presence of administrative office buildings nearby. After independence, the center of the plaza was made pedestrian, but its periphery was cluttered randomly with lorries and bus stops. Place des Martyrs, whether forum or parking lot, historic center or "embarrassing witness of a recent national past," was the product of "the lack of a clear idea of what to do with this space." Even its present name carried an "ideological content," and its function as the "place of demonstrations" par excellence testified to its special status. Tombarel called attention to the extension of the square to the north by the demolition of several houses in 1963 in order to make room for the "fêtes de l'Indépendence." Curiously, he overlooked a major change that is visible in one of the photographs included in his portfolio and that marked the end of the French era: the glaring absence of the Duke of Orleans on his horse—an absence made particularly prominent by the still-remaining base of the statue (fig. 7.19).

As a gesture to the precolonial fabric in his attempt to address the turbulent history of Algiers, Tombarel proposed incorporating into the place des Martyrs new souks specializing in arts and crafts. At the same time, the souk complex, an essential feature of "Islamic" cities lacking in Algiers, would play a crucial role in the tourism industry (fig. 7.20). He used the complicated topography of the plaza (and the existing vaulting beneath it) to create a shopping level below the main one, the latter envisioned as a landscaped open space. The souks would extend under the boulevard on the waterfront and terminate in restaurants with views over the harbor. One more level underground, Tombarel reserved a large parking area for the predicted increase in motor traffic (fig. 7.21).

7.19 Place des Martyrs, photograph showing the base of the statue of the Duke of Orleans (on the right), photograph (Tombarel, "Proposition")

In its essential characteristics, Tombarel's project pursued the long tradition of French planning in Algiers but twisted the forms to accommodate the political, social, and cultural framework of independent Algeria and appended an economic program to it. Place des Martyrs was enhanced as a space that represented and celebrated the nation. It was also heralded as a theater of history that repossessed the colonial space by bringing back the precolonial fabric erased by the French army engineers. However, the gesture to connect postcolonial Algiers to its roots produced an image in conflict with the search for an identity glorifying the newly independent nation. Rather than reviving and celebrating the precolonial fabric, the proposed souks buried it, clearing the ground level for neutral, manicured sets of open spaces. With implicit references to Le Corbusier's proposals that had engraved the colonial power relationship onto Algiers by placing Europeans above and the old city below, Tombarel's thesis project reveals the complexities of the postcolonial condition and the persistence of the old power relations, repackaged to evoke a sense of national pride in Algeria. It also stands as testimony to the persistence of France's conflicted attachment to its former colony.

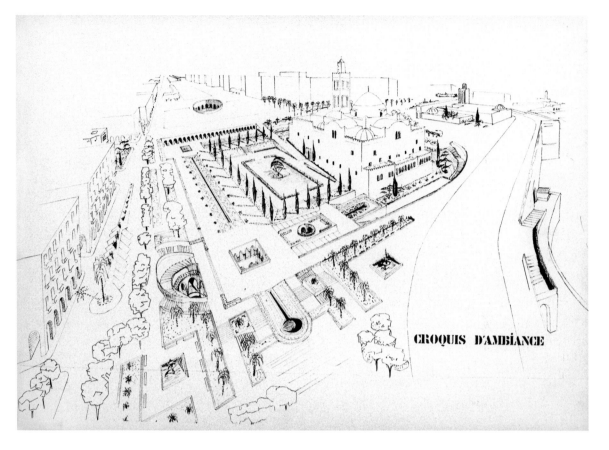

7.20 *(Above)* "Croquis d'ambience" for place des Martyrs, ink on paper (Tombarel, "Proposition")

7.21 *(Below)* Proposal for underground souks and parking, ink on paper (Tombarel, "Proposition")

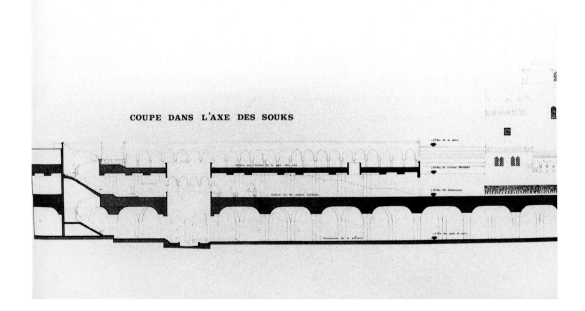

NOTES

1 John Summerson, "Urban Forms," in *The Historian and the City*, ed. O. Handlin and J. Burchard (Cambridge, MA: MIT Press, 1963), 165–66.

2 For the Ottoman city, see André Raymond, "Le centre d'Alger en 1830," *Revue de l'Occident musulman et de la Méditerranée* 31, no. 1 (1981): 73–84; reprinted as "La région centrale d'Alger en 1830," in *Alger: Paysage urbain et architectures, 1800–2000*, ed. Jean-Louis Cohen, Nabila Oulebsir, and Youcef Kanoun (Paris: Éditions de l'Imprimeur, 2003), 46–63; and Sakina Missoum, *Alger à l'époque ottomane: La médina et la maison traditionnelle* (Aix-en-Provence: Édisud, 2003).

3 André Raymond, *Grandes villes arabes à l'époque ottomane* (Paris: Sindbad, 1985), 173–74; Tal Shuval, *La ville d'Alger vers la fin du XVIIIème siècle: Population et cadre urbain* (Paris: Éditions du Centre National de Recherche Scientifique, 1998), 163.

4 For a detailed analysis of the markets, see Shuval, *La ville d'Alger vers la fin du XVIIIème siècle*, 177–90.

5 Ibid., 197.

6 Diego de Haëdo, *Topographie et histoire générale d'Alger*, ed. Dr. Monnereau and Al Berbrugger, trans. Jocelyne Dakhlia (Paris: Éditions Bouchène, 1998), 211–15.

7 Missoum, *Alger à l'époque ottomane*, 146–50; Shuval, *La ville d'Alger vers la fin du XVIIIème siècle*, 197.

8 For the Ottoman mansions, see Lucien Golvin, *Palais et demeures d'Alger à la période ottomane* (Aix-en-Provence: Édisud, 1988); and Missoum, *Alger à l'époque ottomane*, 188–253.

9 Haëdo, *Topographie et histoire générale d'Alger*, 78, 217.

10 For the barracks, see Missoum, *Alger à l'époque ottomane*, 138–44.

11 Louis-André Pichon, *Alger sous la domination française; son état présent et son avenir* (Paris: Théophile Barrois et Benjamin Duprat, 1833), 118–19.

12 Quoted in René Lespès, *Alger: Étude de géographie et d'histoire urbaines* (Paris: Librairie Félix Alcan, 1930), 205.

13 Ibid., 207.

14 The early Ottoman mosques have a continuous colonnade along their main façades. However, the colonnades do not belong to streets as in the case of rue de la Marine but are used as adjacent spaces to the main prayer halls—as indicated by their qualification as "*son cemaat yeri*" (place for latecomers to prayer).

15 "Rapport au Comité du Génie: Séance du 11 octobre 1831," Service Historique de la Défense, Château de Vincennes, Paris (hereafter cited as Défense), Génie, Alger, art. 8, section 6.

16 For a plan of this project, see Cohen, Oulebsir, and Kanoun, *Alger*, 66.

17 This discussion is derived from my article "Colonial/Postcolonial Intersections: *Lieux de mémoire* in Algiers," *Third Text* 49 (January 2000): 63–72; reprinted in *Histori-*

cal Reflections/Réflexions historiques 28, no. 2 (Summer 2002), and in *The Third Text Reader on Art, Culture and Theory,* ed. Rasheed Araeen, Sean Cubitt, and Ziauddin Sardar (London: Continuum, 2002).

18   For a plan of this project, see Cohen, Oulebsir, and Kanoun, *Alger,* 67.

19   Lespès, *Alger,* 333.

20   Charles Desprez, *L'hiver à Alger* (Paris: Éditions d'Essai, 1861), 87.

21   Charles Desprez, *Extraits de L'akhbar* (Algiers: Imprimerie Typographique de L'akhbar, 1867), 7:69, 117-19.

22   Desprez, *L'hiver à Alger,* 86.

23   Desprez, *Extraits de L'akhbar,* 7:66, 68.

24   Lespès, *Alger,* 336.

25   Guy Tombarel, "Proposition d'aménagement des abords de la Casbah pour une re-valorisation du vieil Alger," 1969 (Getty Research Institute, 2003.M.10).

26   "Rapport du Comité des Fortifications: Séance du 14 mars 1884," Défense, Génie, Alger, art. 8, section 6.

27   On the projects and debates of the 1930s, see Zohra Hakimi, "René Danger, Henri Prost et les débuts de la planification urbaine à Alger," in Cohen, Oulebsir, and Kanoun, *Alger,* 140-59.

28   M. Molbert, "L'urbanisme et son application à Alger," *Bulletin municipal officiel de la ville d'Alger,* May 1951, n.p.

29   Jean Alazard, "L'urbanisme à Alger," *Le monde colonial illustré,* no. 80 (April 1930): 93.

30   Le Corbusier's projects for Algiers have been studied by many scholars. For selected references, see Patricia M. E. Lorcin, "Historiographies of Algiers: Critical Reflections," in this volume.

31   Jean-Pierre Faure, *Alger capitale* (Paris: Société Française d'Éditions Littéraires et Techniques, 1936), 30.

32   Jean-Jacques Deluz, *L'urbanisme et l'architecture d'Alger* (Liège: Pierre Mardaga; Algiers: Office des Publications Universitaires, 1988), 74.

33   P. Luviconi, "La transformation du quartier de l'ancienne préfecture," *Bulletin municipal officiel de la ville d'Alger* 11 (September 1949): 11.

34   André Bronner, "Comment garder le souvenir du vieil Alger," *Le monde colonial illustré,* no. 189 (March 1939): 64.

35   *Tribune d'Alger républicain,* 16 August 1946.

36   Jacques Chevallier is best known for his collaboration with architect Fernand Pouillon. See Jacques Chevallier, *Nous algériens* (Paris: Calmann-Levy, 1958); and Fernand Pouillon, *Mémoires d'un architecte* (Paris: Éditions du Seuil, 1968). I examined Chevallier's tenure in my *Urban Forms and Colonial Confrontations: Algiers under French Rule* (Berkeley and Los Angeles: University of California Press, 1997), chap. 5.

37   *Travaux nord-africains,* 19 March 1959.

38   Lespès, *Alger,* 335.

39 Nassima Dris, *La ville mouvementée: Espace public, centralité, mémoire urbaine à Alger* (Paris: L'Harmattan, 2002), 144.

40 Tombarel, "Proposition d'aménagement des abords de la Casbah pour une revalorisation du vieil Alger." The following discussion is based on this document.

41 I am deeply grateful to Guy Tombarel for giving me a telephone interview from his office in Marseilles on 4 June 2007. I thank Jean-Louis Cohen for directing me to him.

42 Note, for example, the impact of the film on historian David Prochaska's academic career in Prochaska, "This Was Then, This Is Now: The Battle of Algiers and After," *Radical History Review* 85 (Winter 2003): 133–49.

43 For a perspective rendering of Coquerel and Renaud's project, see Cohen, Oulebsir, and Kanoun, *Alger,* 147.

HISTORIOGRAPHIES OF ALGIERS

CRITICAL REFLECTIONS

Patricia M. E. Lorcin

The image of Algiers has always been Janus-faced. From one perspective *Alger la blanche* suggests its attraction as a city of great beauty and character, a place that, through the ages, has drawn admirers to enjoy its multiple pleasures. From the other, "Algier [*sic*], the Whip of the Christian World, the terror of Europe,"[1] highlights the anxieties it has engendered across time, first as the nest of corsairs, who raided and plundered the northern shores of the Mediterranean, and more recently as a breeding ground of "fanatics" and terrorists. These images are, consciously or unconsciously, woven into the Western narratives that have emerged about the city in the past two hundred years.

The literature on Algiers is both varied and extensive, and it is impossible to do justice to it in a brief essay. The historiography of a time and place, like other types of literature, reflects the ideologies, circumstances, and even the anxieties of the age in which it is written. Thus, for much of the period covered in this essay, when Algiers was the site of struggle, conquest, and colonization, a Western vision predominated and the voices of Algerians were ignored or marginalized. It was only in the twentieth century that those voices were allowed to be heard and formed an essential part of the portrayals of the city. The discussion below centers on the moments in the city's history when the struggles to impose Western dominance were at their most intense and the identity of the city was at stake. First, I will consider the seventeenth and eighteenth centuries, when European privateers and Ottoman corsairs struggled for supremacy in the Mediterranean, and then I will discuss the nineteenth and early twentieth centuries, which were marked by demographic changes in the city unleashed by the ever-increasing influx of Europeans, who sought to claim Algiers as their own. What follows is an introduction to the changing narratives of the West and a small sample of the historiographies and eventual responses they engendered.

EARLY INTERPRETATIONS

The best historical account of Algiers in the early modern period is J. P. Morgan's *A Complete History of Algiers*, published in 1731.[2] Comprehensive in its historical treatment of the area from the time of the Greeks to the eighteenth century, it includes descriptions of the inhabitants of the region as well as their political and diplomatic activity. The period under the Turks is especially well covered, a reflection no doubt of the existing tensions between the European powers and the Ottomans. Appendices include the articles of peace and commerce established between Charles II of Great Britain and the dey of Algiers. It is, however, as a primary source for an eighteenth-century view of, and relations with, the Maghreb that the book is of special interest.

The image of Algiers during this period was, of course, most influenced by captivity narratives. The Ottoman corsairs, whose activities were similar in many ways to European privateers and buccaneers, patrolled the waters of the Mediterranean, raiding both shore and ships for Christian captives to sell into slavery or imprison for ransom in Algiers. The narratives of freed captives served purposes of titillation and propaganda for Western audiences. The contemporary popularity of such accounts stemmed, more often than not, from their sensationalist dimension. Although their veracity is now open to question, many such accounts were deemed realistic by contemporaries and thus became incorporated into the received wisdom of the time.

The most famous of these captives was Miguel de Cervantes, who allegedly kept a diary during his five years of captivity in Algiers (1575–80) and whose subsequent work was greatly influenced by his experiences.[3] Less well known to the general public but of importance to any scholar dealing with the development of the corsair community are the works of Fra Diego de Haëdo and Emanuel d'Aranda. Haëdo was a Benedictine monk who spent four years in captivity in Algiers (1578–81) and wrote several works on his return to freedom.[4] Although these sources have an obvious Christian bias, they are nonetheless invaluable sources for the period. D'Aranda, who was born in Bruges in 1614, was captured by Turkish corsairs off the coast of Brittany in 1640 and spent two years in captivity; he published his narrative sixteen years later, in 1656.[5] Although written as autobiographical reminiscences, the time of its actual writing is unknown, so it must be used with care. D'Aranda's text appeared in three languages and several editions over thirty years, which underlines the appeal such works had.[6] D'Aranda's reminiscences contain many of the religious and social prejudices of his time, but the text is valuable for the light it throws on both life in Algiers, as seen by an outsider, and the seventeenth-century attitudes of Europeans toward the Algerines.[7]

A comparison between d'Aranda's reminiscences and the early-nineteenth-century reflections of William Shaler, an American, provides insight into changing perceptions and interpretations of life in Algiers. Shaler first went to Algiers as one of the U.S. representatives involved in the negotiations for the Barbary Treaties of 1815, which followed the resolution of hostilities between the United States and the dey. He returned three years later as U.S. consul, and his *Sketches of Algiers* was written during his tenure there (1818–30).[8] Although reflecting a diplomatic mind, Shaler's text is invaluable for the detailed information it provides on the social, political, diplomatic, and military activities and institutions of the period just prior to the French conquest.

By the time Shaler was writing his *Sketches*, Algiers had lost much of its aura of fierceness and was attracting adventurers and geographers who were responding to the rising Western taste for travel literature. Among these, Thomas Shaw's book on the Barbary Coast and the Levant, first published in 1738, is the best known, but it is only one in a growing genre of literature that was to blossom in the nineteenth and twentieth centuries.[9]

COLONIAL AND CONTEMPORARY VIEWS
OF PRECOLONIAL ALGIERS

Ridding the Mediterranean of the "Barbary pirates" was one of the rationales — albeit spurious by 1830 — for the French expedition to Algiers. Interest in the activities of the Barbary corsairs and in the Ottoman period did not wane after French conquest. Although much of the initial literature that emerged after the conquest was related to French military activities, by the 1850s the French had established a historical society, the Société Historique Algérienne. Its monthly journal, the *Revue africaine*, published articles on all aspects of Algeria's past, including work that focused on Algiers.[10] The colonial historian best known for his study of the Ottoman period is Henri-Delmas de Grammont, whose history of Algiers under the Ottomans, for all its colonial bias, is still an important resource.[11] Grammont, who was a member and president of the Société Historique Algérienne, wrote or translated numerous works on Algiers.[12] French interest in the Ottomans was of course predicated as much by a desire to understand the functioning of the Ottoman occupation as it was to produce works of scholarly appeal.[13] The Ottomans had been powerful antagonists to the Europeans, and the desire to understand their slow decline as an imperial power was an incentive to delve into their activities in the Regency.

The French were not the only Europeans who had had relations with the Regency prior to the colonial period. Economic and diplomatic relations between the Algerines and the British developed as a result of the establishment in 1585 of the Barbary Company and its acquisition of a monopoly on trade with North Africa, as authorized by Elizabeth I. Diplomatic ties followed as much to create a united front against their common enemy, Philip II of Spain, as to ensure the smooth running of the company. The strategic relationship between Britain and Algiers lasted until Elizabeth's death in 1603, when hostilities between Spain and Britain ceased. Subsequently, the British became targets of corsair activity, and British narratives during the French colonial period continue to reflect, in their titles if not in their content, the anxieties created during this era.[14]

Recent works on the corsair period are a product of renewed academic interest in slavery and redemption narratives and a desire to dissipate the Manichean Western myths that contrasted heroic Europeans with barbaric Muslim pirates. Daniel Vitkus has edited a useful collection of extracts from British captivity narratives of the early modern period.[15] The volume is introduced by Nabil Matar, who provides the historical framework by means of a fine analysis of the significance of the different narratives. In *Christian Slaves, Muslim Masters*, Robert Davis argues that the difference between slavery in the Americas and in the Maghreb was the difference between economics and ideology.[16] As his title implies, there is a clash-of-civilizations element to the work insofar as Davis sees the motivation of the Maghreb slavers as one of revenge—"almost *djihad*" (p. xxv)—for the wrongs to which the Muslims were subjected during the Crusades and again in 1492 when the Spaniards defeated them at Granada. Although the Mediterranean slave trade outproduced the transatlantic trade during the sixteenth and seventeenth centuries, Davis suggests that it was the market-oriented nature of the transatlantic trade that gave it more "staying power" than its Mediterranean counterpart. The book is essentially a social history of Christian slaves and as such is useful for its detailed information on the capture, labor, and lives they led. William Spencer's *Algiers in the Age of the Corsairs* is now somewhat dated but makes some good points.[17] Spencer emphasizes the social cohesion and cultural achievements of the Regency and, unlike Davis, emphasizes the economic nature of corsair activity and its role in the enrichment of the city. Despite its age, John Wolf's *The Barbary Coast: Algiers under the Turks* remains one of the most, if not the most, authoritative work on the Ottoman period in English.[18] It is a thoroughly researched, engagingly written, and nuanced account of the city from its conquest by the Turks to the arrival of the French, which put an end to the Regency. Wolf is especially strong on the often-tumultuous political and economic relations between the Algerines and the Europeans, highlighting the events and personalities in both groups that shaped the perception of the Regency over time.

Fears, often exaggerated, for the safety of shipping in the Mediterranean provoked European powers to attack the Regency at intervals with the aim of counteracting rising Ottoman power or of cleaning out the "corsair nest" in order to make the Mediterranean a safer space for European shipping. The 1571 battle of Lepanto is usually seen as the watershed event in this process, but James Tracy argues that Charles V of Spain's campaigns against Tunis (1535) and Algiers (1541) were important contributing factors in checking rising Ottoman power.[19] With the help of the Genoese admiral Andrea Doria (1466–1560), Charles V conducted operations against the Ottomans, which, Tracy suggests, forced them to send out large fleets and armies in response. On the one hand, this proved to be another thorn in the Ottoman side, and on the other, it promoted cooperation among often-antagonistic Christian states, thus enabling them to create a more united front.

Daniel Panzac's *Corsaires barbaresques*, now translated into English, shifts the story to the nineteenth century.[20] Although Panzac covers only the century's first two decades, his examination of the tensions between Europeans and North Africans is comprehensive. He provides a fascinating account of the social, economic, and political background to the activities of the Barbary corsairs and details the issues that created the situation that led to European invasion. Using a wide array of French and Ottoman sources, he dispels the Western myths of North African barbarism and demonstrates the economic cynicism of the Europeans in their dealings with the Ottoman seafarers. The volume, which contains numerous illustrations and maps, focuses on the whole of the Maghreb, but its chapters on Algiers are an excellent introduction to the buildup of tensions between Algerines and Europeans that precipitated the French invasion.[21]

Roger Perkins and K. J. Douglas-Morris's *Gunfire in Barbary* focuses on one aspect of this buildup, namely Lord Exmouth's battle against Algiers in 1816.[22] The most interesting issues touched upon, in an otherwise-pedestrian book, have to do with the British abolitionist William Wilberforce and the antislavery movement and the activities of the corsairs of Malta. In the first case, the authors wonder why Wilberforce focused only on the slavery of Africans and not on the slavery of Christians and whites. In the latter case, they draw parallels between the activities of the Algerine Corsairs and those of Malta, who sailed under the standard of the Knights of the Order of St. John of Jerusalem and plundered and enslaved on an even greater scale than the Algerines. Unfortunately, the book is primarily concerned with the background and development of Exmouth's exploits and so does not develop these two potentially provocative leads. Scholars interested in Exmouth and the battle will find this to be a well-researched narrative history with useful appendices, which include a diary of events and a number of useful statistics about marine activity at the time.

VISIONS OF THE FRENCH CONQUEST

The first three decades of the nineteenth century were marked by skirmishes and conflicts of varying severity among the Algiers Regency, Great Britain, France, or the United States, of which Exmouth's campaign was the most intense prior to the French invasion in 1830. When the French landed in Sidi Ferruch in June of that year, they had little idea their "punitive" expedition, as they termed it, would last 132 years and deeply transform the histories of both states. The literature on the fall of Algiers is extensive, starting with contemporary accounts by French or Algerian participants.[23] Alf Heggoy has edited an English translation of a collection of Algerian oral accounts of the fall of Algiers that were originally compiled by the French.[24] Although they gathered many of these texts with the aim of trying to understand and hence dominate their subjects better, Heggoy rightly points out that for text analysis purposes the motives are immaterial; what is important is that the oral traditions surrounding the fall of Algiers have been fixed in print, thus providing an insight into the sentiments of the "common" people. Heggoy's introduction situates the selections and demonstrates that the narratives were as often directed against the failings of Algerian leaders and notables as they were in praise of their accomplishments.[25]

As would be expected, most of the works by colonial authors on the fall of Algiers analyzed the event as the necessary prelude to the advent of French civilization in the area or else described the exploits of the military campaign.[26] There are, however, some colonial accounts that analyze the French expedition in more complex terms. In *Une cause de l'expédition d'Alger* (1955), Marcel Emerit suggested that pillaging the coffers of the Regency was the main motive for the French expedition.[27] Emerit was the first historian to call into question the standard narrative that the expedition was a punitive, if belated, response to the insult of the French consul by the dey in 1827 and the need to put an end to Algerine piracy.[28] The looting, which was presented at the time as caused by the excesses of a limited number of men, was in fact a calculated operation to fill Charles X's depleted coffers to "buy" support for his flagging regime, a goal that the 1830 revolution short-circuited. Emerit drew his conclusions from a report by the *préfet de police* that was based on the findings of the head of a commission established to look into the pillaging but whose findings had been suppressed. Amar Hamdani reaches a similar conclusion in *La vérité sur l'expédition d'Alger*, published in 1985.[29] Colonial interpretations of the conquest of Algiers were, he suggests, mythologized to create modern-day *chansons de geste*, thus erasing the ulterior motives of the campaign. Hamdani goes further than Emerit, claiming that Louis-Philippe, who as an Orléans was a member of the richest family in France, did not dip into the family fortune to augment his allotment from the civil list but rather was able to maintain his lifestyle by other means—that is to say, the treasure of Algiers. Hamdani provides seventy-nine pages of diagrams, police reports, official dispatches, letters, and financial inventories. A racier and more speculative account is that of the investigative journalist Pierre Péan.[30] Part history, part personal research odyssey, part personal "treasure hunt," Péan's interest in the project was stimulated by the knowledge that one of his ancestors had been part of the expedition. Along the way he discovered that the pillaging of Algiers had been hushed up and an inquiry had been undertaken to find out whether it had taken place or not. Although from a historiographical point of view the account leaves something to be desired, it brings the unfortunate saga to life and is an engaging read.[31] Péan rightly points out that it is impossible to estimate the extent of the pillaging, as all the documentary evidence, mentioned by numerous contemporaries, has disappeared.

FROM CONQUEST TO COLONY

As the French presence in Algiers was transformed from a "punitive" sortie to a long-term occupation anchored by settler colonization, interest in the city focused on its social, economic, and cultural dimensions. Algiers had always appealed to foreign adventurers, merchants, travelers, and diplomats, and the change in regime did not dispel the attraction. With a European power in control, some of the age-old anxieties associated with the region dissipated as Westerners traveled about in relative safety. It was, furthermore, the beginning of the high period of what we now know as Orientalism, and artists, travelers, and missionaries wasted no time in crossing the Mediterranean to find inspiration of one sort or another. The British artist William Wyld (1806–89) arrived in 1833 with his friend Horace Vernet. While Vernet concentrated on military scenes and battles, Wyld wandered through the Casbah sketching and painting. He exhibited his work on Algiers at the Paris Salon from 1839 to 1848 and, like many artists who came after him, published an illustrated album of his artistic travels.[32] By the mid–nineteenth century, Algeria had attracted some of Europe's most renowned artists, all of whom found inspiration in its capital city.[33]

During the colonial period, interest in the arts flourished as the European settlers sought to establish Algeria as a region of France, with regionally specific art forms. Works on certain artists, exhibition catalogues, and conference collections increased as the settler colony grew and artistic life started to take shape.[34] In the postcolonial period, influenced by Edward Said's *Orientalism* and the "cultural turn" it engendered, scholars have reassessed the significance of Algiers to artistic creation and reexamined the work of its artists in relation to colonial expansion and the power structures of France's imperial enterprise.[35] In tandem with this trend, a more nostalgic literature emphasizes the aesthetic achievements of colonial artists while predictably leaving aside the colonial implications of their works.[36] Recently, the works of Algerian artists have been rediscovered and interpreted as alternative perspectives to the work of mainstream colonial artists. Of these, Mohammed Racim (1896–1975), considered to be the father of the Algerian miniaturist school and arguably the best Algerian artist of the colonial era, is now enjoying a revival as a national symbol. He depicted idealized scenes of the city before the French occupation in a medium inspired from Islamic miniature painting.[37]

FROM ARTISTRY TO ARCHITECTURE

If the aesthetic values of art occluded the destruction of Ottoman and Arab monuments and masked the appropriation of space and culture inherent in the works of the artists who made pilgrimages to colonial Algeria, architecture was a more blatant expression of the way in which an occupation can reorganize the structure of a city. André Raymond's "Le centre d'Alger en 1830" remains the authoritative text on the Ottoman city just before the French occupation and has been recently revised and reproduced.[38]

Sakina Missoum's two-part work, *Alger à l'époque ottomane,* deals with the Ottoman city and its residential architecture.[39] She traces the history of the construction of the medina, which was built on the Roman ruins of Icosium, by looking at the successive occupations and immigrations and the impact they had on its structural development. The medina's economic significance, its transformation into an urban organization, its politico-military infrastructure, and its ethnic quarters all form part of this history, and although it is geared to situate the work architecturally, it serves as useful background for researchers interested in the French colonial period.

A classic history of the city during French rule is René Lespès's *Alger: Étude du géographie et d'histoire urbaines*. Published on the occasion of the centennial of the occupation, it is based on documents drawn from governmental, army, and municipal archives and is a detailed chronicle of one hundred years of urban interventions. As such, it continues to serve as an indispensable reference.[40] Maria Sgroï-Dufresne's *Alger, 1830–1984* makes some useful points about the construction strategies employed to reshape Algiers at various key moments.[41] She argues that the two main urbanist debates occurred at times when the city was undergoing an identity crisis: that is to say, 1930–42 and 1968–70. The former was the period when Le Corbusier's vision was to transform Algiers into a capital at the head of Africa and open it to the Mediterranean; the latter was when the Algerian Republic wanted to make Algiers a symbol of reclaimed national sovereignty. Zohra Hakimi expands on the first period, which was often associated solely with Le Corbusier's projects, to include those of the urbanists René Danger and Henri Prost and makes a case for the early use of "master plans."[42]

Recent works on the colonial period by Zeynep Çelik, Jacques Deluz, Karim Hadjri and Mohamed Osmani, and Jean-Louis Cohen, Nabila Oulebsir, and Youcef Kanoun, among others, have extended earlier analyses to include the ways in which architectural and spatial forms were used as tools of racial, class, and gender segregation.[43] Yasser Elsheshtawy's *Planning Middle Eastern Cities*, of which Hadjri and Osmani's article on Algiers forms a part, reflects the latest trend of comparison in a global context. Although Hadjri's and Osmani's article on Algiers reiterates the power structures emphasized through urban planning that recent works on the colonial period highlight, the authors point to the success of colonial viticulture in generating the funds for increased urbanization in the colony as a whole. The marginalization of the indigenous proletarians, who could no longer afford housing in the overcrowded "indigenous" Casbah, created the *bidonvilles* that eventually ringed the city. The postcolonial period is divided into two chronological segments: the social period of the 1970s, when foreign architects such as Oscar Niemeyer built large-scale projects, and the 1980s and 1990s when "internationalization passed the city by."[44] Local politics, they argue, played a role in the city's isolation and its inability to interact globally.

The importance of architecture to the creation of a city's image is emphasized in works devoted to individual architects of the colonial period, of whom Le Corbusier is the best known.[45] Whereas the continued scholarly interest in Le Corbusier focuses on his unrealized projects to renovate Algiers, the work of other architects, such as Fernand Pouillon and Roland Simounet, has been the subject of both well-illustrated monographs and exhibitions.[46] The postindependence period, from 1968 to the present, is the focus of a work by Nora Semmoud, who argues that "Islamic fanaticism" has created a society functioning on two levels: one open, the other secret.[47] This duality shapes the way in which the city is being restructured spatially and socially.

ALGIERS SOCIETY

Architecture and urban planning are of course a reflection of the way in which the society living within the city's spaces views itself or would like outsiders to view it. In Algiers, society was fluid in that it was a cosmopolitan mix of peoples from different parts of the Mediterranean. Tal Shuval's *La ville d'Alger vers la fin du XVIIIème siècle* is an introduction to the demographic and sociological situation of the city on the eve of French colonization.[48] Shuval starts with an overview of the population and goes on to deal with the different ethnic and social groups of which it was comprised. In the first section of the book he discusses economic, social, and political factors that came into play, as well as types of wealth, housing, and social hierarchies. In the second part, he examines the structure of the city itself. Shuval has used a wide range of Ottoman, Algerian, and French sources and explicates relevant sections of these sources, as well as providing a number of appendices detailing the distribution, situation, and dates in use, of markets, caravanserais, baths, and other sites of social interaction.

The settler population of Algiers, like that of colonial Algeria as a whole, was made up largely of non-French immigrants, most of whom came from islands or the northern shores of the Mediterranean: Spain, Italy, and Malta.[49] Of these by far the largest group came from Spain, most of whose members settled in Algiers or Oran. It is not surprising, therefore, that they have received the most scholarly attention and are the only group that has been the focus of a monograph. Gérard Crespo and Jean-Jacques Jordi's *Immigration espagnole dans l'Algérois* looks at their contribution to the colonial development of Algiers and its immediate vicinity from conquest to the eve of World War I.[50] Essentially a demographic history, the volume is divided into three sections dealing with the actual waves of immigration, the reaction of the colonial authorities to the immigration, and the acculturation of the immigrants to colonial society. It is of interest not only for the demographic information it contains but also for the comparisons it makes between the different urban centers and between different migratory groups.

Pierre Hebey's *Alger, 1898,* is a more political work, which deals with the appalling wave of anti-Semitism that swept the city at the height of the Dreyfus Affair.[51] Although the 1898 events in Algiers coincided with a turning point in the affair, Hebey cautions against interpreting the "anti-Judaïsme" of the colony as a colonial extension of the anti-Semitism engendered by the Dreyfus Affair. Hebey argues that both its characteristics and its causes were quite different from anti-Semitism in the metropole. The circumstances of the affair merely facilitated an opportunistic coming together of intolerant "Algerians" (settlers) and French nationalists, such as Édouard Drummont, who were important instigators of political anti-Semitism in France. It was this coupling that creates the perception of a link between the two anti-Semitic movements. Like Jean-Denis Bredin, whose *L'affaire* remains one of the best judicial accounts of the Dreyfus Affair, Hebey is a lawyer and the strengths of his book mirror this fact. Although Drummont was a central figure for both metropole and colonial anti-Semitism, his success in Algiers depended on the likes of Max Régis, mayor of Algiers, whose *L'antijuif* rivaled Drummont's *La libre parole* in its anti-Semitic intensity. The settlers, unable to admit that the population native to Algeria was not enamored of the French presence, heaped opprobrium on the Jews, especially Arab or North African Jews, and blamed them for the tensions and eruptions that occurred sporadically.[52] Hebey suggests that the virulent fin-de-siècle anti-Semitism of Algeria was conflated with hitherto-less-political anti-Arab sentiments. When the anti-Semitism died down, anti-Arab/Berber racism had acquired the strident political tone that would ensure their exclusion from citizenship and positions of political and social power.

Although a number of works exist on the development of settler society in Algeria and on aspects of *pied-noir*[53] culture, few focus on the situation in Algiers.[54] Even fewer devote as much space to Algerians as to the settlers.[55] Mahfoud Kaddache's *La vie politique à Alger de 1919 à 1939* does both. Kaddache, who has written extensively on Algerian history, outlines the demographic and political framework before focusing on the politics of the era. The value of the work lies in its detailed exploration of both the Algerian and the settler expectations and strategies and the way in which these intersected at key moments, leading to the inevitable hardening of attitudes as each side rejected the aspirations of the other.[56]

The number of works focusing exclusively on Algiers society is small, but those focusing on women's roles in the development of the city are virtually nonexistent. The only groups that have received any attention are prostitutes, missionaries, and domestics.[57] Interest in prostitution in the colonial period was predicated by purported concerns for public hygiene and unstated preoccupations with social control. Édouard-Adolphe Duchesne's 1853 treatise on prostitution in Algiers was, like Parent-Duchâtelet's work on Paris, which it emulated, as concerned with the moral question as it was with the social.[58] Nothing has been published on the subject for Algiers, or indeed focusing on Algeria, since.[59] Missionary activity has always been implicated, to varying degrees, in imperial activities, so it is somewhat surprising that so little has been written about such activity in Algeria. To be sure, the orders founded by Cardinal Lavigerie in the 1860s, the Pères Blancs and the Soeurs Blanches, met with little success in Algeria, apart from the Kabylia, but they fanned out from Algiers to other parts of Africa and this would suggest avenues of research. Algiers was also the base for other female Catholic orders. With the exception of an article by Sarah Curtis, what little has been written about women missionaries to date is essentially hagiographic.[60] Emilie de Vialar and Lilias Trotter, both of whom worked in Algiers, are no exceptions.[61] Unfortunately, there is no recent work that examines the intersection of missionary and colonial structures in Algiers.[62]

Caroline Brac de la Perrière's work on female domestics during the Algerian War of Independence is one of a limited number of studies on Algerian women's labor during the colonial period.[63] The best-known, quasi-stereotypical, images of Algerian women during the independence struggles are those of the bomb planters in Gillo Pontecorvo's movie *The Battle of Algiers*. Brac de la Perrière's study provides a more complex picture by exploring three dimensions of women's lives during this period. First, she considers Algerian women as members of the "underclass" (*sous-prolétariat*); then she examines the ties between these women workers and their employers in the light of relations between the Muslim and European communities; and finally she looks at their role in the war itself. Brac de la Perrière argues that the fact that Algerian women were employed so extensively in domestic service indicates the degree of poverty to which their traditional society had sunk. However, the fact of having to work for a living outside their homes set them apart from other Algerian women, who either did not need to work or worked within the family labor circle. Working provided these women with new-found agency, which came into its own during the war. The war provided them with cultural pride, which colonialism had all but eliminated, empowering them psychologically. Part oral history, part sociological analysis, the study highlights the complexity of relationships in the war period and the imagery these relations produced.

In any multiethnic or cosmopolitan city, language, as an extension of the ethnic culture, can be or can become a political issue. The development and use of language is of as much importance to politicians and administrators as it is to scholars of linguistics or cultural historians. During the colonial period, interest in the Arabic spoken in Algiers was stimulated by the need to administer the Arabic-speaking population with greater ease.[64] French language and culture were promoted to the detriment of Arabic, even if interest in the latter continued at both the cultural and political level. As the settler colony grew, the evolution of language, both French and Arabic, became the focus of interest, and by the early twentieth century the caricature of the settler patois had been personified in the form of the popular and populist tales of Cagayous.[65]

The newly independent state of Algeria emphasized the reclaiming of Arabic as the national language, but 132 years of colonial rule and the postcolonial migratory movements between France and Algeria made it impossible to eradicate French altogether. In addition, the demands for cultural autonomy of the Berber population of Algeria introduced the Berber language, Tamazight, into the linguistic mix. An edited volume, *Alger plurilingue*, examines the polyglot nature of Algiers society, highlighting not just its linguistic variety but also its differences across urban spaces.[66] Finally, a recent work by Aziza Boucherit looks at the sociolinguistic aspects of the Arabic spoken in Algiers.[67] Boucherit traces the history of the immigrations into Algiers, international and national, and the impact they had on the language. She also touches on the political shifts that shaped the linguistic development of Arabic in the city. By deconstructing the Arabic spoken in Algiers, she highlights both the diversity of the languages and dialects that have contributed to its development and its historical significance.

ALGIERS AT WAR

Wars and conflicts have scarred Algiers from its earliest history, and the twentieth century was no exception. Two wars catapulted Algiers into the international arena: World War II and the Algerian War of Independence. In both cases it was, for very different reasons, a battleground for freedom: in the first instance, in the Allied struggle against the Nazi war machine and, in the second, against the colonial power. Until the execution of Operation Torch, the Allied landings in North Africa, Algiers was a pro-Vichy stronghold. Although the British neutralized the French navy by destroying most of its fleet at Mers-el-Kebir in July 1940, over 100,000 Vichy troops were stationed in French North Africa, with their headquarters in Algiers, under Admiral Darlan. Anthony Verrier's *Assassination in Algiers* is the story behind Darlan's assassination on 24 December 1942 by Fernand Bonnier.[68] Verrier argues that the British were behind the assassination because of Churchill's vehement opposition to Vichy and his apprehension of Roosevelt's inclination to collaborate with Darlan, and his supporters, in maintaining Vichy. For Churchill, Darlan was "an odious Quisling" who could not be trusted and was best out of the way definitively. The assassination certainly cleared the way for tighter control of the Vichy element in Algiers and enabled Churchill to maintain his relationship with Roosevelt without the manipulative influence of Darlan.

Jean Pierre-Bloch picks up the story, in a more personal account, and brings it up to the end of 1944.[69] As can be expected from a high-ranking member of the resistance movement and a member of de Gaulle's Free French, Pierre-Bloch's account centers on the activities of the Free French.[70] In the summer of 1943 de Gaulle transferred his government in exile to Algiers, and Pierre-Bloch's account details the politics and intrigues that preoccupied de Gaulle and his associates. Like all personal accounts it needs to be treated with caution, but the passages on anti-Semitism in Algeria, de Gaulle's politics while in Algiers, and the liberation are worth reading. Among the officers who took refuge in Algiers from Vichy was the film director Marcel Aboulker. His account of the four years he spent in Algiers is often anecdotal but has the advantage of having been written at the time and published immediately after the war.[71] It contains useful information on the resistance activities of the Free French and the political intrigues of the Allies. Darlan's assassination was central to the political developments in wartime Algiers. Unlike Verrier, Aboulker attributes the assassination to French royalist machinations, but the end game is the same. Darlan's assassination put an end to U.S. rapprochement with Vichy and cleared the way for de Gaulle's rise to power.[72] It is surprising, given the importance of Algiers to Allied invasion plans during World War II, that there are not more books devoted exclusively to the situation in the city.

A mere nine years separated the end of World War II and the beginning of the Algerian War of Independence. Jean-Jacques Jordi and Guy Pervillé have edited a collection of essays focusing on Algiers and covering the two wars and the period in between.[73] Although the volume as a whole is a French story, its authors suggest that the social and political developments in postindependence Algeria were intricately connected to the period covered by the volume and that its contents are of as much interest to Algerians as to the French. A number of the articles shed new light on familiar territory. Colette Zyntnicki's contribution on the exclusion of Jewish children from public schools, for example, reminds us that anti-Semitism was a constant feature of life in Algiers. Jean-Louis Planche's examination of the Casbah as a site of Communist and nationalist activity in the decade between 1945 and 1954 questions whether it was in fact the seat of Muslim power as it was sometimes depicted to be. And, of course,

Algiers as the centerpiece of the War of Independence is the focus of nearly half of the articles in the volume.

The Algerian War of Independence has been and continues to be the focus of much scholarly attention. While the earlier literature has tended to focus almost exclusively on the French-Algerian dimension of the war, recent scholarship has demonstrated quite decisively that it was an important site of Cold War politics.[74] For nearly forty years, the Algerian War of Independence was considered by the French to be *des opérations de securité et de maintien de l'ordre* (operations for security and the maintenance of order), and it was in this context that Algiers became the focus of the army's most brutal activities. Torture was first used extensively during the Battle of Algiers, and recent revelations by both the torturers and the tortured have once more focused attention on its perpetration and lamentable legacy.[75] In *Alger, capitale de la résistance, 1956–1957*, Benyoucef Ben Khedda responds to General Paul Aussaresses now-notorious book with his own account of the Battle of Algiers. He describes the background and implementation of the eight-day strike organized by the executive branch of the FLN (Front de Libération National) and the way in which it was used by General Jacques Massu and his paratroopers to intimidate the Algerians. He argues that the strike contributed to the buildup to the actual battle for the city and led the Algerians to realize the true nature of the conflict. The ferocious methods used by the French during the Battle of Algiers, Ben Khedda states, prompted the international community to question the reason and morality of their activities. The Battle of Algiers may have been won by the French on the ground, but it was lost morally and led to the French defeat in the diplomatic and political arena.[76]

WRITING ALGIERS AS NOSTALGIA; WRITING ALGIERS AS HYBRIDITY; WRITING ALGIERS AS TERROR

The Evian Peace Accords of 1962 and the mass exodus of 1.2 million *pieds-noirs* in the summer of that year put an end to colonial rule and all but eliminated the settler presence in the territory. The country's administrative, medical, and educational infrastructure, hitherto staffed by *pieds-noirs*, temporarily collapsed. The Algerian war had spawned two new regimes, both of which wanted to, but could not, put the 132 years in which their destinies were intertwined behind them. Whereas the newly independent Algerians were eager to eradicate the signs of colonial presence in the city, the image of *Alger la blanche* continued to haunt the *pieds-noirs*. Waves of nostalgic literature began to emerge almost immediately after independence. Initially marked by anger and bitterness, these narratives slowly gave way to ones seeking to recapture the essence of an imagined past of benevolence and beauty.[77] Coffee table books abound in this type of literature and they are useful references for their illustrations and views of the colonial town or their reproductions of old postcards and cartoons.[78] Many *pieds-noirs* settled in the South of France, where they have created an active cultural community that perceives itself as diasporic. As such it seeks to re-establish links across the Mediterranean. In November 2003, an exhibition at Fort Saint-Jean in Marseilles entitled *Parlez-moi d'Alger* highlighted this trend. The exhibition was staged in the context of "the Year of Algeria" and traced the commercial and cultural relationship between Algiers and Marseilles from Ottoman times to the present. The exhibition catalogue, which is divided into four sections, with scholars contributing articles to each, illustrates the way in which colonial memory is being reinscribed in the postcolonial public sphere.[79] Gone is the imagery of "paradise lost" so dear to the first generation of *pieds-noirs* immigrants, replaced by one of "Franco-Muslim" unity, a unity that eluded colonial Algeria and which the settlers did so much to prevent.

The 2003 Year of Algeria in France, officially called *El Djazaïr*, Arabic for "Algiers," was not of course for the benefit of the *pieds-noirs* community. Rather it was geared to improve Franco-Algerian relations and stress the influence that the French of North African origin and the large North African immigrant community had had and was having on French culture. Like the *pieds-noirs*, they too have a hybrid identity that looks to Algeria, albeit in very different ways. The best-known works of this group are literary or cinematic and deal with the cultural dislocation caused directly or indirectly by the colonial past.[80] The rise of the FIS (Front Islamique du Salut) and the ensuing civil conflict of the 1990s, which claimed thousands of lives and focused attention on fundamentalism in Algeria, have added a new dimension to works on Algiers. The journalist Nina Hayat (Aïcha Belhalfaoui) has written a memoir-novel about the impact of recent events in Algiers on the lives of its inhabitants, especially women.[81] Entitled *La nuit tombe sur Alger la blanche*, it brings the Janus-faced imagery of Algiers, a city of light and torment, full circle.

It is perhaps apt to end with the only recent long-term history of Algiers. Written by Hocine Mezali, a journalist turned historian, it traces the vicissitudes of Algiers from Roman times to the present.[82] Even the best historian could not do justice to thirty-two centuries of history potted into 364 pages, but in spite of its methodological drawbacks and journalist style, it has the advantage of introducing the reader to the richness and complexity of Algiers, a city that has, at one time or another, been the center of events with worldwide repercussions and has spawned an amazing variety of narratives.

Algiers has haunted the Western imagination for centuries, and for much of that time the West has imposed its interpretations on the city. In the years since Algeria was granted independence, a new image of the city has emerged, one that repudiates its colonial past while acknowledging the richness of its history.

NOTES

1   From the impressions of the French nobleman Le Sieur de Gramaye, on an official visit to Constantinople in 1619. Quoted in William Spencer, *Algiers in the Age of the Corsairs* (Norman: University of Oklahoma Press, 1976), xi.

2   J. Morgan, *A Complete History of Algiers, to Which Is Prefixed an Epitome of the General History of Barbary from the Earliest Times, Interspersed with Many Curious Passages and Remarks Not Touched on by Any Writer Whatever* (New York: Negro Universities Press, 1970).

3   See Maria Antonia Garcés, *Cervantes in Algiers: A Captive's Tale* (Nashville, TN: Vanderbilt University Press, 2005).

4   Fra Diego Haëdo, *Topographia e historia general de Argel* (Valladoid, 1612); Fra Diego Haëdo, *Epitome de los reyes de Argel*, trans. H. D. de Grammont (Algiers: A. Jourdan, 1881); Fra Diego Haëdo, *Dialogos de la captividad*, trans. Moliner-Violle (Algiers: A. Jourdan, 1897).

5   Emanuel d'Aranda, *Les captifs d'Alger*, preface and introduction by Latifa Z'Rari (Paris: Jean-Paul Rocher, 1997); originally published as *Relation de la captivité & liberté du Sieur Emanuel d'Aranda, jadis esclave à Alger* (Brussels: J. Mommart, 1656); an English translation by John Davies was published by J. Starkey in London in 1666.

6   Seven editions appeared during this time: four in French, one in English, and two in Flemish. Latifa Z'Rari, preface to Aranda, *Les captifs d'Alger*, 8.

7   A bibliography of English captivity narratives can be found in Daniel J. Vitkus, ed., *Piracy, Slavery, and Redemption: Barbary Captivity Narratives from Early Modern England* (New York: Columbia University Press, 2001).

8   William Shaler, *Sketches of Algiers, Political, Historical and Civil: Containing an Account of the Geography, Population, Government, Revenues, Commerce, Agriculture, Arts, Civil Institutions, Tribes, Manners, Languages, and Recent Political History of That Country* (Boston: Cummings, Hillard, 1826).

9   Dr. Thomas Shaw, *Travels or Observations Relating to Several Parts of Barbary and the Levant*, 2 vols. (Oxford: Printed at the Theatre, 1738). This work was translated into French as *Voyage en Barbarie* (1743) and then as *Voyage dans la Régence d'Alger* (1830) and served as a reference on the area for the French expeditionary force. See also Filoppo Panati, *Narrative of a Residence in Algiers*, trans. Edward Blanquière (London: Henry Colburn, 1818); Elizabeth Broughton, *Six Years Residence in Algiers* (London: Saunders and Otley, 1838); Ernest Feydeau, *Alger, étude* (Paris: Michel Levy, 1862); D. Hartevelt, *Herinneringen uit Algiers* (Arnheim: Thieme, 1865); L. G. Seguin, *Walks in Algiers* (London: Daldy Isbister, 1878); Louis Bertrand, *Nuits d'Alger* (Paris: Flammarion, 1930); Lucienne Favre, *Tout l'inconnu de la Casbah d'Alger* (Algiers: Baconnier Frères, 1933); H. Montherlant, *Il y a encore des paradis (1928-1931)* (Algiers: Soubi-

ron, 1935). In addition to the travel literature that focuses on Algiers, the multitude of travel books on Algeria nearly always each contain at least one chapter on Algiers.

10   E.g., H. D. de Grammont and L. Piesse, "Un mauscrit du Père Dan: Les illustres captifs," *Revue africaine* 27 (1883): 11–35, 191–206, 355–70; J. Desparmet, «L'entrée des Français à Alger par le Cheikh Abdelkader,» *Revue africaine* 71 (1930): 225–56. Issues of the *Revue africaine* in the 1880s contain numerous articles by Grammont on aspects of the history of Algiers.

11   Henri-Delmas de Grammont, *Histoire d'Alger sous la domination Turque, 1515–1830*, with an introduction by Lemnouar Merouche (1887; Condé-sur-Noireau: Éditions Bouchène, 2001).

12   Henri-Delmas de Grammont, *Un académicien captif à Alger* (Algiers: A. Jourdan, 1883); *Études algériennes: La course, l'esclavage et la rédemption à Alger* (Paris: [no publisher], 1885); *Un pacha d'Alger précurseur de M. de Lesseps* (Algiers: A. Jourdan, 1886). Among his translations was one of Haëdo's *Epitome de los reyes de Argel*.

13   See also C. de Rotalier, *Histoire d'Alger et de la piraterie des Turcs dans la Méditerranée*, 2 vols. (Paris: Paulin, 1841).

14   E.g., Robert L. Playfair, *The Scourge of Christendom: Annals of British Relations with Algiers prior to the Conquest* (London: Smith and Elder, 1884) (Playfair was British consul general at Algiers from 1867 to 1896). A trilingual coffee-table book published to commemorate the restoration of the British Embassy buildings in Algiers provides a pictorial overview of four centuries of relations: Osman Benchérif, *The British in Algiers, 1585–2000* (Algiers: RSM Communication, 2001).

15   Vitkus, *Piracy, Slavery, and Redemption.*

16   Robert C. Davis, *Christian Slaves, Muslim Masters: White Slavery in the Mediterranean, the Barbary Coast and Italy, 1500–1800* (London: Palgrave, 2006).

17   Spencer, *Algiers in the Age of the Corsairs.*

18   John B. Wolf, *The Barbary Coast: Algiers under the Turks, 1500–1830* (New York and London: W. W. Norton, 1970).

19   James D. Tracy, *Emperor Charles V's Crusades against Tunis and Algiers: Appearance and Reality,* James Ford Bell Lectures, no. 38 (Minneapolis: University of Minnesota, 2001).

20   Daniel Panzac, *Barbary Corsairs: The End of a Legend, 1800–1820,* trans. Victoria Hobson and John E. Hawkes (Leiden and Boston: Brill, 2005).

21   For more on the lead-up to the French conquest, see Lucette Valensi, *On the Eve of Colonisation: The Maghreb before French Conquest,* trans. Kenneth Perkins (New York: Africana, 1977).

22   Roger Perkins and Captain K. J. Douglas-Morris, *Gunfire in Barbary: Admiral Exmouth's Battle with the Corsairs of Algiers in 1816; The Story of the Suppression of White Christian Slavery* (Havant: Kenneth Mason, 1982).

23   E.g., Jean Toussaint Merle, *La prise d'Alger; racontée par un témoin* (Paris: Jonquières, 1930); Amable Thiébault Matterer, *Journal de la prise d'Alger par le Capi-*

taine de frégate "Matterer," 1830 (Paris: Éditions de Paris, 1960); Louis-Auguste-Victor de Ghaisne Bourmont, *Rapport official de la prise d'Algér* (Paris: J. Lebreton, 1830); Général Berthezène, *18 mois à Alger* (Montpellier: Auguste Ricard, 1834); Aimable-Jean-Jacques Pélissier, duc de Malakoff, *Mémoire sur les opérations de l'armée française sur la côte d'Afrique depuis le 14 juin, jour du débarquement jusqu'à la prise d'Alger, le 5 juillet 1830* (Algiers: Typographie Duclaux, 1863); M. Bensadek, *La prise d'Alger: Récit d'un officier français, 1830* (Algiers: Édition At-Tabyin/Al-Jahidhiya, 2000). Among the more bizarre works in praise of the expedition was a cantata composed by Ferdinando Paër, *La prise d'Alger* (Paris: Pacini, 1830). Setting exploits to music was in vogue at the time. Exmouth's campaign had produced a comic opera, written by the American poet and lyricist John Howard Payne and Sir Henry Bishop: *The Fall of Algiers* (London: J. Cumberland, 1925).

24 Alf Andrew Heggoy, *The French Conquest of Algiers, 1830: An Algerian Oral Tradition*, Monographs in International Studies, Africa Series, no. 48 (Athens: Ohio University Press, 1986). The selections are from collections made by Eugène Daumas, Ottocar De Schlechta, and Jean Desparmet.

25 Ibid., 9.

26 See, e.g., M. Fioupou, *La prise d'Alger* (Toulon: A. Bordato, 1907); Gabriel Esquer, *Les commencements d'un empire: La prise d'Alger, 1830* (1923; Paris: Larose, 1929); Henriette Celarié, *La prise d'Alger* (Paris: Hachette, 1929); Gabriel Rouquerol, *Expédition de 1830 et prise d'Alger par les français: Organisation et rôle de l'artillerie du corps expéditionnaire* ([no publisher], 1894); E. Déchaud, *La marine à la prise d'Alger* (Paris: Libr. Militaire R. Chapelot, 1906).

27 Marcel Emerit, *Une cause de l'expédition d'Alger, le trésor de la Casbah* (Paris: Imprimerie Nationale, 1955).

28 The dey flicked the consul with a fly whisk following an arrogant tirade by the Frenchman.

29 Amar Hamdani, *La vérité sur l'expédition d'Alger* (Paris: Balland, 1985).

30 Pierre Péan, *Main basse sur Alger: Enquête sur un pillage, juillet 1830* (Paris: Plon, 2004).

31 See also Pierre Serval, *La ténébreuse histoire de la prise d'Alger* (Paris: Table Ronde, 1980).

32 E. Lessore and W. Wyld, *Voyage pittoresque dans la Régence d'Alger exécuté en 1833 et lithographié* (Paris: C. Motte, 1835). See also Adolphe Otth, *Esquisses africaines, dessinées pendant un voyage à Alger et lithographiées* (Berne: J. F. Wagner, 1839).

33 The best known are of course Théodore Chassériau, Eugène Delacroix, Eugène Fromentin, Jean-Léon Gérôme, Jean Auguste Ingres, Henri Matisse, and Auguste Renoir, but many now lesser known artists made the pilgrimage in search of light and exoticism. Other artists, the most notable of whom was Pablo Picasso, never went to Algiers but were inspired by its exotic eroticism.

34 See, e.g., *Actes du XIVe Congrès international des orientalistes, Alger, 1905* (Paris:

E. Leroux, 1906); George Marçais, *L'exposition d'art musulman d'Alger* (Paris: Thorin, 1906); *Les peintres de l'Orient au XIXème siècle: Expositions artistiques du centenaire de l'Algérie* (Algiers: Musée des Beaux-Arts d'Alger, 1930); Jean Alazard, *Le Musée des Beaux-Arts d'Alger* (Paris: H. Laurens, 1930); Jean Alazard, *L'Orient et la peinture française au XIXe siècle d'Eugène Delacroix à Auguste Renoir* (Paris: Plon, 1930); Jean Alazard, *Catalogue des peintures et sculptures exposées dans les galleries du Musée National des Beaux-Arts d'Alger* (Paris: H. Laurens, 1936).

35 E.g., Roger Benjamin, *Orientalist Aesthetics: Art, Colonialism, and French North Africa, 1880–1930* (Berkeley and Los Angeles: University of California Press, 2003); Roger Benjamin, *Renoir and Algeria* (New Haven, CT: Yale University Press, 2003); Todd B. Porterfield, *The Allure of Empire: Art in the Service of French Imperialism, 1798–1836* (Princeton, NJ: Princeton University Press, 1998).

36 E.g., Marion Bidal-Bué, *Alger et ses peintres, 1830–1960* (Paris: Paris-Méditerranée, 2000); Magali Leroy-Terquem et al., *Alger, la Casbah et Paul Guion* (Mediane: Éditions Publisud, 2005). Guion was also an architect and Terquem et al.'s book deals with both aspects of his creativity.

37 Interestingly, Étienne Dinet, a French convert to Islam, has also generated interest of this sort. He is best known for his paintings of the Algerians of the south. On Racim, see Benjamin, *Orientalist Aesthetics*, 235–48. On Dinet, see François Pouillon, *Les deux vies d'Étienne Dinet* (Paris: Éditions Balland, 1997).

38 André Raymond, "Le centre d'Alger en 1830," *Revue de l'Occident musulman et de la Méditerranée* 31, no. 1 (1981): 73–84. The revised version of the article contains new data from Tal Shuval's *La ville d'Alger* (see below) and is included in Jean-Louis Cohen, Nabila Oulebsir, and Youcef Kanoun, eds., *Alger: Paysage urbain et architectures, 1800–2000* (Paris: Imprimeur, 2003).

39 Sakina Missoum, *Alger à l'époque ottomane: La medina et la maison traditionnelle* (Aix-en-Provence: Edisud, 2003).

40 René Lespès, *Alger: Étude du géographie et d'histoire urbaines* (Paris: Félix Alcan, 1930).

41 Maria Sgroï-Dufresne, *Alger, 1830–1984: Stratégies et enjeux urbains* (Paris: Éditions Recherche sur le Civilisations, 1986).

42 Zohra Hakimi, "René Danger, Henri Prost et les débuts de la planification," in Cohen, Oulebsir, and Kanoun, *Alger*, 140–60.

43 Zeynep Çelik, *Urban Forms and Colonial Confrontations: Algiers under French Rule* (Berkeley and Los Angeles: University of California Press, 1997); Jean-Jacques Deluz, *L'urbanisme et l'architecture d'Alger* (Liège: Pierre Mardaga; Algiers: Office des Publications Universitaires, 1988); Jean-Jacques Deluz, *Alger, chronique urbain* (Paris: Éditions Bouchène, 2001); Karim Hadjri and Mohamed Osmani, "Special Development and Urban Transformation of Colonial and Postcolonial Algiers," in *Planning Middle Eastern Cities: An Urban Kaleidoscope in a Globalizing World*, ed. Yasser Elsheshtawy (London and New York: Routledge, 2004); Cohen, Oulebsir, and Kanoun, *Alger*

(published in conjunction with an exhibition of the same name held at the Palais de la Porte Dorée in Paris from June to September 2003).

44 Kadjri and Osmani, "Special Development and Urban Transformation of Colonial and Postcolonial Algiers," 51.

45 The groundbreaking study on Le Corbusier's projects in Algiers is Mary McLeod, "Urbanism and Utopia: Le Corbusier from Regional Syndicalism to Vichy" (PhD diss., Princeton University, 1985). See also Mary McLeod, "Le Corbusier and Algiers," *Oppositions,* nos. 19/20 (Winter/Spring 1980): 54–85; Zeynep Çelik, "Le Corbusier, Orientalism, Colonialism," *Assemblage* 17 (Spring 1992): 59–77; Michèle Lamprakos, "Le Corbusier and Algiers: The Plan Obus as Colonial Urbanism," in *Forms of Dominance in the Architecture and Urbanism of the Colonial Enterprise,* ed. Nezar AlSayyad (Aldershot and Brookfield: Avery, 1992), 183–210; F. Sherry McKay, "Le Corbusier, Negotiating Modernity: Representing Algiers, 1930–1942" (PhD diss., University of British Columbia, 1994); and Jean-Louis Cohen, "Le Corbusier, Perret et les figures d'un Alger moderne," in *Alger,* ed. Cohen, Oulebsir, and Kanoun, 160–85.

46 See, e.g., Jean-Lucien Bonillo, ed., *Fernand Pouillon, architecte méditerranéen* (Marseille: Éditions Imbernon, 2001); Danièle Voldman, *Fernand Pouillon, architecte* (Paris: Payot, 2006); Richard Klein, ed., *Roland Simounet à l'oeuvre: Architecture, 1951–1996* (Villeneuve-d'Ascq: Musée d'Art Moderne Lille Métropole/Institut Français d'Architecture, 2000).

47 Nora Semmoud, *Les stratégies d'appropriation de l'espace à Alger* (Paris: L'Harmattan, 2001).

48 Tal Shuval, *La ville d'Alger vers la fin du XVIIIème siècle: Population et cadre urbain* (Paris: Éditions du Centre National de Recherche Scientifique, 1998). For an early-nineteenth-century account of the demographic situation in Algiers, see *Alger: Topographie, population, forces militaires de terre et de mer, acclimatement, et ressources que le pays peut offrir à l'armée d'expédition: précédé d'un résumé historique: suivi d'un précis sur le service des troupes pendant un siège: et orné d'un plan très-exact de la ville et des environs, par un français qui a résidé à Alger* (Marseille: Typographie de Feissat aîné de Demonchy, 1830).

49 There was also a significant group of Germans.

50 Gérard Crespo and Jean-Jacques Jordi, *L'immigration espagnole dans l'Algérois de 1830 à 1914* (Versailles: Éditions de l'Atlanthrope, 1991).

51 Pierre Hebey, *Alger, 1898: La grande vague antijuive* (Paris: Nil Éditions, 1996). Hebey has written several books that deal directly or indirectly with anti-Semitism, including the prize-winning *La N.R.F. des années sombres, juin 1940–juin 1941, des intellectuels à la dérive* (Paris: Gallimard, 1992), on the intellectuals involved in *La nouvelle revue française.*

52 The Kabyle Rebellion of 1871 was attributed to the fact that the Kabyles resented the Crémieux Decree of 1870, which granted the Jews French citizenship, a citizenship that predated by nearly twenty years the granting of citizenship to the children born

in Algeria of non-French immigrants. See Patricia M. E. Lorcin, *Imperial Identities: Stereotyping, Prejudice and Race in Colonial Algeria* (London: J. B. Tauris, 1995).

53 Originally a pejorative term for the European settlers of French North Africa, it was adopted by them to distinguish themselves from the metropole French.

54 E.g., Jonathan K. Gosnell, *The Politics of Frenchness in Colonial Algeria, 1930–1954* (Rochester, NY: University of Rochester Press, 2002); Patricia M. E. Lorcin, "Rome and France in Africa: Recovering Algeria's Latin Past," *French Historical Studies* 25, no. 2 (2002): 295–329; Pierre Bourdieu, *The Algerians* (Boston: Beacon Press, 1962); Charles-Robert Ageron, ed., *L'Algérie des Français* (Paris: Seuil, 1993).

55 The exceptions examine Algerian society as a whole or focus on individuals. See, e.g., Mahfoud Kaddache, *L'Algérie des Algériens: De la préhistoire à 1954* (Paris: Éditions Paris-Méditerranée, 2003); Charles-Robert Ageron, *Les Algériens musulmans et la France (1871–1919)*, 2 vols. (Paris: Presses Universitaires de France, 1968); Patrick Weil, *Le statut des musulmans en Algérie coloniale: Une nationalité française dénaturée* (San Domenico: European University Institute, 2003); Benjamin Stora and Zakya Daoud, *Ferhat Abbas, une utopie algérienne* (Paris: Denoël, 1995).

56 Mahfoud Kaddache, *La vie politique à Alger de 1919 à 1939* (Algiers: Société Nationale d'Édition et de Diffusion, 1970).

57 Édouard-Adolphe Duchesne, *De la prostitution dans la ville d'Alger depuis la conquête* (Paris: J. B. Ballière, 1853); I. R. Govan Stewart, *Lilias Trotter of Algiers* (London: Lutterworth Press, 1958); Caroline Brac de la Perrière, *Derrière les héros: Les employés de maison musulmanes en service chez les Européens à Alger pendant la guerre d'Algérie, 1954–1962* (Paris: L'Harmattan, 1987).

58 On Duchesne, see Julia Clancy-Smith, "Islam, Gender, and Identities in the Making of French Algeria, 1830–1962," in *Domesticating the Empire: Languages of Gender, Race, and Family Life in French and Dutch Colonialism, 1830–1962*, ed. Julia Clancy-Smith and Frances Gouda (Charlottesville: University Press of Virginia, 1998), 154–74; Duchesne, *De la prostitution dans la ville d'Alger*; A.-J.-B. Parent-Duchâtelet, *De la prostitution dans la ville de Paris, considérée sous le rapport de l'hygiène publique, de la morale et de l'administration: Ouvrage appuyé de documens statistiques puisés dans les archives de la Préfecture de police* (Paris: J. B. Baillière, 1836).

59 The only recent work in which prostitution in colonial Algeria forms a part is Christelle Taraud, *La prostitution coloniale: Algérie, Tunisie, Maroc (1830–1962)* (Paris: Payot, 2003).

60 Sarah Ann Curtis, "Emilie de Vialar and the Religious Conquest of Algeria," *French Historical Studies* 29, no. 2 (2006): 261–92.

61 Stewart, *Lilias Trotter*; Miriam Huffman Rockness, *A Passion for the Impossible: The Life of Lilias Trotter* (Wheaton: Harold Shaw, 1999). The hagiographic literature on de Vialar is extensive. She founded the order Soeurs Saint-Joseph de l'Apparition and moved the order to Algiers in 1835, from whence she fanned out across the Levant. She was beatified in 1951.

62 Sarah Ann Curtis is working on a collective biography of Emilie de Vialar and two other French women missionaries, but neither her study nor her article "Emilie de Vialar and the Religious Conquest of Algeria" are exclusively about Algeria, let alone Algiers.

63 Besides Brac de la Perrière, *Derrière les héros*, see, e.g., Charles Maurin, "Le travail de la femme dans l'évolution de la Casbah d'Alger," *Terres d'Afrique* 3 (1946): 25; Farouk Benatia, *Le travail féminin en Algérie, département d'Alger* (Algiers: Société Nationale d'Édition et de Diffusion, 1970).

64 Jean-Honorat Delporte, *Principes de l'idiome Arabe en usage à Alger* (Algiers: J. B. Philippe, 1836).

65 Marcel S. R. Cohen, *Le parler arabe des Juifs d'Alger* (Paris: H. Campion, 1912); [Auguste Robinet] Musette, *Cagayous, ses meilleures histoires,* 4th ed., introduction, notes, and glossary by Gabriel Audiso (Paris: Gallimard, 1931). For a postcolonial analysis of Cagayous, see David Prochaska, "History as Literature, Literature as History: Cagayous of Algiers," *American Historical Review* 101, no. 3 (June 1996): 671–711.

66 Dalila Morsly and Ali Silem, *Alger plurilingue* (Paris: Centre d'Études et de Recherches en Planification Linguistique, 1996).

67 Aziza Boucherit, *L'Arabe parlé à Alger: Aspects sociolinguistiques et énonciatifs* (Paris and Louvain: Éditions Peeters, 2002). See also Habiba Deming, "Language and Politics: A New Revisionism," in *Algeria and France, 1800–2000: Identity, Memory, Nostalgia,* ed. Patricia M. E. Lorcin (Syracuse, NY: Syracuse University Press, 2006), 181–98.

68 Anthony Verrier, *Assassination in Algiers: Churchill, Roosevelt, de Gaulle, and the Murder of Admiral Darlan* (London: Macmillan, 1990).

69 Jean Pierre-Bloch, *Alger, capitale de la France en guerre: 1942–1944,* preface by Jacques Chaban-Delmas (Paris: Éditions Universal, 1989).

70 Pierre-Bloch served as undersecretary of the interior on the French Committee of National Liberation.

71 Marcel Aboulker, *Alger et ses complots* (Paris: Les Documents Nuit et Jour, 1945).

72 Ibid., 238–61.

73 Jean-Jacques Jordi and Guy Pervillé, eds., *Alger, 1940–1962: Une ville en guerres* (Paris: Éditions Autrement, 1999).

74 Matthew Connelly, *A Diplomatic Revolution: Algeria's Fight for Independence and the Origins of the Post–Cold War Era* (Oxford: Oxford University Press, 2003); Irwin W. Wall, *France, the United States, and the Algerian War* (Berkeley and Los Angeles: University of California Press, 2001).

75 Louisette Ighilahriz, *Algérienne: Récit recueilli par Anne Nivat* (Paris: Fayard/Calmann-Lévy, 2001) (Ighilahriz was one of a number of women tortured during the war; others include Djamila Boupacha and Djamila Bouhired); Paul Aussaresses, *The Battle for the Casbah: Terrorism and Counter-terrorism, 1955–1957* (New York: Enigma Books,

2002) (this is a translation of *Services speciaux, Algérie, 1955–57* [Paris: Perrin, 2001], in which Aussaresses justifies torture and admits to involvement in it himself).

76 Benyoucef Ben Khedda, *Alger, capitale de la résistance, 1956–1957* (Algiers: Houma, 2002).

77 Some early examples are Gabriel Conesa, *Bab-el-Oued: Notre paradis perdu* (Paris: R. Laffont, 1970); André Trives, *Bab-el-Oued, mon quartier, figé dans sa mort* (Paris: La Pensé Universelle, 1975); Roland Bacri, *Le beau temps perdu: Bab-el-Oued retrouvé* (Paris: J. Lanzmann and Seghers, 1978). More recently, see Alain Vircondelet, *Alger, Alger* (Martel: Éditions du Laquet, 1998).

78 See, e.g., Teddy Alzieu, *Alger autrefois* (Saint-Cyr-sur-Loire: Alan Sutton, 2003).

79 See especially Michel Levallois, "Marseille et l'Algérie franco-musulmane du saint-simonien Ismaÿl Urban"; Michèle Baussant, "Le ressentiment: Les pieds-noirs ou le silence de la double rupture"; Jean-Jacques Jordi, "Les harkis ou briser la chape de silence du refus de mémoire"; Abderhamanne Moussaoui, "Un pays enfanté par la guerre"; all in *Parlez-moi d'Alger: Marseille-Alger au miroir des mémoires; ouvrage publié à l'occasion de l'exposition du 7 novembre 2003 au 15 mars 2004* (Paris: Éditions de la Réunion des Musées Nationaux, 2003).

80 The works of Assia Djebar and Leila Sebbar are too well known to be introduced here. The number of French writers of North African descent increases each year. Djebar recently became the first North African to be elected to the Académie Française. It was a tribute not only to her work but also to the great influence that writers of Maghrebi origin have had on Francophone literature. Furthermore, intermarriage between North African French of different national origin (Tunisia, Morocco, or Algeria) produced a hybridity of an even more complex sort. Kebir Ammi is of Algerian-Moroccan origin and writes about this triple hybridity in *Alger la blanche: Les terres contraries* (Carnières-Morianweiz, Belgium: Lansman, 2003).

81 Nina Hayat, *La nuit tombe sur Alger la blanche: Chronique d'une Algérienne* (Paris: Éditions Tirésias, 1995). See also Khalida Messaoudi's *Une Algérienne debout* (Paris: Flammarion, 1995).

82 Hocine Mezali, *Alger: Trente-deux siècles d'histoire* (Algiers: Synergie/ENAG, 2000).

SELECTED BIBLIOGRAPHY

Abdou, B. "Alger au cinéma, de *Pépé le Moko* à *Bab-el-Oued City*." *La pensée de Midi*, no. 4 (Spring 2001): 90–97.

Aboulker, Marcel. *Alger et ses complots*. Paris: Les Documents Nuit et Jour, 1945.

Actes du XIVe Congrès international des orientalistes, Alger, 1905. Paris: E. Leroux, 1906.

Adès, Marie-Claire. *Photographes en Algérie au XIXe siècle*. Paris: Musée Galerie de la Seita, 1999.

Ageron, Charles-Robert, ed. *L'Algérie des Français*. Paris: Seuil, 1993.

———. *Les Algériens musulmans et la France (1871–1919)*. 2 vols. Paris: Presses Universitaires de France, 1968.

———. *Modern Algeria: A History form 1830 to the Present*. 9th ed. Translated and edited by Michael Brett. London: Hurst, 1991.

———. "Le mouvement jeune algérien de 1900 à 1923." In *Études maghrébrines, mélanges Charles-André Julien*, 217–43. Paris: Presses Universitaires de France, 1965.

Alazard, Jean. *Catalogue des peintures et sculptures exposées dans les galleries du Musée National des Beaux-Arts d'Alger*. Paris: H. Laurens, 1936.

———. *Le Musée des Beaux-Arts d'Alger*. Paris: H. Laurens, 1930.

———. *L'Orient et la peinture française au XIXe siècle d'Eugène Delacroix à Auguste Renoir*. Paris: Plon, 1930.

———. "L'urbanisme à Alger." *Le monde colonial illustré*, no. 80 (April 1930): 93.

Allouache, Merzak, and Vincent Colonna, eds. *Algérie, 30 ans: Les enfants de l'indépendance*. Éditions Autrement, hors série, no. 60. Paris: Autrement, 1992.

Alloula, Malek. *Alger: Photographiée au XIXe siècle*. Paris: Marval, 2001.

Althabe, Gérard, and Jean-Louis Comolli. *Regards sur la ville*. Paris: Centre Georges Pompidou, 1994.

Alzieu, Teddy. *Alger autrefois*. Saint-Cyr-sur-Loire: Alan Sutton, 2003.

Ammi, Kebir. *Alger la blanche: Les terres contraries*. Carnières-Morianweiz, Belgium: Lansman, 2003.

Amrane, Djamila. *Les femmes algériennes dans la guerre*. Paris: Plon, 1991.

Anon. "Beaux Arts: Panorama d'Alger par Ch. Langlois." *La France nouvelle*, no. 2038 (20 March 1833).

Anon. "Panorama d'Alger." *L'artiste* 7, 1st series (1834): 150.

Anon. "Panorama d'Alger, par M. Langlois." *L'artiste* 5, 1st series (1833): 45.

Anon. "Peinture: Alger." *Journal des artistes* 2 (11 July 1830): 25–28.

Aranda, Emanuel d'. *Les captifs d'Alger*. Paris: Jean-Paul Rocher, 1997.

Armes, Roy. *Postcolonial Images: Studies in North African Film*. Bloomington: Indiana University Press, 2005.

Aussaresses, Paul. *The Battle for the Casbah: Terrorism and Counter-terrorism, 1955–1957*. New York: Enigma Books, 2002.

Bacri, Roland. *Le beau temps perdu: Bab-el-Oued retrouvé*. Paris: J. Lanzmann and Seghers, 1978.

Bahloul, Joëlle. *The Architecture of Memory*. Cambridge: Cambridge University Press, 1996.

Bapst, Germaine. *Essai sur l'histoire des panoramas et des dioramas*. Paris: G. Masson, 1891.

Barbier, Jules. "Des droits et obligations entre propriétaires d'héritages voisins." *Revue algérienne, tunisienne et marocaine de législation et jurisprudence* 16 (1900): 9–15, 17–23, 42–56, 93–104, 113–44; 17 (1901): 65–84, 89–108.

———. *Itinéraire historique et descriptif de l'Algérie*. Paris: Librarie Hachette, 1855.

Barioli, Marc. *La vie quotidienne des Français en Algérie, 1830–1914*. Paris: Hachette, 1967.

Barré, François. "Le vrai-faux passeport." In *Cités-cinés*, 9. Paris: La Villette/La Grande Halle, 1987.

Bavoux, Évariste. *Alger: Voyage politique et descriptif dans le nord de l'Afrique*. 2 vols. Paris: Chez Brockhaus et Avenarius, 1841.

Beaussier, Marcelin. *Dictionnaire pratique arabe-français contenant tous les mots employés dans l'arabe parlé en Algérie et en Tunisie*, 1887.

Benatia, Farouk. *Le travail féminin en Algérie, département d'Alger*. Algiers: Société Nationale d'Édition et de Diffusion, 1970.

Benchérif, Osman. *The British in Algiers, 1585–2000*. Algiers: RSM Communication, 2001.

Benhassine, Karima. "Vie associative en milieu colonial et nostalgie du terroir." In *Constantine, une ville, des héritages*, 95–111. Constantine: Media Plus, 2004.

Benjamin, Roger. *Orientalist Aesthetics: Art, Colonialism, and French North Africa, 1880–1930*. Berkeley and Los Angeles: University of California Press, 2003.

———. *Renoir and Algeria*. New Haven, CT: Yale University Press and Williamstown, MA: Sterling and Francine Clark Art Institute, 2003.

Ben Khedda, Benyoucef. *Alger, capitale de la résistance, 1956–1957*. Algiers: Houma, 2002.

Bensadek, M. *La prise d'Alger: Récit d'un officier français, 1830*. Algiers: Édition At-Tabyin/Al-Jahidhiya, 2000.

Berque, Jacques. *Structures sociales du Haut-Atlas*. 2d ed. Paris: Presses Universitaires de France, 1978.

Berthezène, Général. *18 mois à Alger*. Montpellier: Auguste Ricard, 1834.

Bertrand, Louis. *Nuits d'Alger*. Paris: Flammarion, 1930.

Bidal-Bué, Marion. *Alger et ses peintres, 1830–1960*. Paris: Paris-Méditerranée, 2000.

Bignardi, Irene. "The Making of the Battle of Algiers." *Cineaste* 25, no. 2 (Spring 2000): 14–22.

Blonnel, Capitaine. "Comment finit Ali La Pointe." *Historia* 233 (January 1958): 1201–7.

Bonillo, Jean-Lucien, ed. *Fernand Pouillon, architecte méditerranéen*. Marseille: Éditions Imbernon, 2001.

Bordas, Jeannine. *Le peuplement algérien: Essai démographique*. Oran: Fonque, 1958.

Boucherit, Aziza. *L'Arabe parlé à Alger: Aspects sociolinguistiques et énonciatifs*. Paris and Louvain: Éditions Peeters, 2002.

Boulanger, Pierre. *Le cinema colonial: De "L'Atlantide" à "Lawrence d'Arabie."* Paris: Seghers, 1975.

Bourdieu, Pierre. *The Algerians*. Translated by Alan C. M. Ross. Boston: Beacon Press, 1962.

Bourguet, M.-N., B. Lepetit, D. Nordman, and M. Sinarellis. *L'invention de la Méditerranée: Egypte, Morée, Algérie*. Paris: Éditions de l'École des Hautes Études en Sciences Sociales, 1998.

Bourseul, E.-Ch. *Biographie du colonel Langlois*. Paris: P. Dupont, 1874.

Brac de la Perrière, Caroline. *Derrière les héros: Les employées de maison musulmanes en service chez les Européens à Alger pendant la guerre d'Algérie, 1954–1962*. Paris: L'Harmattan, 1987.

Brahmi, Denise. «Le cinéma colonial revisité.» *Cinémas du Maghreb, CinémAction* 111 (2004): 36–48.

Bridgman, Frederick Arthur. *Winters in Algeria*. New York: Harper and Brothers, 1890.

British Consul's Logbook. Public Record Office, London, Foreign Office series, Algeria, 113/5, 1829–30.

British Valour Displayed in the Cause of Humanity: Being a Description of Messrs. Marshall's Grand Marine Peristrepic Panorama of the Bombardment of Algiers. Manchester: M. Wilson, 1822.

Bronner, André. "Comment garder le souvenir du vieil Alger." *Le monde colonial illustré*, no. 189 (March 1939): 64.

Broughton, Elizabeth. *Six Years Residence in Algiers*. London: Saunders and Otley, 1838.

Bruller, Isabelle. *Algérie romantique des officiers de l'armée française, 1830–37*. Paris: Service Historique de l'Armée de Terre, 1994.

Brunschvig, R. "Urbanisme médiéval et droit musulman." *Revue des études islamiques*, 1947, 127–55.

C. A. "Photography in Algeria." *Photographic News*, October 1858, 53–54.

Calmes, Alain. *Le roman colonial en Algérie avant 1914*. Paris: L'Harmattan, 1984.

Camus, Albert. *The First Man*. Translated by David Hapgood. New York: Knopf, 1995.

———. *Le premier homme*. Paris: Gallimard, 1994.

Cardon, Émile. Review of *Le gouvernement de l'Algérie de 1852 à 1858*, by F. Ribourt. *Revue du monde colonial* 1 (1859): 50–55.

Cardon, Émile, and A. Noirot. "Visite à l'Exposition Permanente de l'Algérie et des Colonies." *Revue du monde coloniale* 3 (1860): 60–67.

Carette, Capitaine [Ernest]. *Algérie*. In *L'univers pittoresque: Histoire et description de tous les peuples, de leurs religions, moeurs, coutumes, industrie, &*. Paris: Firmin Didot, 1850.

Carlier, Omar, and Fanny Colonna, eds. *Lettrés intellectuels et militants en Algérie, 1880–1950*. Algiers: Office des Publications Universitaires, 1988.

Cavasino, Agnès. *Emilie de Vialar, fondatrice*. Dourgne: L'Abbaye Sainte-Scholastique, 1987.

Celarié, Henriette. *La prise d'Alger*. Paris: Hachette, 1929.

Çelik, Zeynep. "Colonial/Postcolonial Intersections: *Lieux de mémoire* in Algiers." *Third Text* 49 (January 2000): 63–72.

———. "Framing the Colony: Houses of Algeria Photographed." *Art History* 27, no. 4 (September 2004): 616–26.

———. "Learning from the Bidonville: CIAM Looks at Algiers." *Harvard Design Magazine*, Spring 2003, 69–74.

———. *Urban Forms and Colonial Confrontations: Algiers under French Rule*. Berkeley and Los Angeles: University of California Press, 1997.

Chabaud-Arnault. "Attaque des batteries algériennes par Lord Exmouth en 1816." *Revue africaine* 19 (1875): 194–202.

Chaïr, Omar. "Ali La Pointe, un terroriste a l'état pur." *Historia* 208 (1971): 468–69.

Chambre des Députés. "Séance du Mardi 29 avril." *Moniteur universel*, no. 120, supplement (5 April 1834): 1074.

Cherry, Deborah. "Earth into World, Land into Landscape: The Worlding of Algeria in Nineteenth-Century British Feminism." In *Orientalism's Interlocutors: Painting, Architecture, Photography*, edited by Jill Beaulieu and Mary Roberts, 103–30. Durham, NC: Duke University Press, 2002.

Chevallier, Jacques. *Nous algériens*. Paris: Calmann-Levy, 1958.

Christian, Pierre. *L'Afrique française, l'empire de Maroc, et les déserts du Sahara*. Paris: A. Barbier, 1846.

Clancy-Smith, Julia. "The Colonial Gaze: Sex and Gender in the Discourses of French

North Africa." In *Franco-Arab Encounters*, edited by L. Carl Brown and Matthew Gordon, 201–28. Beirut: American University of Beirut Press, 1996.

———. "Europe and Its Social Marginals in 19th-Century Mediterranean North Africa." In *Outside In: On the Margins of the Modern Middle East*, edited by Eugene Rogan, 149–82. London: I. B. Tauris, 2002.

———. "Gender in the City: The Medina of Tunis, 1850–1881." In *Africa's Urban Past*, edited by David Anderson and Richard Rathbone, 189–204. Oxford: Currey, 2000.

———. *Rebel and Saint: Muslim Notables, Populist Protest, Colonial Encounters (Algeria and Tunisia, 1800–1904)*. Berkeley and Los Angeles: University of California Press, 1994.

Cohen, Jean-Louis, Nabila Oulebsir, and Youcef Kanoun, eds. *Alger: Paysage urbain et architectures, 1800–2000*. Paris: Éditions de l'Imprimeur, 2003.

Cohen, Marcel S. R. *Le parler arabe des Juifs d'Alger*. Paris: H. Campion, 1912.

Comité du Vieil Alger. *Feuillets d'El-Djezaïr*. Reprint, Blida: Éditions du Tel, 2003.

Conesa, Gabriel. *Bab-el-Oued: Notre paradis perdu*. Paris: R. Laffont, 1970.

Connelly, Matthew. *A Diplomatic Revolution: Algeria's Fight for Independence and the Origins of the Post–Cold War Era*. Oxford: Oxford University Press, 2003.

Côte, Marc. *L'Algérie, ou l'espace retourné*. Paris: Éditions Flammarion, 1992.

Crespo, Gérard. *Les Italiens en Algérie, 1830–1960: Histoire et sociologie d'une migration*. Calvisson: Éditions Jacques Gandini, 1994.

Crespo, Gérard, and Jean-Jacques Jordi. *L'immigration espagnole dans l'Algérois de 1830 à 1914*. Versailles: Éditions de l'Atlanthrope, 1991.

Crowdus, Gary. "Terrorism and Torture in *The Battle of Algiers*: An Interview with Yacef Saadi." *Cineaste* 29, no. 3 (Summer 2004): 30–37.

Curtis, Sarah Ann. "Emilie de Vialar and the Religious Conquest of Algeria." *French Historical Studies* 29, no. 2 (2006): 261–92.

Dalles, Edouard. *Alger, Bou-Farik, Blidah et leurs environs*. Algiers: Librairie Adolphe Jourdan, 1888.

Davis, Robert C. *Christian Slaves, Muslim Masters: White Slavery in the Mediterranean, the Barbary Coast and Italy, 1500–1800*. London: Palgrave, 2006.

Déchaud, E. *La marine à la prise d'Alger*. Paris: Libr. Militaire R. Chapelot, 1906.

Déjeux, Jean. *La littérature Algérienne contemporaine*. Paris: Presses Universitaires de France, 1975.

———. *La littérature féminine de langue française au Maghreb*. Paris: Karthala, 1994.

Delporte, Jean-Honorat. *Principes de l'idiome Arabe en usage à Alger*. Algiers: J. B. Philippe, 1836.

Deluz, Jean-Jacques. *L'urbanisme et l'architecture d'Alger*. Liège: Pierre Mardaga; Algiers: Office des Publications Universitaires, 1988.

Desparmet, Joseph. "Naissance d'une histoire 'nationale' de l'Algérie." *Bulletin du Comité de l'Afrique Française*, July 1933, 387–92.

Desprez, Charles. *Alger naguère et maintenant*. Algiers: F. Maréchal, 1868.

———. *Extraits de L'akhbar*. Algiers: Imprimerie Typographique de L'akhbar, 1867.

———. *L'hiver à Alger*. Paris: Éditions d'Essai, 1861.

———. "La photographie à Alger." In *Miscellanées algériennes*. Algiers: Jules Breucq, 1864/65. (Originally published in *L'akhbar*, 7 May 1865.)

Direche-Slimani, Karima. *Chrétiens de Kabylie, 1873–1954: Une action missionaire dans l'Algérie coloniale*. Paris: Éditions Bouchène, 2004.

Donato, Marc. *L'émigration des Maltais en Algérie au XIXème siècle*. Montpellier: Collection Africa Nostra, 1985.

Dris, Nassima. *La ville mouvementée: Espace public, centralité, mémoire urbaine à Alger*. Paris: L'Harmattan, 2002.

Dubuisson, Serge, and Jean-Charles Humbert. "Jean Geiser, photographe-editeur: Alger, 1848–1923, chronique d'une famille." In *L'image dans le monde arabe*, 275–84. Paris: Éditions du Centre National de la Recherche Scientifique, 1995.

Duchesne, Édouard-Adolphe. *De la prostitution dans la ville d'Alger depuis la conquête*. Paris: J. B. Baillière, 1853.

Dwyer, Philip G. *Napoleon: The Path to Power, 1769–1799*. London: Bloomsbury, 2006.

Emerit, Marcel. *Une cause de l'expédition d'Alger, le trésor de la Casbah*. Paris: Imprimerie Nationale, 1955.

Esquer, Gabriel. *Les commencements d'un empire: La prise d'Alger, 1830*. 1923; Paris: Larose, 1929.

———. *Iconographie historique de l'Algérie depuis le XVIe siècle jusqu'à 1871*. Paris: Plon, 1929.

Exposition universelle de 1867 à Paris: Rapports du jury international publiés sous la direction de Michel Chevalier. Paris: P. Dupont, 1868.

F. P. "Peinture: Panorama d'Alger, par M. Ch. Langlois." *Moniteur universel*, no. 59 (28 February 1833), 3d supplement, 557.

Fanon, Franz. *The Wretched of the Earth*. Translated by Constance Farrington. New York: Grove Press, 1968.

Faure, Jean-Pierre. *Alger capitale*. Paris: Société Française d'Éditions Littéraires et Techniques, 1936.

Favre, Lucienne. *Tout l'inconnu de la Casbah d'Alger*. Algiers: Baconnier Frères, 1933.

Feydeau, Ernest. *Alger, étude*. Paris: Michel Levy, 1862.

Fioupou, M. *La prise d'Alger*. Toulon: A. Bordato, 1907.

Fisquet, Honoré-Jean-Pierre. *Histoire de l'Algérie depuis les temps anciens jusqu'à nos jours*. Paris: A la Direction, 1842.

Flamand, Thierry. "Adapter la ville à l'écran." In *Visions urbains: Villes d'Europe à l'écran*, 8–13. Paris: Centre Georges Pompidou, 1994.

Fletcher, Yaël Simpson. "Irresistible Seductions: Gendered Representations of Colonial Algeria around 1930." In *Domesticating the Empire: Race, Gender, and Family Life in French and Dutch Colonialism, 1830–1962*, edited by Julia Clancy-Smith and Frances Gouda, 193–210. Charlottesville: University Press of Virginia, 1998.

Fredet, Estelle. "L'Algérie photographiée (1856–57) de Félix-Jacques-Antoine Moulin, et la politique algérienne de l'Empire." In *Mémoire de maitrise*. N.p.: Université de Provence, 1993–94.

Garcés, Maria Antonia. *Cervantes in Algiers: A Captive's Tale*. Nashville, TN: Vanderbilt University Press, 2005.

Gautier, Théophile. *Voyage pittoresque en Algérie*. Edited by Madeleine Cottin. Geneva: Droz, 1973.

Genty de Bussy, Pierre. *De l'établissement des Français dans la Régence d'Alger*. Paris: Firmin Didot, 1835.

Ghaisne Bourmont, Louis-Auguste-Victor de. *Rapport officiel de la prise d'Algér*. Paris: J. Lebreton, 1830.

Golvin, Lucien. *Palais et demeures d'Alger à la période ottomane*. Aix-en-Provence: Édisud, 1988.

Gomot, F. *Guide du voyageur en Algérie*. Paris: J. DuMaine, 1844.

Gosnell, Jonathan K. *The Politics of Frenchness in Colonial Algeria, 1930–1954*. Rochester, NY: University of Rochester Press, 2002.

Grammont, Henri-Delmas de. *Un académicien captif à Alger*. Algiers: A. Jourdan, 1883.

———. *Études algériennes: La course, l'esclavage et la rédemption à Alger*. Paris: [no publisher], 1885.

———. *Histoire d'Alger sous la domination Turque, 1515–1830*. Condé-sur-Noireau: Éditions Bouchène, 2001.

———. *Un pacha d'Alger précurseur de M. de Lesseps*. Algiers: A. Jourdan, 1886.

Grangaud, Isabelle. "Alger, au miroir de ses sources." In *Actes du colloque international du 4 au 6 mai 2002 à l'École Polytechnique d'Architecture et d'Urbanisme*. Algiers: Éditions Dalimen, 2004.

———. "Autour des villes de la Régence d'Alger, le cas de Constantine." *Antiquités africaines* 40–41 (2004–5): 289–99.

———. *La ville imprenable: Une historie sociale de Constantine au 18e siècle*. Paris: Éditions de l'École des Hautes Études en Sciences Sociales, 2002.

Haëdo, Diego de. *Topographie et histoire générale d'Alger*. Edited by Dr. Monnereau and Al Berbrugger. Translated by Jocelyne Dakhlia. Paris: Éditions Bouchène, 1998.

Hamdani, Amar. *La vérité sur l'expédition d'Alger*. Paris: Balland, 1985.

Hamdan Khûdja. *Le miroir, aperçu historique et statistique sur la Régence d'Alger*, edited by S. Djeghloul. Paris: Sindbad, 1985.

Hartevelt, D. *Herinneringen uit Algiers*. Arnheim: Thieme, 1865.

Hayat, Nina. *La nuit tombe sur Alger la blanche: Chronique d'une Algérienne*. Paris: Éditions Tirésias, 1995.

Hebey, Pierre. *Alger, 1898: La grande vague antijuive*. Paris: Nil Éditions, 1996.

Heffernan, Michael. "French Colonial Migration." In *The Cambridge Survey of World Migration*, edited by Robin Cohen, 33–38. Cambridge: Cambridge University Press, 1995.

Heggoy, Alf Andrew. *The French Conquest of Algiers, 1830: An Algerian Oral Tradition.* Athens: Ohio University Center for International Studies, Africa Studies Program, 1986.

Hennebelle, Guy. *Le cinéma colonial de "L'Atlantide" à "Lawrence d'Arabie."* Paris: Seghers, 1975.

Henry, Jean-Robert. Introduction to *French and Algerian Identities from Colonial Times to the Present: A Century of Interaction.* Edited by Alec G. Hargreaves and Michael J. Heffernan, 1–18. Lewiston, NY: Edwin Mellen Press, 1993.

———. "La norme et l'imaginaire: Construction de l'altérité juridique en droit colonial algérien." *Procès* 18 (1987–88): 13–27.

Histoire populaire contemporaine de la France. Paris: A. Lahure, 1864.

Hutchinson, John, and Anthony D. Smith, eds. *Nationalism.* Oxford: Oxford University Press, 1994.

Icheboudene, Larbi. "De la Houma à la cité: Une évolution historique de l'espace social algérois." *Revue algérienne des sciences juridiques, économiques et politiques* 40 (2002): 59–74.

Idrissi Janati, M'hammed. "Les images identitaires à Fès: Divisions de la société, divisions de la ville." In *Les divisions de la ville,* edited by C. Topalov, 347–72. Paris: UNESCO and Maison des Sciences de l'Homme, 2002.

Ighilahriz, Louisette. *Algérienne: Récit recueilli par Anne Nivat.* Paris: Fayard/Calmann-Lévy, 2001.

Ilbert, Robert. "La ville islamique: Réalité et abstraction." *Les cahiers de la recherche architecturale* 10/11 (1982): 6–14.

Jacobson, Ken. *Odalisques and Arabesques: Orientalist Photography, 1839–1925.* London: Quaritch, 2007.

Jal, Augustin. *Panorama d'Alger, peint par M. Charles Langlois, Chef de Bataillon au corps royal d'état major, officier de la Légion-d'Honneur auteur du panorama de Navarin.* Paris: [no publisher], 1833.

Jennings, James. *Description of Lord Exmouth's Attack upon Algiers Painted by Henry Aston Barker: Now Exhibiting in His Panorama.* London: Jas. Adlard and Sons, 1818.

Jordi, Jean-Jacques, and Guy Pervillé, eds. *Alger, 1940–1962: Une ville en guerres.* Paris: Éditions Autrement, 1999.

Julien, Charles-André. *Histoire de l'Algérie contemporaine.* Vol. 1, *La conquête et les débuts de la colonisation (1827–1871).* 2d ed. Paris: Presses Universitaires de France, 1979.

Julien, G. "L'Algérie photographiée." *L'illustration* 31 (1858): 200.

Jungmann, R. *Costumes, moeurs et usages des Algériens.* Strasbourg: J. Bernard, 1837.

Kaddache, Mahfoud. *L'Algérie des Algériens: De la préhistoire à 1954.* Paris: Éditions Paris-Méditerranée, 2003.

———. *La vie politique à Alger de 1919 à 1939.* Algiers: Société Nationale d'Édition et de Diffusion, 1970.

Khalil, Andrea. "The Myth of Masculinity in the Films of Merzak Allouache." *Journal of North African Studies* 12, no. 3 (September 2007): 329–45.

Klein, Henri. *Feuillets d'El-Djezaïr*. Algiers: L. Chaix [1937].

Landau, Paul S. "Empires of the Visual: Photography and Colonial Administration in Africa." In *Images and Empires: Visuality in Colonial and Post-colonial Africa*, edited by Paul S. Landau and Deborah Kaspin, 141–71. Berkeley and Los Angeles: University of California Press, 2002.

Laugier de Tassy. *Histoire du royaume d'Alger*. 2d ed. Paris: Chez Piltan, 1830.

Lefebvre, Henri. *The Production of Space*. Translated by Donald Nicholson-Smith. Oxford, UK, and Cambridge, MA: Blackwell Publishers, 1991.

Leprun, Sylviane. *Le théâtre des colonies*. Paris: L'Harmattan, 1986.

Lerebours, Noël-Marie-Paymal. *Excursions Daguerriennes*. Paris: Rittner et Goupil, 1841.

Leroy-Terquem, Magali, et al. *Alger, la Casbah et Paul Guion*. Mediane: Éditions Publisud, 2005.

Lesbet, Djaffar. *La Casbah d'Alger: Gestion urbain et vide sociale*. Algiers: Publications Universitaires, 1985.

Lespès, René. *Alger: Étude du géographie et d'histoire urbaines*. Paris: Félix Alcan, 1930.

Lessore, E., and W. Wyld. *Voyage pittoresque dans la Régence d'Alger exécuté en 1833 et lithographié par E. Lessore et W. Wyld*. Paris: C. Motte, 1835.

Letourneau, Roger. *Fès avant le protectorat*. Casablanca: Société Marocaine de Librairie et d'Édition; Paris: Firmin Didot, 1949.

———. *Les villes musulmanes de l'Afrique du Nord*. Algiers: La Maison des Livres, 1957.

Lorcin, Patricia M. E., ed. *Algeria and France, 1800–2000: Identity, Memory, Nostalgia*. Syracuse, NY: Syracuse University Press, 2006.

———. *Imperial Identities: Stereotyping, Prejudice and Race in Colonial Algeria*. London: J. B. Tauris, 1995.

———. "Rome and France in Africa: Recovering Algeria's Latin Past." *French Historical Studies* 25, no. 2 (2002): 295–329.

Lorent, Jakob August. *Egypten, Alhambra, Tlemsen, Algier: Reisebilder aus den Anfängen der Photographie*. Compiled by Wulf Schirmer, Werner Schnuchel, and Franz Waller. Mainz: P. von Zabern, c. 1985.

Maire, Joseph. *Souvenirs d'Alger*. Paris: Challamel, 1884.

Marçais, George. *L'exposition d'art musulman d'Alger*. Paris: Thorin, 1906.

Marchand, Henri. *La Musulmane algérienne*. Algiers: Éditions Subervie, 1960.

Margerie, Laure de, et al. *Charles Cordier, 1827–1905: L'autre et l'ailleurs*. Paris: La Martinière, 2004.

Matterer, Amable-Thiébault. *Journal de la prise d'Alger par le Capitaine de frégate "Matterer," 1830*. Paris: Éditions de Paris, 1960.

McDougall, James. *History and the Culture of Nationalism in Algeria*. Cambridge: Cambridge University Press, 2006.

———. "The Shabiba Islamiyya of Algiers: Education, Authority, and Colonial Control, 1921–1957." *Comparative Studies of South Asia, Africa, and the Middle East* 24, no. 1 (2004): 149–57.

Megherbi, Abdelghani. *Les Algériens au miroir du cinéma colonial*. Paris: Société Nationale d'Édition et de Diffusion, 1982.

Melon, Paul. *Problèmes algériens et tunisiens: Ce que disent les chiffres*. Paris: Challamel, 1903.

Ménerville, M. P. De. *Dictionnaire de la législation algérienne: Code annoté et manuel raisonné des lois, ordonnances, décrets, décisions et arrêtés publiés au bulletin officiel des actes du gouvernement suivi d'une table alphabétique des matières et d'une table chronologique des lois, décrets, etc. . . . 1. 1830–1860*. Paris, 1866.

Merad, Ali. *Le réformisme musulman en Algérie de 1925 à 1940: Essai d'histoire religieuse et sociale*. Paris: Mouton, 1967.

Merle, Jean-Toussaint. *La prise d'Alger, racontée par un témoin*. Paris: Jonquières, 1930.

Messaoudi, Khalida. *Une Algérienne debout*. Paris: Flammarion, 1995.

Meynier, Gilbert, and Ahmed Koulaksis. *L'émir Khaled, premier za'im? Identité algérienne et colonialisme français*. Paris: L'Harmattan, 1987.

Mezali, Hocine. *Alger: Trente-deux siècles d'histoire*. Algiers: Synergie/ENAG, 2000.

Miller, Peter Benson. "By the Sword and the Plow: Théodore Chassériau's Cour des Comptes Murals and Algeria." *Art Bulletin* 86, no. 4 (December 2004): 690–718.

Ministère de l'Instruction Publique. "Extrait du registre des delibérations du conseil royal de l'instruction publique." *Moniteur universel*, no. 120 (30 April 1834).

Missoum, Sakina. *Alger à l'époque ottomane: La médina et la maison traditionnelle*. Aix-en-Provence: Édisud, 2003.

Moch, Leslie Page. *Moving Europeans: Migration in Western Europe since 1650*. 2d ed. Bloomington: Indiana University Press, 2003.

Molbert, M. "L'urbanisme et son application à Alger." *Bulletin municipal officiel de la ville d'Alger*, May 1951, n.p.

Mondenard, Anne de. "L'Algérie, terre oubliée des photographes en Orient." In *Delacroix à Renoir: L'Algérie des peintres*, 109–14. Paris: Hazan, 2003.

Montherlant, H. *Il y a encore des paradis (1928–1931)*. Algiers: Soubiron, 1935.

Morell, John Reynell. *Algeria: The Topography and History, Political, Social, and Natural of French Africa*. London, 1854. New ed., London: Darf, 1984.

Morgan, J. *A Complete History of Algiers, to Which Is Prefixed an Epitome of the General History of Barbary from the Earliest Times, Interspersed with Many Curious Passages and Remarks Not Touched on by Any Writer Whatever*. New York: Negro Universities Press, 1970.

Morin, Edgar. *Le cinéma ou l'homme imaginaire*. Paris: Seuil, 1962.

Morsly, Dalila, and Ali Silem. *Alger plurilingue*. Paris: Centre d'Études et de Recherches en Planification Linguistique, 1996.

Moulin. "La photographie en Algérie." *Lumière* 6, no. 12 (22 March 1856): 46.

Münsterberg, Hugo. *The Film, a Psychological Study: The Silent Photoplay in 1916*. New York: Dover Publications, 1970.

Musette, [Auguste Robinet]. *Cagayous, ses meilleures histoires*. 4th ed. Introduction, notes, and glossary by Gabriel Audiso. Paris: Gallimard, 1931.

Nejmeddine, H. "La rue dans la ville de l'occident musulman médiéval d'après les sources juridiques malikites." *Arabica* 50, no. 3 (2003): 273–305.

Niney, François. *Visions urbaines: Villes d'Europe à l'écran*. Paris: Centre Georges Pompidou, 1994.

Nora, Pierre. *Les Français d'Algérie*. Paris: René Julliard, 1961.

Oms, Marcel. "L'imaginaire coloniale au cinéma." In *Images et colonies: Regards sur l'Afrique; Actes du colloque 22 janvier 1993 à la Bibliothèque Nationale à Paris*, 103–7. Paris: Syros/ACHAC, 1993.

Otth, Adolphe. *Esquisses africaines dessinées pendant un voyage à Alger et lithographiées par Adolphe Otth*. Berne: J. F. Wagner, 1839.

Oulebsir, Nabila. *Les usages du patrimoine: Monuments, musées et politique colonial en Algérie, 1830–1930*. Paris: Éditions de la Maison des Sciences de l'Homme, 2004.

Paër, Ferdinando. *La prise d'Alger*. Paris: Pacini, 1830.

Panati, Filoppo. *Narrative of a Residence in Algiers*. Translated by Edward Blanquière. London: Henry Colburn, 1818.

Panzac, Daniel. *Barbary Corsairs: The End of a Legend, 1800–1820*. Translated by Victoria Hobson and John E. Hawkes. Leiden and Boston: Brill, 2005.

Parent-Duchâtelet, A.-J.-B. *De la prostitution dans la ville de Paris, considérée sous le rapport de l'hygiène publique, de la morale et de l'administration: Ouvrage appuyé de documens statistiques puisés dans les archives de la Préfecture de police*. Paris: J. B. Baillière, 1836.

Parlez-moi d'Alger: Marseille-Alger au miroir des mémoires; ouvrage publié à l'occasion de l'exposition du 7 novembre 2003 au 15 mars 2004. Paris: Éditions de la Réunion des Musées Nationaux, 2003.

Payne, John Howard, and Sir Henry Bishop. *The Fall of Algiers*. London: J. Cumberland, 1925.

Péan, Pierre. *Main basse sur Alger: Enquête sur un pillage, juillet 1830*. Paris: Plon, 2004.

Les peintres de l'Orient au XIXème siècle: Expositions artistiques du centenaire de l'Algérie. Algiers: Musée des Beaux-Arts d'Alger, 1930.

Pélissier, Aimable-Jean-Jacques, duc de Malakoff. *Mémoire sur les opérations de l'armée française sur la côte d'Afrique depuis le 14 juin, jour du débarquement jusqu'à la prise d'Alger, le 5 juillet 1830*. Algiers: Typographie Duclaux, 1863.

Perkins, Roger, and Captain K. J. Douglas-Morris. *Gunfire in Barbary: Admiral Exmouth's Battle with the Corsairs of Algiers in 1816; The Story of the Suppression of White Christian Slavery*. Havant: Kenneth Mason, 1982.

Perrot, A. M. *Alger: Esquisse topographique et historique du royaume et de la ville*. Paris: Librairie Ladvocat, 1830.

———. *Alger: Topographie, population, forces militaires de terre et de mer, acclimatement, et ressources que le pas peut offrir à l'armée d'expédition par un français qui a résidé à Alger.* Marseille: Typographie de Feissat aîne et Demonchy, 1830.

Petit, Marie-Paule. *L'oeuvre algérois de Jean-Charles Langlois.* 3 vols. Thèse de troisième cycle en esthéthique. Université de Paris I, n.d. [c. 1983].

Pichon, Louis-André. *Alger sous la domination française; son état présent et son avenir.* Paris: Théophile Barrois et Benjamin Duprat, 1833.

Pierre-Bloch, Jean. *Alger, capitale de la France en guerre: 1942-1944.* Paris: Éditions Universal, 1989.

Playfair, Robert L. *The Scourge of Christendom: Annals of British Relations with Algiers prior to the Conquest.* London: Smith and Elder, 1884.

Pontecorvo, Gillo. *The Battle of Algiers.* New York: Scribners, 1973.

Porterfield, Todd B. *The Allure of Empire: Art in the Service of French Imperialism, 1798-1836.* Princeton, NJ: Princeton University Press, 1998.

Prochaska, David. "L'Algérie imaginaire: Jalons pour une histoire de l'iconographie coloniale." *Gradhiva* 7 (Winter 1989): 29-38.

———. "History as Literature, Literature as History: Cagayous of Algiers." *American Historical Review* 101, no. 3 (June 1996): 671-711.

———. *Making Algeria French: Colonialism in Bône, 1870-1920.* Cambridge: Cambridge University Press, 1990.

Rathbone, Richard, and David M. Anderson, eds. *Africa's Urban Past.* Oxford: Currey, 2000.

Raymond, André. "Le centre d'Alger en 1830." *Revue de l'Occident musulman et de la Méditerranée* 31, no. 1 (1981): 73-84.

———. *Grandes villes arabes à l'époque ottomane.* Paris: Sindbad, 1985.

Rockness, Miriam Huffman. *A Passion for the Impossible: The Life of Lilias Trotter.* Wheaton: Harold Shaw, 1999.

Rotalier, C. de. *Histoire d'Alger et de la piraterie des Turcs dans la Méditerranée.* 2 vols. Paris: Paulin, 1841.

Rouquerol, Gabriel. *Expédition de 1830 et prise d'Alger par les français: Organisation et rôle de l'artillerie du corps expéditionnaire.* [No publisher], 1894.

Rozet, Claude-Antoine. *Algérie.* Paris: Firmin Didot, 1850.

———. *Voyage dans la Régence d'Alger.* 3 vols. plus atlas. Paris: Arthus Bertrand, 1833.

Salle, Eusèbe de. "Le panorama d'Alger." *Revue de Paris* 49 (1833): 173-81.

Seguin, L. G. *Walks in Algiers.* London: Daldy Isbister, 1878.

Semmoud, Nora. *Les stratégies d'appropriation de l'espace à Alger.* Paris: L'Harmattan, 2001.

Serval, Pierre. *La ténébreuse histoire de la prise d'Alger.* Paris: Table Ronde, 1980.

Sessions, Jennifer Elson. "Making Colonial France: Culture, National Identity, and the Colonization of Algeria, 1830-1851." PhD diss., University of Pennsylvania, 2005.

Sgroï-Dufresne, Maria. *Alger, 1830-1984: Stratégies et enjeux urbains.* Paris: Éditions Recherche sur le Civilisations, 1986.

Shaler, William. *Sketches of Algiers, Political, Historical and Civil: Containing an Account of the Geography, Population, Government, Revenues, Commerce, Agriculture, Arts, Civil Institutions, Tribes, Manners, Languages, and Recent Political History of That Country.* Boston: Cummings, Hillard, 1826.

Shuval, Tal. "Households in Ottoman Algeria." *Turkish Studies Association Bulletin* 24, no. 1 (Spring 2000): 41–64.

———. *La ville d'Alger vers la fin du XVIIIème siècle: Population et cadre urbain.* Paris: Éditions du Centre National de Recherche Scientifique, 1998.

Soufi, Fouad. "Les archives, une problématique de patrimonialisation." In "Le patrimoine." *Insaniyat: Revue algérienne d'anthropologie et de sciences sociales,* no. 12 (September–December 2000): 129–50.

Spencer, William. *Algiers in the Age of the Corsairs.* Norman: University of Oklahoma Press, 1976.

Stafford, Barbara Maria, and Frances Terpak. *Devices of Wonder: From the World in a Box to Images on a Screen.* Los Angeles: Getty Research Institute, 2001.

Stewart, I. R. Govan. *Lilias Trotter of Algiers.* London: Lutterworth Press, 1958.

Stora, Benjamin, and Zakya Daoud. *Ferhat Abbas, une utopie algérienne.* Paris: Denoël, 1995.

Taraud, Christelle. *La prostitution coloniale: Algérie, Tunisie, Maroc (1830–1962).* Paris: Payot, 2003.

Thompson, Virginia. "'I Went Pale with Pleasure': The Body, Sexuality, and National Identity among French Travelers to Algiers in the Nineteenth Century." In *Algeria and France, 1800–2000: Identity, Memory, Nostalgia,* edited by Patricia M. E. Lorcin, 18–32. Syracuse, NY: Syracuse University Press, 2006.

Tlemçani, Rachid. "Islam in France: The French Have Themselves to Blame." *Middle East Quarterly* 4 (1997): 31–38.

Tocqueville, Alexis de. "Notes on the Voyage to Algeria in 1841." In *Writings on Empire and Slavery,* edited and translated by Jennifer Pitts, 36–37. Baltimore, MD: Johns Hopkins University Press, 2001.

———. *Oeuvres complètes.* Vol. 3, *Écrits et discours politiques.* Paris: Gallimard, 1991.

Tracy, James D. *Emperor Charles V's Crusades against Tunis and Algiers: Appearance and Reality.* James Ford Bell Lectures, no. 38. Minneapolis: University of Minnesota, 2001.

Trémaux, Pierre. *Parallèles des édifices anciens et modernes du continent africain.* Paris: L. Hachette, 1861.

Trives, André. *Bab-el-Oued, mon quartier, figé dans sa mort.* Paris: La Pensé Universelle, 1975.

Tudury, Guy. *La prodigieuse histoire des Mahonnais en Algérie.* Nîmes: C. Lacour, 1992.

Valensi, Lucette. *On the Eve of Colonisation: The Maghreb before French Conquest.* Translated by Kenneth Perkins. New York: Africana, 1977.

Van Staëvel, Jean-Pierre. "Le Qâdî au bout du labyrinthe: L'impasse dans la littérature jurisprudentielle mâlikite (al-Andalus et Maghreb, 3/IX–9/XV siècles)." In

L'urbanism dans l'Occident au Moyen Age, edited by P. Cressier, M. Fierro, and J.-P. Van Staëvel, 39–63. Madrid: Casa de Velâzquez–CSIC, 2000.

———. "Les usages de la ville dans l'occident musulman médiéval (9ème–14ème siècle)." PhD diss., Université de Lyon II, 2001.

Verrier, Anthony. *Assassination in Algiers: Churchill, Roosevelt, de Gaulle, and the Murder of Admiral Darlan.* London: Macmillan, 1990.

Vilar, Juan. *Los Espagnoles en la Argelia Francesa (1830–1914).* Murcia: Universidad de Murcia, 1989.

Vincendeau, Ginette. *Pépé le Moko.* London: British Film Institute, 1998.

Vircondelet, Alain. *Alger, Alger.* Martel: Éditions du Laquet, 1998.

Vitkus, Daniel J., ed. *Piracy, Slavery and Redemption: Barbary Captivity Narratives from Early Modern England.* New York: Columbia University Press, 2001.

Wall, Irwin W. *France, the United States, and the Algerian War.* Berkeley and Los Angeles: University of California Press, 2001.

Weil, Patrick. *Le statut des musulmans en Algérie coloniale: Une nationalité française dénaturée.* San Domenico: European University Institute, 2003.

Wirth, E. "Villes islamiques, villes arabes, villes orientales." In *La ville arabe en Islam,* edited by A. Bouhdiba and D. Chevallier, 193–225. Tunis: Cérès, 1982.

Wolf, John B. *The Barbary Coast: Algiers under the Turks, 1500–1830.* New York and London: W. W. Norton, 1970.

Zarobell, John. "Jean-Charles Langlois's Panorama of Algiers (1833) and the Prospective Colonial Landscape." *Art History* 26, no. 5 (2003): 638–68.

———. "Framing French Algeria: Colonialism, Travel, and the Representation of Landscape, 1830–1870." PhD diss., University of California at Berkeley, 2000.

INDEX

CONTRIBUTORS

ERIC BREITBART is a writer and documentary filmmaker whose work includes film portraits of artists Diego Rivera (*I Paint What I See*) and Robert Indiana (*American Dreamer*), photographer Louis Stettner (*Times Square*), art historian Aby Warburg (*The Archive of Memory*), and industrial engineer Frederick Winslow Taylor (*Clockwork*). *A World on Display*, his film about the 1904 Louisiana Purchase Exposition, was adapted as a book (1997). He has given presentations about film and popular culture at academic conferences and film festivals in Europe, the United States, and North Africa and has published numerous articles and reviews in journals such as *Cinemascope*, *New England Review*, *Metropolis*, *Cinéaste*, and *American Film*. His recent article "Cinema Power/Labor Power" was translated into German and published in Freunde der deutschen Kinemathek's *Work in Progress: Kinematografien der Arbeit* (2007). His latest film is *Cinepingle: la mémoire du geste*, a feature-length documentary about work and creativity.

OMAR CARLIER is Professor of History at the Université de Paris VII. He is the author of *Espace maghrébin: La force du local?* (with Nadir Marouf, 1996), *Entre nation et jihad: Histoire sociale des radicalismes algériens* (1995), *Imache amar, un itinéraire militant* (1987; 2007). He has edited several volumes, including *La construction corporelle du leadership politique dans les pays du Sud à l'époque contemporaine* (2007), *L'oralité au Maghreb* (1992), and *Lettrés, intellectuels, et militants en Algérie, 19e–20e siècle* (1987), and published numerous articles on the social and political history of Algeria during the colonial and postcolonial eras.

He serves on the editorial boards of *Cahiers du Gremamo* (Paris) and *Insaniyat* (Algiers).

ZEYNEP ÇELIK is Distinguished Professor of Architecture at the New Jersey Institute of Technology. She works on the architectural and urban history of the Middle East and North Africa in the nineteenth and twentieth centuries. Her publications include *The Remaking of Istanbul* (1986; 1993), *Displaying the Orient: Architecture of Islam at Nineteenth Century World's Fairs* (1992), *Urban Forms and Colonial Confrontations: Algiers under French Rule* (1997), *Streets: Critical Perspectives on Public Space* (1993 — coeditor), and *Empire, Architecture, and the City: French-Ottoman Encounters, 1830-1914* (2008), as well as articles on cross-cultural topics. She has served as the editor of the *Journal of the Society of Architectural Historians* (2000-2003). Currently, she is working on the historiography of archaeology in the late Ottoman Empire and a comparative study of visual culture, c. 1900.

JULIA CLANCY-SMITH is Professor of History at the University of Arizona, Tucson. She is the author of *Rebel and Saint: Muslim Notables, Populist Protest, Colonial Encounters (Algeria and Tunisia, 1800-1904)* (1994). She coauthored *Domesticating the Empire: Gender, Race, and Family Life in the Dutch and French Empires* (1998), coedited *Writing French Colonial Histories,* a special issue of *French Historical Studies* (2004), and edited *North Africa, Islam, and the Mediterranean World from the Almoravids to the Algerian War* (2001). Her latest book, *Mediterranean Odysseys: Migrants and Migrations in 19th-Century North Africa,* will be published in 2009. She is currently working on a monograph on colonial education for Muslim girls in French North Africa as well as two textbooks, *The Modern Middle East and North Africa* and *The History of North Africa in the Modern Era.*

ISABELLE GRANGAUD is a researcher at the Centre National de la Recherche Scientifique (CNRS) and an associate at the Institut de Recherches et d'Études sur le Monde Arabe et Musulman (IREMAM) in Aix-en-Provence. She is the author of *La ville imprenable: Une histoire sociale de Constantine au 18° siècle* (2002; 2004). She works on the cities of the Maghreb from the sixteenth to the nineteenth centuries, especially Constantine and Algiers, concentrating on social practices and urban institutions. She also examines the production of archives, on which she has written several articles. The proceedings of a workshop that she organized on comparative perspectives on legal registers will be published under the title *La justice et ses écrits.*

PATRICIA M. E. LORCIN is Associate Professor of History at the University of Minnesota—Twin Cities and editor of *French Historical Studies*. She is the author of *Imperial Identities: Stereotyping, Prejudice, and Race in Colonial Algeria* (1995; 1999; French translation, 2005), editor of *Algeria and France, 1800–2000: Identity, Memory, Nostalgia* (2006), and coeditor of *Migrances, diasporas et transculturalités francophones: Littératures et cultures d'Afrique, des Caraïbes, d'Europe et du Québec* (2005) and *Transnational Cultures and Identities in the Francophone World* (forthcoming). She has written numerous articles on French imperialism and colonialism, one of which was awarded the 2002 William Koren Prize for the best article on French history published by a North American scholar. She is at present working on a comparative study of European women writers in the colonies of Algeria and Kenya and coediting *War and Its Spaces: France and the Francophone World*.

FRANCES TERPAK is Curator of Photographs at the Getty Research Institute, where she has developed their photographic and optical devices collections. Her research specialties include popular entertainment and optical devices in the early modern period and the history of photography—particularly as practiced in the French colonies, the Ottoman Empire, and China. She curated the 1998 exhibition "Framing the Asian Shore: Nineteenth-Century Photographs of the Ottoman Empire," and co-curated with Barbara Stafford the 2001 exhibition "Devices of Wonder: From the World in a Box to Images on a Screen," which received numerous awards, including, for its catalogue, a Katherine Kyes Leab/Daniel J. Leab Award from the Association of College and Research Libraries. She is currently working on photography in the Middle East and an exhibition on nineteenth-century photography in China.